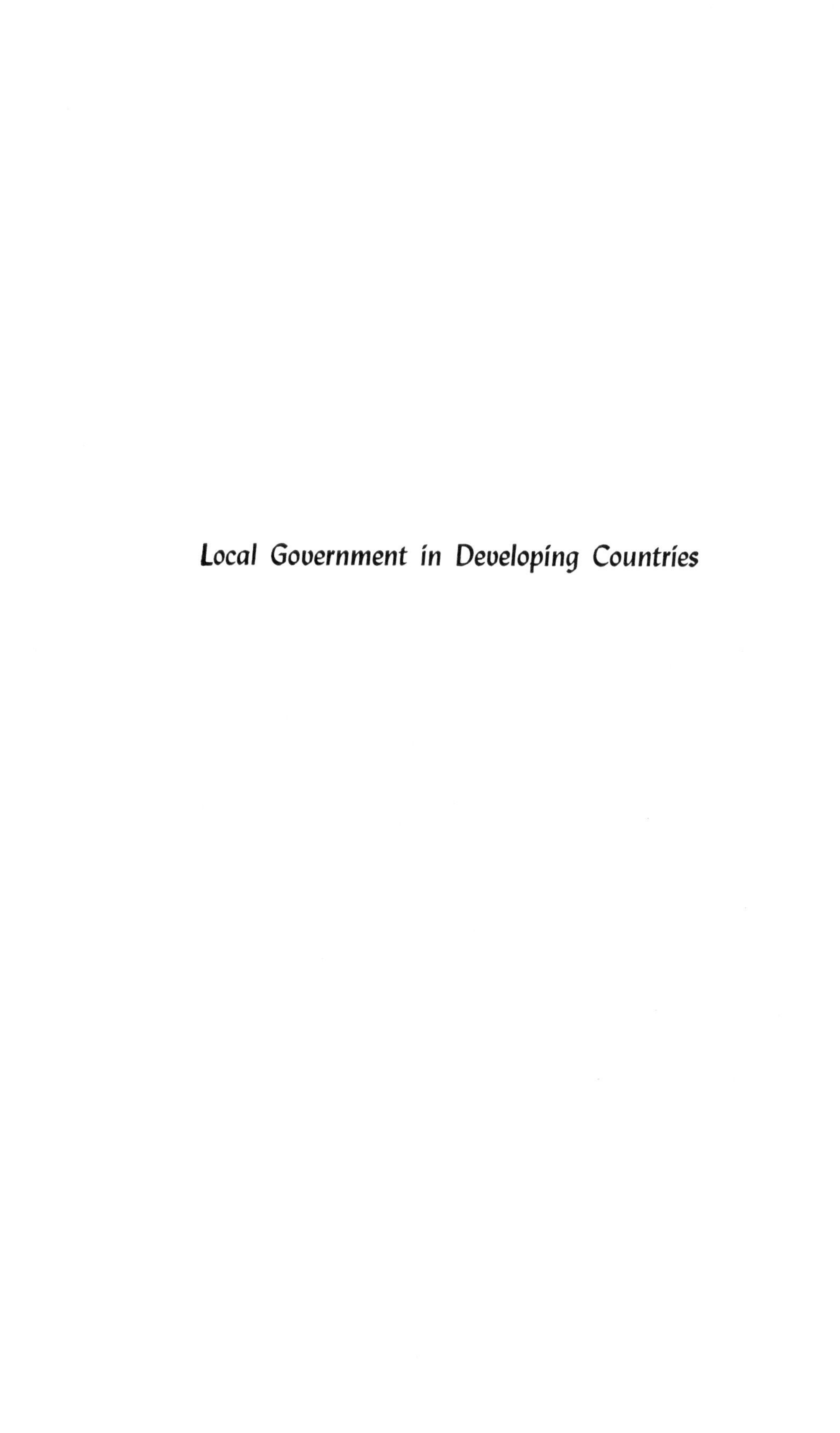

Local Government in Developing Countries

McGRAW-HILL SERIES IN INTERNATIONAL DEVELOPMENT

ALDERFER • *Local Government in Developing Countries*
BRYCE • *Industrial Development: A Guide for Accelerating Economic Growth*
DUNN • *International Handbook of Advertising*
EICHER AND WITT • *Agriculture in Economic Development*
HARBISON AND MYERS • *Education, Manpower and Economic Growth: Strategies of Human Resource Development*
POWELSON • *Latin America: Today's Economic and Social Revolution*
WALINSKY • *The Planning and Execution of Economic Development: A Non-technical Guide for Policy Makers and Administrators*

Local Government in Developing Countries

HAROLD F. ALDERFER

Professor Emeritus of Political Science,
The Pennsylvania State University
Educational and Research Associate,
Fels Institute of Local and State Government,
University of Pennsylvania

McGRAW-HILL BOOK COMPANY

New York Toronto London

LOCAL GOVERNMENT IN DEVELOPING COUNTRIES

 Library of Congress Catalog Card Number 63–20718

00987

Preface

THIS VOLUME is designed to describe the general pattern of local government in developing nations. These nations include both those that are new chronologically and those that are emerging in the Western sense of the term. Their European or American backgrounds, as well as the traditional foundations, are described in order to explain their evolving form and structure. Their major problems in the fields of national-local relationships, finance, elections, and general administration are explored in terms of their ability to function with effectiveness and to render necessary services to their people. Special attention is paid to metropolitan government problems and to community development in the more rural areas. Suggestions are made to point out the road to improvement and greater efficiency.

At no time in history has the field of local government been so important to national development. With the phenomenal rise of independent states in the nineteenth and twentieth centuries, especially since the end of World War II, and the increasing availability to the peoples of the world of the fruits of modern technology and organization, the place of local government in national progress is being recognized for its own merit and for what it can do for the general welfare of the people.

We wish to acknowledge with deep appreciation the work of Mrs. Esther LeeDecker as research librarian, and that of Miss Dorothy Bittle and Mrs. Marguerite Steiner, who aided in the preparation of the type-written manuscript. We also would like to record our indebtedness to the Pennsylvania State Library at the Capitol in Harrisburg, Pennsylvania, for the use of its excellent research facilities and for the efforts of the staff in making available materials, both in the library and in exchange with other libraries, that were used in writing this book. For all defects of omission and commission, the author himself is alone responsible.

Harold F. Alderfer

Contents

1 Four Basic Patterns

FOUR BASIC PATTERNS of local government are found in the world today: the French, the English, the Soviet, and the traditional. Each one has variants and there are partial combinations of patterns, but essentially any particular system in present operation belongs to one of these classes. For example, the Turkish is not exactly like that of France, but it belongs in that category; the Indian is not English in all details, but it could not be placed under any of the others; the Yugoslavic is much more decentralized than the Soviet, but it is unmistakably communistic. No matter what traditional local government is examined, the chief and the council of elders are omnipresent in some sort of arrangement.

Except for the traditional, local government as it is today is a product of Western civilization—even the Soviet with all of its revolutionary and socialistic institutions and practices has features not only from prerevolutionary Russia but also from nineteenth century continental Europe. In all the area that was once a part of the Ottoman Empire, there is little left of the local government system that for centuries existed under the sultanate. Of the Byzantine Empire which preceded it, not only nothing remains but little is actually known of its local government. Of the Greco-Roman world before it, the Greek city-state and the Roman municipium have long since passed into historical oblivion. In China, Japan, Korea, India, and Southeast Asia, as in the Moslem Middle East not within the sphere of the late Ottoman Empire, Western institutions have been superimposed on what still remains of traditional institutions which are today no more than fragmentary residues. In the North and South American continents, any indigenous local institutions of government that existed before the coming of the white man are gone beyond memory. The same may be said about Australia, New Zealand, and the Antipodes. In Africa, native institutions, some still viable, have been integrated in some measure into the European colonial systems of the powers which in the nineteenth century took over the hegemony of the Black Continent.

As a general rule, colonizing powers upon gaining sovereign rights in foreign places have concentrated upon establishing national and top provincial administrations to carry out their political, economic, and social objectives. They have either neglected the local field, being satisfied to accept local leadership if found to be cooperative, or have half-heartedly tried to remake local institutions in their own image. As a result, these colonial governments, even when ultimately independent and manned by native officials and personnel, tend to be centralized in the national, colonial, and provincial capitals. This is also true in many places where a transfer of sovereignty was not involved but where major powers exercised quasi-governmental functions within their spheres of influence, for example, in League of Nations mandated and United Nations trust territories, and in nations which received substantial foreign military and economic aid since World War II. On the other hand, recent changes in India, Pakistan, the United Arab Republic, and Yugoslavia have been in the direction of decentralization of local government institutions.

Local government as defined for the purposes of our consideration consists of all units of government under the national level in unitary states and under national and state levels in federal systems. Complete coverage will include all levels: provinces, districts, subdistricts, municipalities, villages—whatever their functions may be. In many instances, the governments of the higher local levels not only control many activities of the lower; they also serve the people directly. Furthermore, national-local relations are also part of the picture. No matter what nation is examined, it is important to keep in mind the essential unity of government as a whole. The Western nation-state as a concept and as a going reality is predicated upon a legal sovereignty that is indivisible and a social wholeness that is complete. Nations that lack either of these or substantial parts thereof are usually beset with the possibility of disintegration and dissolution.

THE FRENCH IMAGE

The French system of local government is established in a large portion of the world today. In fact, outside of the Anglo-American nations and the Soviet world, along with their respective spheres of influence, it is practically supreme. This includes West Europe, the Near, Middle, and Far East, Central and South America, and large portions of the African continent. While it is not the task here to trace the historical reasons for its proliferation throughout the world during the nineteenth and early twentieth centuries, this system of local administration was brought forth by the French Revolution and was given solid foundations in Napoleonic legislation. Both had profound effects upon the existing feudal and monarchical systems of Europe. In European countries, in their sometimes shattered but always shocked condition, the new system of French local government gained either immediate foothold or later acceptance in whole or in part in delayed action which awaited propitious events.

This system of local government was an integral part of the new and modern state fashioned by French revolutionary and nationalistic ideas, and it followed these ideas wherever they went. In the early nineteenth century, France was the chief imperial power of continental Europe in Asia and North Africa. Other nations in Europe with colonial interests at that time were Spain, Belgium, and Holland, and their possessions felt the French influence through their own mother colonial administrations. The English system of local government began its democratic modernization with the Municipal Reform Act of 1835, but this was not completed before the late decades of the century. Its influence in the non-Anglo-American world was negligible. Therefore, the French system of local government had little competition in the changing world of the early nineteenth century, and as the century wore on, even English dependencies, faced with the problems of colonial administration of "backward" peoples, took over much of the centralized and hierarchical mechanics of French administration.

Although modern French local government stems from the Revolution and the empire of Napoleon, they did not make a clean sweep of French governmental institutions of the *ancien régime*. The past was not altogether ignored, it could not be entirely forgotten. During the preceding Bourbon monarchies, the chief administrative district was the *généralité*, which was governed by an intendant appointed by the king and responsible to him alone.[1] While no bureaucratic uniformity existed from one district to another, the power of the ruler over the ruled was in theory absolute, and it was translated from word into deed by the intendant and his staff. By the eve of the Revolution, the old medieval independence of communes, municipalities, and provinces had long disappeared. *L'état c'est moi,* said Louis XIV. Yet the commune remained not only a geographic place and a sociological unit; it never lost the loyalty and affection of its citizens. After the Revolution, it again became the foundation of French local government.

But in another way, the past was not forgotten. The French monarchy had built a strong, unified nation, the strongest in Europe at one time, and the leadership of the Revolution in Paris, after watching with fear the anarchy and chaos that might result from unbridled revolutionary activities in the provinces and communes, defeated the forces of federalism and local autonomy before they had a chance to take root. The French nation of the Revolution remained unified and its government unitary. A month after the storming of the Bastille, the Constituent Assembly ruled that "a national constitution and public liberty are more

[1] The official title of intendants was *intendant de justice, police, et finances, et commissaires départis dans les généralités du Royaume pour l'exécution des ordres du Roi.* Quoted from Brian Chapman, *The Prefects and Provincial France,* George Allen & Unwin, Ltd., London, 1955, p. 11.

advantageous to the provinces than the privileges which some of them now enjoy, and whose sacrifice is now necessary for the intimate union of all parts of the Empire. It is therefore decreed that all the particular privileges of the provinces, principalities, cities, corps and communities, be they financial advantages or of any other kind, are henceforth abolished, and merged in the common law of all the French." [2]

All France was then divided into 83 departments, each governed by an elective assembly of 36 councilors who nominated an executive committee of eight from their own number. Central inspection was provided for in the persons of itinerant officers of the king, and an elected supervisor was empowered to see that the decisions of the assembly and executive committee were carried out. Within the departments, 44,000 or more communes were established as local units with self-governing powers. Each commune was to have a mayor and council elected by the citizens, only the poorest of whom were denied the right to vote. Thus while the French nation remained unitary, local government became in one fell swoop democratic and decentralized. But the new system did not work well. The Revolution was in full swing; the Red Terror swept the nation; law and order disappeared. In thousands of communes, officials were oppressive, corrupt, and capricious. In 1795 the Directory sought to bring the communes under stricter state control. The canton was made the unit of local government; it included a number of communes except the largest which were made separate cantons. While this stemmed the tide of anarchy, it was an artificial entity with no appeal to French sentiment.[3]

When Napoleon came into power, he thoroughly revised the organization of local government. In the law of February 17, 1800, he set up a system that was to last, except for minor changes, to the present day. It was orderly, symmetrical, and logical—the product of a great military mind operating in a civil framework. An unbroken chain of command functioned from the national government through departments and *arrondissements* down to the smallest commune. A corps of adjutants—loyal, trained, competent, and disciplined—the prefects of the depart-

[2] Quoted in Chapman, *ibid.*, p. 14.

[3] William Bennett Munro, *The Government of European Cities,* The Macmillan Company, New York, 1927, pp. 211–212.

ments, and the subprefects of the *arrondissements* carried out the will of the central government. Ministerial regulations, from which there should be no deviation, made government throughout France uniform and precise. A body of noncommissioned officers—the communal mayors and councilmen—obedient, loyal, and indigenous to the community and of the soil of France, constituted the lowest rung of the hierarchy. While this was not the democracy of the Revolution, still it was not a throw-back to the absolutist monarchy; it was the new French state, aggressively nationalist but deep down republican in spirit. It was the first, and to this day perhaps the most perfect, organization of a unitary government in the Western world. But it was a government not of laws but of men.

During the century and a half of its existence, it became gradually more democratic. In 1831, the communal councils were made elective; in 1881, the mayor ceased to be nominated by the central government and became an elective official chosen by and from the membership of the council. By the Municipal Code of 1884, which is still the basic law, the council was given powers of decision in matters of purely local concern but not without an elaborate complex of checks on the part of the higher officials of *arrondissements,* departments, and central ministries.

At present there are in France 90 departments, about 300 *arrondissements,* and approximately 40,000 communes. The communes, large and small, are the villages, towns, and cities of the nation. Governments in each of these levels have an executive—prefect, subprefect, or mayor. The executive is powerful in his domain but is responsible to the next higher executive, while the prefect is responsible to the Minister of Interior. At the provincial and communal levels, there is an elective council with limited powers.[4]

Certain legal principles and practices are basic in French local government. Local units are organs of the central government to a much greater extent than in England or the United States. They have no powers that are not granted to them by a constituted authority. Further-

[4] Each *arrondissement* is divided into cantons which exist only for judicial and electoral purposes. Neither the *arrondissements* nor the cantons have corporate status. The *arrondissements* handle much of the routine work of the departments; the sub-prefects are called the "letter boxes" of the prefects.

more, as the executive power in France has its own rights and duties distinct from those granted by the legislative authority, local government is subject to the executive branch, for example in such fields as police, security, hygiene, and safety. In fact, all public services come under executive jurisdiction. This gives the mayor of a commune, for example, a dual capacity—as an agent of the central executive and an official following the directives given him by his local council. Finally, the executive branch, although administratively independent of both the legislative and judicial branches, is still not independent of law. Administrative courts are set up to deal with cases that arise between citizens and administrative agencies and officials. The highest of these courts is the *Conseil d'État,* while the lower courts are the *conseils de préfecture.* These courts are another of the Napoleonic inventions which have been copied in many of the nations of the world.[5]

In summary, French local government is characterized by centralization, chain of command, hierarchical structure, executive domination, and legislative subordination. We shall find these in some relative degree in all local governments that have followed the French pattern.

THE ENGLISH PATTERN

English local government goes back in an unbroken line through the centuries to Anglo-Saxon times before the Norman invasion in 1066. In fact, many English boroughs antedate the national government itself; they were not creations of the central government, although they came to be integrated into the national system. But their basic history is that of the municipal corporation possessing corporate powers and relative independence from the jurisdiction of central government functionaries. Boroughs were governed by charters given them by the Crown and had their own officers, in many cases even their own justices of the peace. They had a broad range of powers and held the right to send their own representatives to Parliament. During the seventeenth and eighteenth centuries they deteriorated as community institutions, being governed by self-perpetuating boards consisting of a mayor and aldermen who ad-

[5] Brian Chapman, *Introduction to French Local Government,* George Allen & Unwin, Ltd., London, 1953, p. 27.

ministered the "close" corporations for their own narrow economic or political interests. But the nineteenth-century democratic breakthrough led to the passage of the Municipal Corporation Act of 1835, which extended the notion of incorporation to the electors, called burgesses, as well as to the mayor and aldermen. The governing authority came to be an elective council, members holding office for three years.[6]

For five hundred years before 1888, justices of the peace, superseding the sheriffs as general administrative officers of the Crown in local areas outside the borders of incorporated boroughs, carried on county functions and the control of officials in the urban towns and the rural parishes. Having no modern administrative staffs, they governed by means of the judicial method of detecting negligence and violations of the law, and by bringing persons into court and before jury, fining or passing a judgment upon the officer or authority in question. In 1888, the method of governing counties through justices of the peace was abolished. It was replaced by elective county councils with broad powers, and with some supervision over urban and rural districts.

Modern English local government was established during the latter decades of the nineteenth century. It consists of *county boroughs* (founded in 1888) which possess a full range of borough and county functions and are independent of all other local authorities; *administrative counties* (founded in 1888) which include both town and county areas and administer such functions as health, public assistance, police, roads, and elementary and secondary education; *municipal boroughs* (founded in 1835 and 1882) which have a free body of powers except those exercised by administrative county councils; *urban districts* (founded in 1872) which also have a free body of powers except those exercised by administrative county councils; *rural districts* (founded in 1872) which have less extensive functions, never education or police and hardly ever roads; and *parish meetings or councils* (founded in 1894) with few, if any, functions.[7]

One of the basic characteristics of English local government is that, except for few and minor exceptions, the local units are free from control

[6] Herman Finer, *English Local Government,* Columbia University Press, New York, 1934, pp. 42–46, 56–64.

[7] *Ibid.*, p. 34.

of other local authorities. There is no authority between them and the national ministries and Parliament. This contrasts sharply with the hierarchical system of French local government, where higher local units have administrative and financial controls over the lower echelons. Likewise, and again in contrast with the French system, English local government is decentralized rather than deconcentrated. Decentralization means that there are local decision-making agencies with more or less independent existence and powers; deconcentration, on the other hand, means that all governmental power lies with the central government, and local units, even in the case of elective officials, act simply as agents of the central government. English local authorities are generally multipurpose, or as Herman Finer puts it, "compendious"—they are not *ad hoc,* confined to one function, like school districts in the United States. However, all these traits are tempered by the modern drive for national integration and increased state control.[8] In English local government, moreover, the unpaid elective council is the dominant power. The bulk of its work is done by committees which loom large in the administrative process and wield power in depth unmatched in councils following the French pattern. Councils direct the salaried and wage employees through committees rather than through executives such as the city managers who are found in the United States. Furthermore, the principle of co-option is freely used. This is the inclusion in council committees, either by permissive or mandatory provisions, of persons who have not been elected as councilors, but because of their training, experience, or background can contribute in a substantial way to the work of the local units. This principle recognizes that democratic elections do not necessarily assure full representation of all elements of the community or professional competence. As the councilors are part-time as well as unpaid, and as they cannot delegate responsibilities to chief executives or allow their work to be carried out by agents of the central government, the services of co-opters are extensively utilized and recognized.[9]

While English local government is more decentralized than that of France, central authorities are gaining increased powers in local administration. Such administrative control is exercised through various na-

[8] *Ibid.,* pp. 19–22.
[9] *Ibid.,* p. 220.

tional ministries, especially the Ministry of Health. It consists of the approval of some appointments, the threat of substitute administration, the making of regulations to implement parliamentary statutes, the refusal to approve certain local actions, the granting of provisional orders, and the giving of advice and information. But especially important is inspection, which is the characteristic English mode of central administrative control. Most of the national agents dealing with lower levels are known as inspectors.[10]

In summary, English local government is characterized by decentralization, legislative dominance, co-option through the committee system, multipurpose activity, and voluntary citizen participation.

THE SOVIET MODEL

Before the 1917 Revolution, Russia was divided into provinces and regions, each headed by a governor whose powers were severely limited by the ministries of the central government. There were also districts in each province headed by a chief of police and his deputies. Within each district were cantons which included a number of villages and which had an assembly whose members were elected by the village communes which composed it. So far the system shows a similitude to the French, which may be evidence that the czarist regime copied continental models during the nineteenth century. In fact, by terms of the Municipal Act promulgated in 1870, which was modeled after the Prussian system, all local taxpaying citizens were granted the right to vote and hold positions on the municipal boards, although the central state authorities controlled their administration.

The village, the mir of the ancient regime, had in its turn a local assembly of the householders who elected a headman. The mir, the unbreakable atom of Russian life, was the ideal of Tolstoi in seeking a community that was simple, democratic, and sociologically whole. It is surprising to know that much freedom existed in the mir when all the higher units of Russian government were rigidly controlled from above. "Every student of Russian life and institutions under the Tsars, whether

[10] R. K. Gooch, "Local Government in England," in William Anderson (ed.), *Local Government in Europe*, Appleton-Century-Crofts, Inc., New York, 1939, pp. 76–79.

Russian or foreign, was forcibly struck by the apparent anomaly of the existence of the utmost democratic government in the village commune in the midst of the most perfectly autocratic central government," says Karl Borders.[11] In the face of absentee landlordism and absentee central bureaucracy, rents and taxes were levied against the mir and divided internally by the commune, which also handled all the local and minor details of government without supervision.

The Revolution inaugurated great changes in the system of Russian local government. It became a system of soviets, a term that means councils. In the beginning, these soviets were composed of delegates or deputies elected by workers employed in factories, by soldiers in the Red Army, and by peasants in villages and agricultural districts. They trace their origin to the Revolution of 1905, when a council of workers in an outlying city instigated a strike and took over the administration of some municipal functions. While this particular soviet did not last long in the face of central government opposition, the concept was not forgotten and was made basic after the communistic revolution.

The present system of local government in the Soviet Union is made up of several levels of administration. All levels under the All Union, Union Republic, and Autonomous Republic levels are considered as local government. The first and highest level is composed of the administrative units directly subordinate to the Republic governments: the *krais,* the *oblasts,* the *okrugs,* and the larger cities. In 1957 there were 160 of these. The second level consists of rural *raions,* towns of intermediate size, and city *raions.* In 1957 there were 4,363 rural *raions* and 505 city *raions.* The third level includes the village soviets, settlement soviets, and small-town soviets. In 1957 there were about 54,000 of these.[12]

The theoretical basis of Soviet local government is "democratic centralism." This concept was transferred from the organization of the Communist party, which calls for the election of all leading party bodies from the lowest to the highest, periodical reports of party bodies to party organizations, strict party discipline in which the minority is subordinate to the majority, and the binding character of the decisions of higher

[11] Karl Borders, "Local Autonomy in Russian Village Life under the Soviets," *Social Forces,* March, 1929, pp. 409–414.

[12] L. G. Churchward, "Continuity and Change in Soviet Local Government, 1947–1957," *Soviet Studies,* January, 1958, pp. 256–285.

bodies upon the lower. In government, all organs are links in one continuous chain of governmental power. Local agencies are not intended as lawmaking agencies in the full sense of the term, but as agencies directed from the center. Higher organs may direct lower agencies, and the executive committees of the lower soviets are responsible not only to the soviets of their level but to the executive committee of the next higher level. Local soviets elect a chairman, a deputy chairman, a secretary, members of the executive committee, and members of standing committees. Within the executive committee is a presidium which acts as the executive for the deliberative executive body. It is composed of full-time municipal, district, or regional officials who supervise the work of the soviet's regular departments. For example, in the city of Leningrad the city soviet has 550 deputies, the executive committee numbers 25, while the presidium consists of a chairman, eight vice-chairmen, and a secretary. Local soviet members receive no salary, but the pay they receive on other jobs goes on while they attend the occasional meetings of the soviets.[13]

Increasingly since 1940, stress is placed upon the participation of citizens in the actual process and work of governmental agencies. Reliance on standing committees or commissions and an enlargement of the scope of local powers is noted especially in the decentralization of control over industries and agriculture. Furthermore, there has been a reduction in numbers of local government officials and personnel. The overall objective of all governmental agencies, including the local, is socialistic planning for the economic and social development of the community. This makes the scope of local government much broader than it is in France, England, or the United States. The trend in all aspects of Soviet government in recent years has been the emphasis upon socialist legality in the work of the state apparatus, that is, the soviet system has been developing its own law and uniform regulations upon which to set standards for performance and procedure. For example, the book of regulations for executive committees of local soviets is a tome of 1,800 pages. This establishment of legal norms for administration is based upon the constitution, statutes, directives of the party, and the regulations devised by the higher levels of government, and it can be assumed

[13] Robert C. Tucker, "Field Observations on Soviet Local Government," *The Slavic and East European Review,* December, 1959, pp. 526–538.

that the interpretation and application of this complex involves increasing reliance upon bureaucracy from above.

But the outstanding feature of Soviet local government is the Communist party direction and leadership at all levels of government. This is especially evident in the manner in which elections are held. As one observer, H. N. Brailsford, said as early as 1927: "What is elsewhere a riot of discord is here a desire for registering unanimity. In other countries the sovereign electors choose their governors. In Russia they ratify their governors' choice." The pattern of elections, established in 1936, calls for the biennial elections of deputies or delegates to the soviets on a territorial rather than a place-of-work basis. There are uniform suffrage for those eighteen years of age or over, a direct and secret ballot, election by simple majority, and an absence of residence requirements. The election procedure is strictly regulated and formal, but it is strange to Western eyes in that there is only one candidate for each office. Nominations are made by worker, occupational, and peasant groups, but these nominations are screened by party secretaries and ratified at meetings of the Communist party. While public opinion has limited influence, and the candidates are given an opportunity to discuss their qualifications and ideas, the choices are always controlled. However, effort is made, especially at the lowest level, to include nonparty persons, recognizing those who have made constructive contributions to the economic and social life of the community where there is no danger that subversive elements will get into power.

The mass of local government personnel is impressive: in 1961, more than 1,800,000 deputies were elected to the 54,000 soviets. Of the total, 40 per cent were women, 45 per cent party members, and 62 per cent workers. Out of the whole list, only 249 candidates listed were not elected. But in the Soviet system, deputies are not wielders of political power, nor are they important in the overall governmental process, and the elections are important only because of their show of "solidarity." [14] One observer thinks it is difficult to say how far Communist party control of local government involves a restriction of Soviet democracy because this control has been both stimulating and stultifying. Close party

[14] Howard R. Swearer, "The Functions of Soviet Election," *Midwest Journal of Political Science,* May, 1961, pp. 129–149.

control has dampened the initiative of citizens who wait upon the pronouncements of party leadership to set local policy, but on the other hand has stirred otherwise lethargic persons into enthusiastic activity in order to gain personal credit with the powers that be. Furthermore, the increase of local bureaucracy is noted as party committees parallel local government units.[15] In 1958, 103 regional economic councils which take away some of the economic functions from local government were established. Since the death of Stalin, there has been a restoration of collective leadership, rather than the dictatorial administrative methods which that leader encouraged. However, unanimity of decision is usually sought, and the concept of a simple majority remains dead.

In summary, Soviet local government is characterized by Communist party control under the name of democratic centralism, single-candidate elections, hierarchical chain of command, and a broad scope of governmental powers to local councils.

TRADITIONAL RESIDUES

The term "traditional local government," as far as we are concerned here, means that a government is indigenous to the place where it exists. But in all the world today, it is difficult to point to any governmental system that is unaffected by Western culture, so for our purposes "traditional" means non-Western. In other words, all governmental institutions and practices are either Western or traditional; there is no other category.

Western influences are much stronger on the national or overall level than on the grass-roots side. The Western colonizer came in the front door rather than the rear. There he put on the pressure to get government in his own image, something he could understand and operate. He was not anxious to get down to the people as such; that was for the missionaries. As long as peace, tranquillity, and economic access prevailed, he made no serious effort to change local institutions and habits; in fact, he gladly cooperated. Thus Western overall and traditional local institutions worked side by side, each adjusting to the other where necessary and possible. In fact, the native elite, trained in Western schools,

[15] L. G. Churchward, "Soviet Local Government," *Australian Outlook,* September, 1959, pp. 211–222.

returned to be enthusiastically modern, anxious to make their traditional institutions over on Western models. This was the general pattern, but there were many exceptions to the rule, and many combinations and variations are found. But the bifurcation between the dynamic Western center and the static native locality made the drive towards centralization a foregone conclusion.

Traditional local government, in most places, may be described in terms of a chief, a village head, or some kind of local leader, either acting as sole authority or more often assisted by a council of elders. The power structure is in terms of an extended family, clan, tribe, religious elite, or economic class. The functions of government are consonant with the cultural stage of the people, and the jurisdiction is limited to a village or a group of villages in a contiguous geographic area. A substantial part of the land is owned and worked in common, but there is also individual ownership, especially of movable property. Originally, according to Kropotkin, the village community was one of free men, democracy, equality, and the spirit of mutual aid.[16] While such a pattern may seem simple, there is much more than meets the eye. Custom, tradition, ritual, ceremonial, and all the mores run deep; their tangled webs are thick with age, mysterious to the outlander. Some village communities are products of a high degree of sophistication, parts of a larger system that has disintegrated or changed, sometimes older than Western time.

Sociologists and kindred observers have found the village community in many parts of the world, and they believe it existed in others where it is no longer extant. Kropotkin, citing many anthropological studies done in the nineteenth century, finds this institution in the early Slavonian culture as well as in present day Slavic lands; in England during the Saxon and Norman times, partially surviving until the nineteenth century; at the bottom of the social organization of old Scotland, Ireland, and Wales; in France where the village folkmote common ownership of land persisted until Turgot's day; in India, where both Aryans and non-Aryans lived under it. It is found in Afghanistan, Mongolia, Java, Malaya, Abyssinia, the Sudan, the interior of Africa, the Pacific archipelagoes, and North and South America before the coming of the

[16] P. Kropotkin, *Mutual Aid: A Factor in Evolution,* Penguin Books Limited, Middlesex, England, 1902, chaps. 3 and 4.

Westerner. "In short," Kropotkin concludes, "we do not know of one single human race or one single nation which has not had its period of village communities." [17]

G. L. Gomme, British anthropologist, believed that the village community was a product of the backward races of the world, not of the foremost, that its existence amid the more advanced institutions of civilization is due to survival, not to creation, and that its widespread existence shows that it represents a phase of economic development through which all progressive races must have passed. Furthermore, he declares that it is necessary to understand that the village community was primitive and not historical, due to the earliest instincts of race and not to the political thought of a governing class or to the commercial necessities of a trading class. In other words, it is not a modern institution, but one that must have begun far back in the history of the human race.[18]

Oswald Spengler divorces the town from the village, the former representing a particular historical culture, the latter an existence with no history. What distinguishes a town from a village is not size, he declares, but the presence of a soul. The man of the land and the man of the city are different essences.[19]

In summary, traditional residues, usually in the form of village communities, tend to be like each other the world over. They do not have the hallmarks of a specific culture; they are inclined to be simple in political structure, which is backed up by complex sociological mores and originally tended in the direction of democracy and freedom. But the residues which exist now are fragmentary and appear side by side with the political institutions of a more highly developed culture, namely the Western.

[17] *Ibid.*, pp. 106–107.

[18] G. L. Gomme, *The Village Community,* Charles Scribner's Sons, New York, 1890, pp. 16, 290.

[19] Oswald Spengler, *The Decline of the West,* Alfred A. Knopf, Inc., New York, 1934, vol. 2, p. 91.

2 The Evolution of Form and Structure: Latin America and Africa

THE FORM and structure of local government throughout the world today are the product of a history that covers many centuries. In them are found the hard facts of community life, the hopes and aspirations of peoples, the rubble of wars and invasions, the ideologies of philosophers, and the ambitions of leaders. Form and structure are part and parcel of the civilizations through which local government lived, whether they be frail remnants of those long since dead or full-blown frameworks of living cultures. While there are many variations, there are no accidents; each and every beam or column has a meaning of its own.

This is not to say that the form and structure of local government are always the outward show of inward reality. Many times they belie what actually happens in real life. Yet because they are there, they tell about how things once were, or about what people thought should be, or perhaps what might be in the future if all went well. And so knowledge of form and structure is important to understand local government in depth as well as its surface lineaments.

Furthermore, form and structure make a pattern of points of power;

the relationships of these points indicate the path of activity of people in local government. They chart the outside ranges of the operation; they determine inward possibilities. They do not, however, indicate the intensity with which local government is carried on. That depends on the people involved: the officials, the subordinate personnel, the constituencies and the higher authorities.

In this and the next four chapters, we shall try to outline the basic features of local governments in various parts of the world and to tell briefly something about their evolution. This will provide a backdrop for understanding present problems and exploring future possibilities.

LATIN AMERICA

Spain was the first colonial power among Western nations, the first to establish a colonial empire, which it governed for three hundred years. Its vast domain in the Americas included all the land from Mexico down through Central and South America with the exception of the extensive domain of Brazil which, by terms of a treaty signed in 1494 between Spain and Portugal, went to Portugal.

At the time of the discovery of America the power of the Spanish monarchy had reached its highest level, while the medieval institutions of the Cortes, the assemblies of the three social classes—the nobility, the clergy, and the delegates from chartered towns and cities—and the *municipios* had lost a greater part of their former power. The agency of the first importance in colonial affairs, after the king himself, was the Council of the Indies appointed by and responsible to him. From the time of its establishment in 1493, it made all laws for the Spanish possessions, acted as the court of last resort, and advised the king on all colonial matters. Its jurisdiction embraced all functions of government: legislative, financial, military, ecclesiastical, commercial, and legal. It nominated to the king all the civil and ecclesiastical officers in these possessions. Another agency was the *Casa de Contratación,* subordinate to both the king and the Council of the Indies, established in 1503 to give the king a rigid monopoly on all colonial trade. The colonial possessions were considered to be the property of the Spanish sovereign and not of the nation. When the colonies were fully organized in 1574, the Spanish possessions in America were divided into two kingdoms: New Spain, which included Mexico, Central America, and the islands; and Peru, which embraced all of South America except Brazil. Each was governed by a viceroy, who ruled with the authority of the king, and under him were captains general, governors, and *corregidores,* each governing a smaller area. At the lowest rung of the central hierarchy was the *alcalde mayor,* who was administrative officer of the *partidos,* exercising police, military, and judicial powers. Another governing institution in the Americas was the *audiencia,* a body of magistrates acting both as a supreme court and a board of administration.

In characterizing the Spanish colonial system, Prof. C. H. Haring points out that there was no clear division of powers between the various functionaries but a division of authority which prevented effective administration. All appointments were made directly from Spain, minute regulations and laws emanated from the king and his council, all activities of colonial officials were investigated and evaluated by the central authorities, and each official could report and appeal directly with the authorities in Seville. There was no chain of command. The result was overlapping of functions, delay, and red tape that frustrated the development of orderly progress.[1]

But along with the administrative network of the centralized monarchy came another institution of government, the municipality. Castilian in origin, it stemmed from the days after the reconquest of Spain from the Moors when the Spanish monarchy was faced with the need to repopulate lands vacated by the enemy. Walled towns were built as military outposts to protect the agricultural units and villages located in these areas, and special privileges, called *fueros municipales,* were granted to attract new settlers. Residents who were heads of families and property owners were given the right to meet in an assembly called the *consejo,* and in this assembly municipal officers were elected, frequently being drawn by lot. These were called *regidores,* who had supreme municipal authority. Also elected were two alcaldes or magistrates, and other officers.

[1] William Warren Sweet, *A History of Latin America,* Abingdon Press, Nashville, Tenn., 1919, pp. 94–101. Miguel Jorrin, *Governments of Latin America,* D. Van Nostrand Company, Inc., Princeton, N.J., 1953, pp. 3–17. C. H. Haring, *The Spanish Empire in America,* Oxford University Press, Fair Lawn, N.J., 1947, p. 121.

In America, the municipal corporation was called *cabildo* (chapter) with *regidores* chosen by the inhabitants, and alcaldes or mayors chosen by the *regidores* along with other local officials. In times of trouble and perplexity, the officers still convoked an assembly of important citizens and clergy to deliberate with the *cabildo*. But this democratic institution suffered like its progenitor in Spain. *Regidores* were named by the king, and his functionaries infringed upon local authority.

Frederick B. Pike describes the system of checks and balances devised by the Hapsburg kings to govern their overseas holdings as it applied to municipalities.[2]

First, the *residencia* was a system whereby the administration of local officials might be investigated by an official of higher level, such as a governor or *corregidor,* even after the local official's term of office had expired. If found delinquent the derelict official might be removed from office if still acting, or he or his heirs might be fined. Furthermore, the *audiencia* had broad power of supervision and control of municipal operations, especially as to finance and public works. Viceroys and other government officials also had controls over municipal business when they wanted to exercise them. On the other hand, the *cabildos* possessed some powers to curb the higher authorities. They could send *procuradores* to the Council of the Indies and even to the king to voice their complaints and plead their cases, and many times the Crown came to the aid of the municipalities. Thus, in spite of the imposing list of possible cases for intervention on the part of viceroys, governors, *corregidores* or *alcaldes mayores* such as confirmation of elections and ordinances, formulation of budgets and financial administration, execution of public works, imposition of taxes, market control, price fixing, bestowal of private property, and local decisions of judges, actually the *cabildo* enjoyed general freedom of action. Cooperation with the municipalities was usually offered by the higher levels of government. Professor Pike states, "these checks and balances may be judged as a brilliantly conceived means of maintaining under colonial status a vast overseas empire . . . and served to prevent the rise of an unchecked spirit of local

[2] Frederick B. Pike, "The Municipality and the System of Checks and Balances in Spanish-American Colonial Administration," *The Americas,* October, 1958, pp. 139–158.

autonomy while tending to preserve sentiments of loyalty to the Crown."

Portugal never developed a system comparable to that of Spain. The Council in Lisbon dealt with affairs in Brazil, dividing the country into feudal districts called captaincies in which the proprietor acted as governor. In 1548 a captain general was appointed for the entire province, and in 1763 a viceroy with subordinate captains general under him, succeeded him, with Rio de Janeiro as the seat of government. Here too, a centralizing monarchy strove to control ambitious local oligarchs.[3]

In periods of revolution, the municipalities of South America took things in their own hands. The year 1810 was when revolution got under way. City officials turned to the old medieval practice of "open meetings" of city councils and citizens, and it was the cities, not the nations, that revolted.[4] The wars of independence were largely "municipal affairs."

The new constitutions stressed the powers of provinces and municipalities, but as it turned out, "strong men" took power in their own hands through party organizations. *Caudillismo,* the concentration of authority in the hands of one man, became the bane of Latin American democracy. Coupled with the colonial legacy of centralization and the ideological stimulus of the French image of national centralism, it became an intense nationalism led by the executive, who often was a virtual dictator. The separation-of-powers concept so prominent in the constitutions was disregarded, and in its place came an exaggerated executive dominance over both the legislature and the judiciary, as well as over local government.[5]

The two types of Latin American government—federal and unitary—in terms of local self-government scarcely differ from each other. In unitary states, the President and the Minister of Interior have a firm hold on subdivisions through constitutional sanctions; in federal nations, while states enjoy a modicum of power, the practice of federal intervention is recognized as a legal and common practice. In both, local government is restricted in power, freedom, and financial resources. The President appoints governors, *corregidores, intendentes,* prefects, and

[3] Sweet, *op. cit.*, p. 100.

[4] John J. Johnson, "The Latin American Municipality Deteriorates," *Inter-American Economic Affairs,* Summer, 1950, pp. 24–35.

[5] Jorrin, *op. cit.,* pp. 65–70, 139–140.

even sometimes municipal mayors (*alcaldes*). Provincial assemblies in federal states, or where they exist in unitary nations, have little or no constitutional power and are submerged informally by the executive. The same can be said for elective municipal mayors and councils.[6]

The basic unit of local government in Latin America is the *municipio* or municipality. In most of the nations, municipalities include both urban and rural settlements and cover the entire country. In some states there are subdivisons of the municipalities. For example, Colombia has *corregimientos,* villages with their own magistrates; *veredas,* smaller enclaves; and *barrios,* neighborhoods in urban centers; the last two without corporate status. In Haiti, French influence is shown in the use of the names of *arrondissement* and commune for local units. In Brazil, the subdivision is the *distrito.*

Capital cities of Latin American nations are usually federal districts governed directly by the national Ministry of Interior and are usually without a local legislative body, although in some cases they have special representation in the national legislative body.

While local government is generally subordinate to national authority in Latin American government, there are exceptions and differences. James T. Busey points out, for example, that legislative and judicial independence are highly developed in Uruguay and Chile, and that unquestioned executive dominance is not assured in all important aspects of political life of Argentina, Brazil, Peru, Colombia, and Panama, and even in some of the Central American states.[7] With this in mind, it may be instructive to mention institutions and practices in local government that differ from the norm. In Argentina, *intendentes* appointed by the provincial governors are the executives of the municipality, but in some provinces they are elected by the people or by the municipal council. In Bolivia, while the mayor is appointed by the president, the choice is made from a panel of three persons recommended by the municipal council from their own members, one of whom must represent the

[6] Russell H. Fitzgibbon, IV, "Constitutional Developments in Latin America: A Synthesis," *American Political Science Review,* June, 1945, pp. 511–521. J. Lloyd Mecham, "Latin American Constitution: Nominal or Real," *The Journal of Politics,* May, 1959, pp. 264, 270.

[7] James T. Busey, *Notes on Costa Rican Democracy,* University of Colorado Studies, Series in Political Science, no. 2, Boulder, Colo., February, 1962, pp. 7–8.

minority. In Chile, provincial assemblies are composed of representatives of municipalities. In Costa Rica, provinces are divided into cantons which elect juntas, the members of which are known as *regidores*. In these units there is a considerable degree of local autonomy and "real authority over an important range of local matters." In Ecuador, the elective municipal council of the canton has a large degree of self-government. In El Salvador, the municipalities control the local police, which must be a civil body. In Guatemala, in communities with large Indian populations, there are free elections and considerable independence. In Honduras, municipal government is not a political entity but a corporation of public law, which confines its activities to economic and administrative areas in which it exercises relative independence. In Panama, the inhabitants of a municipality have rights of initiative and referendum in local matters and may change their form of government from strong mayor to commission.[8]

Brazil illustrates the general structure of Latin American local government. There are three levels of government: federal, state, and municipal, the last being the only agency of local government in the nation. There were 2,755 municipalities in 1962, the number showing a great increase since 1950 as a result of state legislative action establishing new municipalities out of subdistricts. Each municipality, including rural as well as urban territory, has a seat of municipal government located in an urban community called the city (*cidade*). Municipalities may be divided into districts, the chief administrator of which is appointed by municipal authority, but districts have little importance in local adminis-

[8] Jorrin, *op. cit.*, pp. 152–161. Austin F. MacDonald, *Latin American Politics and Government*, Thomas Y. Crowell Company, New York, 1954, various chapters on specific countries. Austin F. MacDonald, *Government of the Argentine Republic*, Thomas Y. Crowell Company, New York, 1942, pp. 398–414. Care, Inc., *Colombia Community Development: A Survey Report*, December, 1960, pp. 53–54. Carl L. Donald, "Brazilian Self-government: Myth or Reality," *The Western Political Quarterly*, December, 1960, pp. 1043–1055. Samuel Humes and Eileen M. Martin, *The Structure of Local Governments*, International Union of Local Authorities, Martinus Nijhoff, The Hague, 1961, pp. 342–361. Oliver G. Ricketson, Jr., "Municipal Organization of an Indian Township in Guatemala," *The Geographic Review*, October, 1939, pp. 643–647. William S. Stokes, *Honduras: An Area Study in Government*, The University of Wisconsin Press, Madison, Wis., 1950, pp. 150–181. William P. Tucker, *The Mexican Government Today*, The University of Minnesota Press, Minneapolis, 1957, pp. 391–408. Leonard Cardenas, Jr., *The Municipality in Northern Mexico*, Southwestern Studies, vol. 1, no. 1, Texas Western College Press, El Paso, Tex., 1963.

tration. All municipalities are governed under a mayor-council system. Both mayor and council are elected at large by universal suffrage in partisan elections and with proportional representation so as to give different political parties equitable distribution. In a few states, however, the mayors are appointed by the governors. Terms of both are for four years. The legislative powers of the council are generally broad, and they include functions generally considered "local." Council ordinances are required for tax levies, the annual budget, the establishment of municipal services, personnel regulations, planning and zoning, and tax exemptions. The council may impeach the mayor, audit his annual financial report, and inspect his administrative actions. Local ordinances need no approval from higher authority except for legality. The mayor has entire responsibility for administration including appointment and removal of personnel in accordance with civil service regulations. He may veto ordinances and make proposals to council. While the power to undertake municipal services is broad, in actual practice they appear to be unsatisfactory, especially in rural areas, largely because of limited finances. As a result, the state and national governments have taken over a larger number of functions.[9]

AFRICA

The tremendous surge of African colonies toward independence since World War II has been a major development of twentieth-century world politics. Where it will lead and what will be the final results cannot be foreseen at this time. The continent of Africa has been described as consisting not of twenty or thirty nation-states but of several hundred native tribes in various stages of civilization. It has been estimated that the total population of Africa is 220 million, among which is a sprinkling of Europeans and Asians in varying but small proportions from place to

[9] United Nations Technical Assistance Programme, *Decentralization for National and Local Development,* New York, 1962, pp. 133–140. W. Hoven and A. van den Elshout, *Central Services to Local Authorities,* International Union of Local Authorities (prepared for the United Nations), The Hague, 1962, part 4, pp. B-1 to B-7. *Local Government in the XXth Century,* International Union of Local Authorities, Martinus Nijhoff. The Hague, 1963, pp. 65–74.

place. In 1960, fifteen new states entered the United Nations. These were not necessarily socially indigenous entities, but were rather areas carved out during the last decades of the nineteenth century by the European powers in the mad scramble for spheres of influence, territories, trade concessions, and natural resources. Before this time most of Africa, except for the regions of the north along the Mediterranean littoral and small coastal and island spots in East Africa south of the Persian Gulf, was unorganized in the Western sense. There were tribes, headed by councils of elders and chieftains in various combinations; there were remnants of former barbaric empires; there were millions of people living as close to that "state of nature" dreamt up by eighteenth-century political philosophers as real people in historical times ever got. While African cities, except those on the northern and eastern fringes, are less than fifty years old, urbanization, industrialization, and Europeanization have been proceeding at various paces and already have made substantial inroads into the original patterns of life. Freetown, in Sierra Leone, an exception, was chartered by the British in 1799.

Before 1950, there were four independent nations in Africa: Liberia, an independent republic since 1847; Egypt, now the United Arab Republic, independent since 1922 and a republic since 1953; Ethiopia, an independent empire since time immemorial; and the Union of South Africa, a sovereign member of the British Commonwealth of Nations from 1910 to 1961, but an independent republic now.

Since 1950, the following nations (generally in order from north to south) obtained their national independence. *Tunisia* (1956) had been a French protectorate since 1881 and is now a republic; *Morocco* (1956) had been a French protectorate since 1912, since 1957 a kingdom with the Sultan of Morocco as king; *Algeria* (1962), after 132 years of French rule; *Libya* (1951) had been a former Italian colony whose General Assembly declared for independence in 1949 and whose King Indris proclaimed it two years later; *Sudan* (1956), conquered by Egypt in the 1820s, rebelled in 1874, reconquered by the British and Egyptians and jointly controlled by them until 1951; *Eritrea* (1952), made an autonomous state in a federation with Ethiopia; *Somalia* (1960), formerly Italian Somaliland, in 1949 given to Italian administration as a trust territory under the United Nations, independence voted by the General Assembly; nations of the French Community in French West and Equatorial Africa (*Togo, Mali, Senegal, Dahomey, Niger, Upper Volta, Ivory Coast, Chad, Mauritania, Gabon, Republic of the Congo, Central African Republic,* and *Malagasy Republic*) all achieving independence in 1960; *Nigeria* (1960), British colony and protectorate, has a federal system of three provinces; *Ghana* (1957), British colony and protectorate, the freeing of which gave impetus to the nationalist movement all over Africa; *Guinea* (1958), loosely confederated with Ghana; *Congo* (1960), a Belgian territory; *Sierra Leone* (1961), a British colony; *Tanganyika* (1961), a British territory; *Uganda* (1962), a British protectorate; *Kenya* (1963), a British colony; the republic of *Ruanda* and the kingdom of *Burundi* (1962), Belgian territories; and the *Federal Republic of Cameroun,* joining the French and British Cameroons (1961). The following territories are still within a colonial system of one of the major European powers: Great Britain—*Gambia, Zanzibar, Northern Rhodesia, Southern Rhodesia, Nyasaland, Basutoland, Bechuanaland, Swaziland,* and *Southwest Africa;* Portugal—*Angola, Mozambique,* and *Portuguese Guinea;* France—*French Somaliland,* and *Comoro Islands;* Spain—*Spanish Sahara, Ifni,* and *Spanish Guinea.*

The indigenous governments or political systems of tropical Africa were based upon the chief, the council of elders, and members of the tribe in relationships depending upon circumstance, personality, and tradition. Sometimes the chief was all-powerful, but usually he was not, for the African society did not breed autocrats. Sometimes the chief was little more than *primus inter pares,* and the authority was the chief in council; sometimes there was no chief at all in the sense of politics, leadership being centered upon familial, religious, or magical mores. In some places, the tribes under one chief or council were large and far-flung; there are legends of great empires during the thirteenth and fourteenth centuries that had a complicated structure of provincial governors, administrative staffs, and vassals. More often, the chiefdoms were

[10] *The New York Times,* Jan. 4, 1960; *1963 Britannica Book of the Year,* "Africa," pp. 125–128, 760. *Keesing's Contemporary Archives,* Aug. 17–24, 1963, p. 19592, as reprinted from *The Times,* of London, Aug. 2, 1963.

small and restricted, actually extensions of family or village for which the chief or governing body had original responsibility to protect the people. The chief and other leaders often had secrets of magic and performed ritualistic ceremonies that had come down through the ages to aid them in the assertion of their authority. In smaller tribes and subdivisions, and in villages, meetings of the entire male population were held to decide on matters of general welfare. In some tribes, administrative responsibilities were given to designated age sets, those groups of young men born within a few years of each other, who acted as market policemen, foresters, or road cleaners. Secret societies flourished with all the paraphernalia common to such groups since the dawn of history. Any sudden or violent change in such a civilization, or its method of government, breaks what was a living and homogeneous social unit, possibly crude and simple in form, but self-respecting and energetic, into a mere scattering of human units, despondent and usually corrupt.[11]

British Africa

The evolution of local government in British Africa is illustrated by the developments in Nigeria, a British colony and protectorate. The Royal Niger Company, a trading company operating in Nigeria during the first two decades of exploration and occupation, turned over to the British Crown its charter and political rights in return for compensation for private rights. The date of this event was January 1, 1900. Sixty years later on October 1, 1960, Nigeria achieved full independence and became the twelfth independent member of the British Commonwealth of Nations.

Nigeria was first administered by a governor and three lieutenant governors—one for the northern provinces, one for the southern, and one for the colony of Nigeria. The governor was assisted by an executive committee made up of members of his staff. Beginning in 1923, two units of the federation, the southern provinces and the colony of Nigeria, were granted a legislative council which was partly elective but contained a majority of government members. The council included representatives

[11] David F. Carney, *Government and Economy in British West Africa*, Bookman Associates, New York, 1961, p. 54.

from nongovernmental organizations and from the otherwise unrepresented African population.[12]

Lord Lugard developed the practice of "indirect rule" as a British administrative policy which began in Northern Nigeria about 1900 and lasted to 1950. It spread to other parts of British Africa. It was based upon the use of native authorities for the purpose of governmental administration of the native peoples. While it was much to be preferred to the "direct rule" used by other powers, if it were to be assumed that native African institutions were valuable and could by evolutionary methods be improved, it posed a number of problems which gave increasing cause for apprehension, and which later led to its abandonment in favor of democratic institutions fashioned on British models.

In Northern Nigeria, the emirs were recognized as integral parts of the governmental machinery but as Lugard stated, the government insisted upon their observance of the "fundamental laws of humanity and justice." An emir who proved unamenable was deposed and another recognized by the people was put in his place. The British residents and district officers were not expected to be executives, but rather sympathetic guides and supervisors directing the path of native institutions to efficiency and democracy by evolutionary methods. Sometimes the institution of "sole native authorities," that is, the emirs or chiefs of the tribe, so recognized by the British, was completely alien to the indigenous institutions where a chief always ruled with a council. The "sole native authorities" system favored the illiterate, conservative, and reactionary chiefs at the expense of the more educated elements which were increasing from year to year. In other parts of Nigeria and in some other areas of British Africa, the existence of strong traditional authorities such as chiefs in council or councils without chiefs, or the absence of central native authorities such as the emirs of the northern territories, constituted an obstacle to a unified administrative structure. The success of indirect rule depended upon an overall, accepted native authority through which the British colonial system could work.

The main criticism leveled at government by native authorities was that the implied assumptions under which it was supposed to work

[12] Royal Institute of International Affairs, *Nigeria, the Political and Economic Background,* London, 1960. *Encyclopaedia Britannica,* vol. 16, pp. 441–442.

were at least partially wrong. Sometimes there was no chief with the kind of authority British officials wanted or needed, and so administrative functions were not carried out, but devolved upon the British colonial staff which as a rule was too small in number for the tasks to be done. Furthermore, "progress" was not an impelling motive either for the chiefs or their constituents, with the exception of the ever-increasing educated elite and those members of tribes who were dissociated from their tribes by the urban and industrial opportunities in the towns. Likewise, the objective of more democracy was not actively sought by the chiefs, who had no desire to broaden the base of authority. Again, positive powers and functions that were allowed, including the building of public works, became the responsibility of the colonial district officers, who did the planning and directing of such activities to the point where "indirect rule" became more and more "direct rule." [13]

An integral part of indirect rule was the manner in which law and order was maintained. In the early states of British occupation, it involved the suppression of tribal conflicts and slave raiding. Later, as these practices died down, order was secured largely by the system by which the native community policed itself. Only the major types of crime were dealt with by the colonial government police force, which was usually a small agency, and the great majority of breaches of the peace and violations of law were dealt with through the native authority police or tribal messengers. The assessment and collection of the native tax, which was viewed by the British as an important part of the education of the native population in the practice of local government, was also a part of the responsibilities of native administration, as was the growing provision of local services in the fields of education, health, and agricultural development which supplemented provincial activities. Such functions as the provisions of markets, the establishment of minor roads, local water supply, and the promotion of local industries had always been strictly local in character.[14]

[13] L. Gray Cowan, *Local Government in West Africa,* Columbia University Press, New York, 1958, pp. 1–13, 23–31. D. Cameron and B. K. Cooper, *The West African Councillor,* Oxford University Press, Fair Lawn, N.J., 1954.

[14] Lord Malcolm Hailey, *Native Administration in the British African Territories,* part 4, "A General Survey of the System of Native Administration," Colonial Office, London, Her Majesty's Stationery Office, 1951, pp. 1–5.

The problems arising out of indirect rule and the general evolution of the African political picture led British authorities to propose radical changes in their colonial policies. Increased political interest and participation in government by Africans was accepted as desirable, and so was the provision of new social services necessitated by the changing mode of living brought on by Western civilization. As a result of this changed attitude, for example, the Native Authority Law of 1945 for Northern Nigeria established a chain of councils for all levels of government. At the bottom, the village councils remained as semitraditional informal gatherings of citizens and as electoral colleges for district councilors. In places with compact populations, district councilors were elected directly by the people. The next higher level was the district council, which carried on functions and activities dictated by their education and interest. These served also as electoral colleges for the native authority councils, the next higher rung in the administrative ladder. The relationship between these native authorities and the British colonial government was that British residents and district officers might examine, record, tender advice, and attend meetings, but have no vote. While Nigerian local government was consciously modeled on the English council system, the existence of a network of centrally appointed officials suggested the French rather than the English system.

The standard administrative pattern of all councils was that the paid staff formed the nucleus and the elected representatives the majority; the former executed, the latter advised. Normally control of native authority administrative departments was exercised through the full-time salaried councilors who were the equivalent of cabinet officers with portfolios and with whom a committee of the council could be associated only in an advisory capacity. Election to these councils was by several methods: by acclamation, the most widespread and traditional method, used especially in villages; by show of hands, the more formal method; or by electors grouping themselves behind the candidate of their choice. In the more educated areas the secret, written ballot was used. In council voting there was a general preference for arriving at a decision acceptable to all rather than asking for a vote which would be decided by a majority. As things worked out, literate Africans were becoming the mainstays on the councils. Under the revised system of local government, the British governor remained the ultimate authority for the establishment of native authorities, and the day-by-day relations between the British regional government and the native authorities were under the jurisdiction of the Minister of Local Government. A council was established by an instrument which specified its composition and functions, and all chartered councils had to have a majority of elected members. Another new institution, one that had a striking resemblance to the English system of co-option, was an "outer council" composed of elected representatives from district councils and nominated educated members, which acted as an advisory body to native authorities. Furthermore, in urban areas, urban councils were established to take care of the local government needs of these newly developed areas.[15]

In other parts of British Africa there was the same general trend toward more democracy and self-government at the local level with some differences from place to place: Eastern and Western Nigeria, the Gold Coast, Kenya, Nyasaland, Uganda, and Tanganyika.[16]

There was one exception, South Africa. Local government history in the Union of South Africa began in 1682, thirty years after Jan van Riebeeck landed on the Cape of Good Hope, but it was confined almost entirely to the Cape until the middle of the nineteenth century. The background of these institutions was pre-Napoleonic Dutch and British. The landdrost and heemraaden were first established by the Dutch East India Company. The office of heemraad was created in thirteenth-

[15] "A Review of the State of Development of the Native Authority System in the Northern Region of Nigeria on the 1st of January, 1955," prepared by the Minister of Local Government, Northern Region, Nigeria, *Journal of African Administration,* April, 1955, pp. 77–86.

[16] E. C. Alderton, "Developments in Local Government in the Eastern Region of Nigeria," *Journal of African Administration,* October, 1956, pp. 169–179. J. D. Livingston Booth, District Officer, "Oiling the Wheels of Local Government in Eastern Nigeria," *Journal of African Administration,* April, 1955, pp. 55–64. Simon Ottenberg, "Comments on Local Government in Afikpo Division, South Eastern Nigeria," *Journal of African Administration,* January, 1956, pp. 3–10. R. E. Brown, "Local Government in the West Region of Nigeria, 1950–1955," *Journal of African Administration,* October, 1955, pp. 180–188. St. J. J. Hannigan, "Local Government in the Gold Coast," *Journal of African Administration,* July, 1955, pp. 116–123. M. N. Evans, "Local Government in the African Area of Kenya," *Journal of African Administration,* July, 1955, pp. 125–127. H. G. Graham-Jolly, "Progress of Local Government in Nyasaland," *Journal of African Administration,* October, 1955, pp. 188–192. Dr. J. Gus Liebenow, "Some Problems in Introducing Local Government Reform in Tanganyika," *Journal of African Administration,* July, 1956, pp. 132–139.

century Holland to form a lower court, and the landdrost had for a long time been a rural district agent of higher authority in judicial, police, civil, and military affairs.[17] The most important development in local government history in South Africa was the Municipal Ordinance of 1838. While it continued many of the established practices, it changed the system from Dutch to English. Municipalities could be established by any group of householders, who then were empowered to draft regulations to be approved by the governor. Commissioners, to be elected by the householders for three-year terms, were given power to appoint police and watchmen; to provide fire engines, lighting systems, roads and streets, water systems, and other public works; to establish markets, abate public nuisances, regulate common pasture land, and enforce other regulations for the general welfare of the community. They could also appoint a treasurer and a rate collector, and were authorized to levy taxes on immovable property. This ordinance became a model for local government throughout South Africa. Self-government was accepted as the basis for local administration. The ordinance separated the judicial functions from the municipality.

The Natal Municipal Government Ordinance of 1854 borrowed much from the English Municipal Corporations Act of 1835. It constituted the inhabitants of the town a corporate body, provided for a mayor, a town clerk and auditors, and established the committee system for council. Taxation was to be by the town council instead of a public meeting. Some changes were made since its adoption, but the general outlines established during the early nineteenth century for municipal government were along English lines, while earlier Dutch practices in rural government remained basic. The system was characterized by continuity of form and practice, self-determination, variety of functions, financial independence, and voluntary service. Local government in South Africa, however, applied only to the European minority of the population. The policy of *apartheid,* whereby this European minority constituted the nation of South Africa, excluded the native colored peoples from participation. South African policy, at least

[17] L. P. Green, *History of Local Government in South Africa,* Juta and Co. Ltd., Capetown, South Africa, 1957, pp. 2–3.

in theory, calls for the colored races to form their own national state.[18]

French Africa

France, having rapidly acquired large territories in Africa during the later decades of the nineteenth century and being a unitary state, organized its colonies under a Governor responsible to the Minister of Colonies in Paris. The area being large, the territories were grouped in two federations, French West Africa and French Equatorial Africa.[19] Each territory in the federation had its own administration, and at the head of all the territories was a Governor General.

The French system of colonial administration was from the beginning "direct rule" in contrast to the British system of using traditional authorities. This was partly because military force had been required to reduce the chiefs within the territories, partly because France had been since the days of Napoleon an aggressively unitary state, but also because "assimilation" had been always a constant policy in French colonial administration. This meant not only that there should be a constant imposition of French culture upon colonial peoples, but also that these colonials should be freed from slavery and enjoy the same rights gained by all French citizens at the time of the French Revolution. One of the by-products of this concept was that there was never any formal color line in French African territories. While the concept of assimilation began to find theoretical and practical opposition as far as colonial policy was concerned, another concept, that of "association," came into being. By this was meant cooperation between colonial administration and native political bodies to provide the leadership to guide Africa along the path of civilization.

Centralization of administration in Paris characterized the French system. The Governor General of the federation, reporting to the Minister

[18] *Ibid.*, pp. 16–21, 90–97. E. P. Erasmus, "The Policy of Apartheid," *African Affairs,* January, 1961, pp. 56–65.

[19] French West Africa included Senegal, French Guinea, Ivory Coast, Dahomey, French Sudan, Upper Volta, Niger, and Mauritania; French Equatorial Africa included Middle Congo, Gabon, Ubangi-Shari, and Chad. In addition, two trust territories, Cameroun and Togoland, were given to France.

of the Colonies, was the supreme head of the government, and it was through him that communications of the lieutenant governors of the provinces and their administrations were channeled. At the local level, the territories were divided into *cercles* and subdivisions, or regions and districts, in which an administrator was supreme. Except for a very small number of civil service posts, the educated African elite created by the policies of assimilation and association found no place in the centralized governmental structure for their services.[20]

Thus, in French Tropical Africa there was little local government. The exception to this was found in certain municipalities. In Senegal, three municipalities—Dakar, Rufisque, and Saint-Louis—were established in 1872, and in 1884 the French municipal law was extended to them. Councils were elected by universal suffrage, and the mayor and his assistant were elected by council. The French colonial administration supervised them. Their main source of revenue was the *octroi de mer,* which they divided with the territorial government. In some other parts of Senegal, there were "mixed" local authorities where councils were appointed by the administration or elected by the people, and in 1947 the Governor General was authorized, after consulting the territorial assembly, to establish such *communes de moyen exercice.* But in rural areas there were no popularly elected councils except a few established in Cameroun and Togoland after 1952. There were, however, advisory councils of notables appointed by administrative officers who chaired these councils.

The issues at stake in local government in French Africa were the granting of full municipal government in urban areas, the need for more representative and efficient government, and the position of the native chiefs in colonial administration.[21]

A most important French colonial development was the formation of the French Community which came into being with the promulgation of the Constitution of the Fifth Republic on October 5, 1958. This included the French Republic itself, and 19 overseas departments, including 13 in Algeria and 2 in Sahara; 11 member states in Africa which

[20] Cowan, *op. cit.,* pp. 35–61.

[21] Kenneth Robinson, "Local Government Reform in French Tropical Africa," *Journal of African Administration,* October, 1956, pp. 179–185.

in 1960 obtained full independence within the Community; and the French Southern and Antarctic overseas territories. The president of the French Republic is the president of the French Community. Other official organs are an executive committee consisting of the heads of government of all member states, the ministers of the central government responsible for colonial affairs, a senate formed of delegates of the national assemblies of the member states, and a court of arbitration. In 1960, the French Constitution was amended to allow the new states to become independent states within the Community.

Belgian Congo

King Leopold II of Belgium called a conference of the leading European powers in Brussels in 1876 for the purpose of exploring and civilizing Africa. At that time the International Association of the Congo was founded, and in 1885, after a conference with the great powers, with the sanction of the Belgian legislature, King Leopold assumed leadership of the new independent state of Congo. After some international agitation about conditions in the Congo, it became a Belgian colony in 1905, which it remained until granted independence in 1960.

From the foundation of the International Association, treaties were made with various native authorities including heads of families, tribal chiefs, and powerful chieftains ruling as sultans. The main colonizing task was to secure effective occupation of the vast country. Once the Congo state and its government were established, many Congo chiefs recognized their authority. In 1891, a decree was promulgated which formulated rules for the governing of the native population through "invested" chiefs who, having original tribal authority, were confirmed by the government. In 1906, a second decree established the *chefferie* as an administrative subdivision and delegated to its chief a small part of the authority of the state. In 1910, a third decree extended the jurisdiction of the *chefferie* to cover the entire Congo population, but many of the chiefs proved either too weak or incapable of providing leadership to obtain improved social and economic conditions. In 1933, a fourth decree created *secteurs* as artificial communities within the *chefferies* to develop their own native authorities or traditional social organizations. Furthermore, concentrations of native populations around the new

European towns and settlements led to the promulgation of a royal decree in 1931 to set up extracustomary centers with municipal organizations, and in 1945, native cities were granted full organizations for local government.

The administration of native areas under the 1933 decree was directed toward regulating the movement and registration of the native population. The native authorities governed the *chefferies* by native custom subject to public law and statutory provisions. The native chief was invested by the Belgian district commissioner, and the *secteur* was placed under the authority of a *secteur* chief, assisted by a native council mandated by legislation. The *secteur* chiefs and their assistants were selected by the district commissioner, their offices acting as intermediaries between the Belgian government and the native peoples. They were paid salaries from the colonial budget.

The administration machinery of extracustomary centers, where Africans detached from tribal organizations lived, was modeled after that of the native areas. The centers were administered by a chief and an advisory council appointed by the district commissioner and chaired by a representative of Belgian authority. The administration of native cities, Leopoldville for example, was headed by native authorities appointed and removed by the district commissioner. The Governor General was granted the power to remove any area from its normal district and make an urban area, granting it the status of a town. The urban area then was governed by a district commissioner who presided over an urban committee composed of eight persons of Belgian nationality appointed for two years and with advisory powers only. The administration was empowered to impose local taxes with the approval of the provincial governor.[22]

Northern Africa

Tunisia was established as a protectorate of France under a resident general in 1883. The Bey remained head of the nation but delegated

[22] Ministry of Colonies, Brussels, Belgium, "The Organization of Native Administration in the Belgian Congo," *Journal of African Administration,* April, 1956, pp. 88–95.

foreign affairs and internal order to the French. In 1956 Tunisia became independent, and in 1957 the Bey was deposed and a republic proclaimed. The Municipal Law of 1957 governs urban municipalities, which number 112. Each municipality has a council ranging from six to thirty members, depending on the population and the tax base. They are elected by a majority vote of all citizens over twenty years of age to serve three-year terms. The executive is the mayor, who is aided by two to six deputies serving as a board. All are elected by the council from its membership. The mayor is both the agent of the state in the municipality and the executive of the local unit. He is the police chief, but the police are employees of the central government. There is extensive central control through the Ministry of the Interior, the provincial governor, and the Secretary of Finance. Local legislation may be declared null and void, many local decisions must receive prior approval, a council may be suspended or dissolved, and its members may be dismissed. Rural Tunisia is organized into basic units called *cheikhats* headed by a *cheik* who is appointed by the Minister of Interior from a list of three nominated by an assembly of electors of the unit, which consists of all adults over twenty years of age. This headman has financial, police, and judicial duties. He is the liaison between the local citizens and the central government. Here again the central government exercises strict control. Directly below the central government are fourteen provinces each composed of four to ten districts. The chief executive is the governor, who is assisted by an administrative council appointed by the central government for three-year terms. The governor may have assistants who head the districts.[23]

Morocco became a French protectorate in 1912, having been recognized as being within the French sphere of influence since 1904. The government has been a constitutional monarchy since 1962 under a King who is also the highest religious authority. There is also a chamber of elected representatives. Since 1960, urban and rural communes have had elected councils. These councils have general competence of decision and advice, but the decisions must be approved by the governor and the Minister of Interior. The president of the council has some executive

[23] Humes and Martin, *op. cit.*, pp. 362–366.

powers, but the pasha who is the agent of the Minister of Interior is in control of the police. The kingdom has 16 provinces, 2 prefectures, and 800 urban and rural communes. Each province is divided into three to five *cercles,* and each *cercle* into two or three *caidats,* and each *caidat* into two or three communes. The two prefectures are the cities of Rabat-Salé and Casablanca, headed by prefects. All large cities are divided into districts; Casablanca has 14, each headed by a caliph appointed by the governor. The Minister of Interior is the chief overseer of local government.[24]

In *Libya,* there is a federal government with three provinces, each headed by a vali who is appointed and may be removed by the King. Libya, an Italian colony since 1912, was constituted as an independent state in 1951 by action of the United Nations. The national government has a bicameral legislature, and each province has an appointive council and an elected legislative assembly. Before 1962, the national and provincial government divided governmental powers between them, but in that year constitutional changes were made which gave a large share of the provincial powers away to the national government.[25]

Senegal has seven regions with a regional assembly elected by universal suffrage, and a governor representing the central government. He is assisted by a deputy in charge of development activities and by the inspector of the regional technical services, both of whom are members of the Regional Development Committee. Within each region there are three to six *cercles,* headed by a commandant who reports to the regional governor. Its officials are responsible for the technical services within the *cercle,* but there is no *cercle* council or assembly. The basic administrative district is the *arrondissement,* the jurisdiction which coincides with the Rural Development Center. The chief of the *arrondissement* is the administrator, while the Rural Development Council organizes the work of community development in the area. At the base are the villages grouped around a central village in rural communities, the local basic

[24] Henry Mourer, *Les Problèmes Administratifs de l'Urbanisation au Maroc,* United Nations, Department of Economic and Social Affairs, Document no. 15, Rabat, January, 1962, pp. 15–16.

[25] *The Constitution of Libya,* the Official Gazette of the United Kingdom of Libya, English translation, the Government Printer, Tripoli, October, 1951. Amendments to the constitution as reported in *Trablus el Ghach,* Dec. 9, 1962.

authority which coincides with the cooperatives which are the basic cells of economic development.[26]

Liberia and Ethiopia

Local government institutions in Liberia have a distinctly American nomenclature although basically they are much like those in British Africa, complete with native authorities. The national government, established as it was under American sponsorship and encouragement, is headed by a President, elected for a term of eight years, and a bicameral legislature. The President is assisted by a cabinet in which there is a Minister of Interior under whom all local government institutions function. First of all, there are five counties and three provinces, the former in charge of a superintendent and the latter under a provincial commissioner. These are responsible to the Minister of Interior but are appointed directly by the President. Advisory councils, composed of the paramount chiefs in the jurisdiction and several elders, assist the superintendents and commissioners.

In each county there are five districts, headed by a county commissioner, who is appointed by the President but recommended by the Minister of Interior. Here too there is an advisory council, made up of paramount chiefs and elders. Within each district there are a number of chiefdoms, headed by a paramount chief, appointed by the President upon recommendation by the Minister of Interior, holding office for a term of four years. An advisory council of the chiefdom is made up of clan chiefs and elders. Within the chiefdoms are clans which are headed by clan chiefs elected by the people, and an advisory council made up of elders. While there are villages within this smallest jurisdiction, they have no legal status although their informal leadership is represented on the clan advisory council.

Elections are conducted by secret ballot. Most of the subordinate personnel both in the national government and in the local units are under civil service protection and regulations.[27]

The ancient empire of Ethiopia is governed under an Emperor, assisted

[26] United Nations Technical Assistance Programme, *Decentralization for National and Local Development, op. cit.,* pp. 175–178.

[27] From a conversation with Hon. John P. Onumah, Special Commissioner on Government Operations, government of Liberia.

by a number of ministries and a council of elders of the Crown. The country is divided into 12 provinces and Eritrea. There are 74 subprovinces which contain 360 districts which in turn are divided into 1,112 subdistricts. All units are directly responsible to the Emperor through his Minister of Interior.

There are two classes of municipalities, some of whose members are appointed by the provincial governor and some elected by municipal immovable-property holders. The chief executive is a mayor (*kantiba*) or a director, appointed by the Emperor, who reports to the Minister of Interior. Villages have headmen who are the Emperor's agents but also the village leaders. Some are hereditary, others appointed by the provincial governor, but generally they are approved by the villagers themselves.[28]

[28] Humes and Martin, *op. cit.*, pp. 405–410.

3 The Evolution of Form and Structure: The Near and the Middle East

WHEN THE REPUBLIC of Turkey was proclaimed on October 29, 1923, the Ottoman Empire, for more than five centuries a world power including many races and nations on three continents, finally disappeared into the pages of history. There were many factors that contributed to its dissolution, chief of which were the governmental incompetence of the sultanate during the nineteenth century and the rising pressure for westernization both from within and from without the empire. The end of World War I in which the Ottoman Empire allied itself with Germany and Austria-Hungary was the death knell. The victorious Allies, great and small, were poised for the dismemberment of the dying colossus. Only the energy of the Young Turks, led by the incomparable Mustafa Kemal Pasha (Kemal Atatürk), saved Turkey proper. Most of the remainder of the empire was broken down into small states, mandated by the League of Nations to France and England or brought within their sphere of influence.

Government under the Ottoman Empire was far different from that of Western Europe. The empire was not a nation in the Western sense but an amalgamation of separate and often hostile peoples under the military sway of a dominant race, the Ottoman Turks. Theoretically, the whole empire was under the personal control of the sultan, who was also caliph or the successor to the Prophet Mohammed, and as such the spiritual head of most of the Moslem world, even of some parts outside the political boundaries of the empire. Thus he carried on the traditions of absolutism implicit in the earlier Arabian caliphate, and in the Byzantine, Roman, and Persian Empires which preceded it as political rulers of the Near and Middle East. It was not only during the five centuries of Ottoman hegemony that the area was governed by all-powerful rulers; absolutism as an accepted governmental concept goes back in an unbroken chain to the dawn of history.

The governmental organization of the empire, centralized as it was, flowed from the person of the sultan through a complicated hierarchy. Three main officials, structured in the form of a triangle, headed the organization. At the apex was the ruler's general deputy called grand vezir. Of the other two principals, one was in charge of correspondence, documents, commands, and regulations; the other supervised revenues and expenditures. The grand vezir was the sultan's "absolute representative" although he had no direct authority over the sultan's household or over the "learned doctors" who were the interpreters of Islamic religious law. He controlled all appointments to the army, the central government, and the provinces, and was also the sultan's chief dispenser of justice. From these three top administrators downward there existed an imposing array of officials that the extensive empire needed to keep law and order and to carry on its multifarious activities.

The empire was divided into administrative districts called eyalets governed by an official called vezir, bey, or emir, as the case might be. When the empire was at its most extensive, there were thirty-six such districts. But while he was the sultan's representative, his authority was not all-embracing, for the Sacred Law (Sharia) was administered by kadis who were judges of the province, and financial matters were handled by special officers independent of the governor, reporting directly to the grand vezir. For it was the constant fear of the sultans and the central government that the provincial governors would usurp their powers, so that checks and balances within the provinces were standard operating procedures.

In general, the Ottoman provincial administration recognized existing institutions of various localities and enclaves where possible and did not seek to reform or revolutionize them. Its main interest was to keep the peace and to collect taxes and revenues to finance the imperial establishment. Each provincial government had to pay its own way in addition to delivering an equitable amount to the central treasury. The village communes of the settled rural population, the tribal organization of the nomad Arabs and Kurds, and the occupational guilds of the towns were recognized by the central administration as the duly constituted local authorities. Non-Moslem peoples within the empire, although not accepted as equals to the Moslems, had the right to have their own religion, language, and courts. In the best days of the empire, Ottoman administration was eminently successful; the accepted policies and objects of government were simplicity of administration, light taxation, and the general welfare of the subjects. As the empire declined, the rule became corrupt, inefficient, and tyrannical, depending on the character of the provincial officials.[1]

During the nineteenth century, Western influences made themselves felt in the governmental system within the Ottoman Empire. The emerging new order called for a modern state, and during the first decades of the century there was only one new model, the French system with its four-tier hierarchy of departments, *arrondissements,* cantons, and communes. In 1820, Egypt was subdivided into four levels: *mudiriyyah, markaz, qism,* and village. Between 1840 and 1860, Ottoman lands were divided into vilayets, *kazas, nahiyes,* and villages.[2] Comparable officials such as the prefect and the mayor went with the system.

The great advantage of such a system in the Near and Middle East

[1] H. A. R. Gibb and Harold Bowen, *Islamic Society and the West,* vol. 1, *Islamic Society in the Eighteenth Century,* Oxford University Press, Fair Lawn, N.J., 1950.

[2] W. Hardy Wickwar, "The Pattern and Problems of Local Administration in the Middle East," *Middle East Journal,* Summer, 1958, pp. 249–260. These subdivisions had different names in different parts of the empire: vilayets were called *liwas* and *muhafazahs* in Arab countries; while *kazas* were called *quadas,* and *nahiyes* were called *nahiyyahs* there.

after the disintegration of the Ottoman Empire was that it allowed the national authority at the top to make itself felt in every local community through an unbroken chain of command. This was especially important because the new nations needed the stability of a unitary government to make firm their existence and continuity. The new national governments were Western institutions; they helped to steer their people to the Western way of life. The provincial and other local officials were appointed by the central government and were responsible for local government in the centralized state. In fact, these nations were often more centralized than was France.

So far it has been difficult to establish elective councils in villages of the Near and Middle East. W. Hardy Wickwar observes that there is always a traditional or customary council of elders, tribal chieftains, or familial authorities who have survived as settlers of disputes, promoters of local projects, and leaders of opinion. But central government officials prefer to work with agents appointed by them who will carry out ministerial directives rather than with the traditional councils. Legally, these councils and local authorities have no existence, and so have no statutory responsibilities. Central governments have established villages of local units on an arbitrary and synthetic basis for the administration of specified functions. Thus, in Egypt before 1960 there were 3,878 fiscal villages under the Ministry of Finance, 4,034 police villages under the Ministry of Interior, and 4,651 sanitation villages under the Ministry of Health.

TURKEY

The Constitution of the Republic of Turkey, adopted January 10, 1945, divides the nation into vilayets, the vilayets into *kazas*, the *kazas* into *nahiyes* which are made up of *kasabas* and villages.[3]

In the vilayets (provinces), numbering 63, a governor, a general provincial assembly, and a permanent provincial council govern. The governor (vali) is the executive representative of the central government on one hand, and the chief representative of the province on the other. He is appointed by the Minister of the Interior. The members of the general

[3] Helen Miller Davis, *Constitutions, Electoral Laws, Treaties of States in the Near and Middle East,* rev. ed., The Duke University Press, Durham, N.C., 1953, p. 462.

provincial assembly are elected from districts. The permanent council, the executive committee, is a body of four elected once a year by the provincial assembly from its own members and presided over by the governor.[4] The districts (*kazas*), numbering 498, are the administrative subdivisions of the provinces, headed by deputy governors (*kaymakams*) appointed by the central government. The commune (*nahiye*) is a lower administrative unit of the central government but is not to be confused with municipalities or villages. The commune is made up of a number of villages. Its governing authority is a communal director, the mudir, appointed by the governor of the province and subject to confirmation by the Minister of Interior. There is a communal assembly chosen for four-year terms by a communal committee composed of elected officials of villages and hamlets. A communal council, composed of four members with the communal director as president, and permanent members including a doctor, an agriculturist, a teacher, and a school director, acts as an executive body. The commune is the lowest level of the central government hierarchy and to it the central ministries assign doctors, veterinarians, agriculturists, and other technicians.[5]

The Turkish village (*koy*) is governed under the village code adopted in 1924; it is a community with less than 2,000 population. There are about 40,000 villages in Turkey.[6] The basic village authority is the village assembly composed of every man and woman over eighteen years of age who has lived in the village for six months or more. This body meets from time to time to discuss village problems and determine village policies; to elect the village headman (mukhtar), the religious leader (imam), and the members of the council of elders, from five to twelve depending upon the size of the village; and to fix salaries of village employees and make other similar decisions. The council of elders is presided over by the headman, elected for a four-year term, who is the executive both of the village assembly and the council of elders, and makes known the new laws and regulations of the central government. He also has duties regarding the registration of births and deaths, conscription, national taxes, and like re-

[4] Turkish Information Office, *Self-government in Turkey*, pp. 16–19.

[5] Orba F. Traylor, *Turkish Local Government and Methods of Financing*, 1951, Economic Cooperation Administration, memorandum of Sept. 12, 1951, Athens, Greece.

[6] Wickwar, *op. cit.*

sponsibilities.[7] There are, in addition, thousands of settlements which are not villages in a legal sense, having customary rather than statutory councils.

More than 600 communities of 2,000 or more population are organized as municipalities (*belediyes*). They are administered by a mayor, a municipal advisory commission, and a municipal council whose members are elected directly from the people for a four-year term. The mayor is appointed by the governor of the province except in capital cities where he is appointed by the central authorities.[8]

IRAN AND AFGHANISTAN

The Fundamental Laws of Iran, dated December 30, 1906, contain no reference to provincial and local government, but in the Supplementary Fundamental Laws of October 7, 1907, amended December 12, 1925, Article 29, there is the following declaration: "The special interests of each province, department and district shall be arranged and regulated, in accordance with special laws on this subject, by provincial and departmental councils (*anjumans*)." Articles 90 to 93 declare that throughout the nation *anjumans* shall be established, the members to be elected by the people, and that they are free to exercise supervision "over all reforms connected with public advantage," always providing that they stay within the limits of the law, and publish full accounts of their expenditures and receipts.[9] However, to date no attempts have been made to establish such councils.

The law of 1937 establishes a four-tier provincial and local government structure with 10 *ostans,* plus separate governorates for Teheran, the capital city, and for Persian Baluchistan. The *ostans* are divided into 92 *sharistans,* which are in turn divided into *bakhshs,* which are made up of a number of villages (*dehs*) and towns. The chief administrator for the

[7] Turkish Information Office, *op. cit.,* pp. 5–6.

[8] Tahir Aktan, "The Basic Structure: Provincial Administration and Local Self-government," *Studies in Turkish Local Government,* Public Administration Institute for Turkey and the Middle East, Ankara, 1955, pp. 15–33. See also Fatma Mansur, "Foundations of Turkish Local Government," *ibid.,* pp. 5–13, for a lucid exposition of the theoretical and practical bases for centralization of authority in the Turkish state. *Local Government in the XXth Century,* International Union of Local Authorities, Martinus Nijhoff, The Hague, 1963, pp. 392–393.

[9] Davis, *op. cit.,* pp. 121, 127.

ostan is the *ostandar,* who is the governor general, appointed by the Minister of Interior. His staff is made up largely of representatives from the central ministries within his province. The *sharistan* is governed under a *fermandar,* and the *bakhsh* under a *bakhshdar.* Both these officials are representatives of the central government appointed by higher authority and approved finally by the Minister of Interior and the Council of Ministers.

On the village level, the *dehar* is the national representative in a rural district (*dehistan*) and may act for a number of villages, while the *kadkhoda,* who must be among the permanent residents of the village, is appointed upon recommendation of the landlord whom he represents. Both these local officials are appointed by order of the *bakhshdar* and *fermandar,* proceeding in the regular chain of command. The *kadkhoda* may be dismissed at the request of the landlord.

There are administrative councils for the first three levels of government—*ostans, sharistans,* and *bakhshs*—made up of officers of the central government located in the particular jurisdiction, but in the *bakhsh,* a required number of landlords and farmers are added. The scope of powers of these councils presided over by the executive officer in each jurisdiction is broad and sweeping, but higher-level control virtually stops all local initiative. The *fermandar* and the *bakhshdar* direct and control both the *kadkhoda* and village *dehar.*[10]

In 1954 under the terms of a law proclaimed by Premier Mossadegh, village councils, the membership of which was appointed by the landlords and the *bakhshdars,* were authorized to be established for purposes of community development. The 1956 census reported that out of 3,501 villages in six census districts (there are 49,000 villages in all of Iran) 41 per cent had village councils. These, of course, were not councils in the strict sense of the word for they had no corporate status, could not raise revenue by taxation, and were not elective. They were, in fact, village development or agricultural societies established under terms of a limiting statute.

Cities and towns, those settlements over 5,000 population, have their own administration headed by a mayor appointed by the Minister of

[10] *The Law of the State Territorial Divisions and the Functions of Fermandars and Bakhshdars,* Alban 16, 1316 (1937).

Interior, and an "elective" council, which may be, and often is, appointed by the same minister.

Afghanistan became a separate and independent state in 1747, but until the accession of Amanullah in 1919, the government was an absolute monarchy. Since then certain democratic institutions and practices evolved, but overall power still rests with the king and his immediate advisers. The present constitution was adopted in 1931 and amended in 1933. It sets up in the chief town of each governor's province an advisory committee of which the mode of election, the number of members, and the duties are subject to regulations of the government. The constitution also declares that the principle of administration of the provinces is based on three fundamental rules: delegation of authority, allotment of duties, and fixation of responsibility. The provincial civil servants are posted to each province from each central ministry separately, and each of these is held responsible to his superior. Furthermore, the formation of municipalities and their duties are to be governed by a special code.[11]

For administrative purposes, Afghanistan is divided into nine provinces, each in charge of a governor, and each is subdivided into districts (*hakumat*). The governor is assisted by local officials in charge of revenue, justice, communications, etc. The ten largest towns are controlled by municipal committees headed by a president.[12]

THE ARAB STATES

Covering most of the area of Arab states, including municipalities, are the local administrative units of the national government: provinces, districts, subdistricts, and villages. Exception must be made of the large areas occupied by nomad tribes, which are governed by their traditional leaders, the sheikhs and councils of elders. Furthermore, many of the larger cities are also provinces where municipal and national functions are carried on by one governmental unit. This pattern is a legacy of the nineteenth-century Ottoman Empire, which copied the French system of local organization as part of its move toward westernization.

[11] *Fundamental Principles of the Government of Afghanistan,* Oct. 31, 1931, with Addendum, Feb. 22, 1933, Articles 71–72, 102–105, from Davis, *op. cit.,* pp. 4–17.

[12] *Encyclopaedia Britannica,* vol. 1, p. 286.

Iraq, Lebanon, Syria, and *Jordan* have almost identical units of local administration with, however, slightly different nomenclature. The province and its governor dominate the local scene. The governor is an appointee of the central government either by the chief executive or the Minister of Interior or of Local Government, as the case may be. In Iraq there is a provincial council, partly appointed, partly elective, with limited powers; in the other three states there is none. Under the province is the district, also headed by a national appointee who reports to the governor, and below the district is a subdistrict (except in Lebanon) whose chief is also nationally appointed and responsible to the next higher level. The fourth or bottom layer is the village or group of contiguous villages, with a chief and sometimes a local council, elective in Lebanon and Syria but mostly appointed in Iraq and Jordan. None of these units have legal personality, and they must be considered as local units of the national administration.[13]

Municipal government is sometimes independent of the national units of local administration, and sometimes a part of them. For example, in Beirut, the capital city of Lebanon, the boundaries of the province and the municipality are identical, and the governor of the province is also mayor of the city. In the other capitals, Damascus, Baghdad, and Amman, while the mayor or chief of administration is not a provincial governor, he reports directly to the national ministry in charge of local government. The municipal council is generally dominated by the administrator and has few powers of its own. The control of municipalities by central authority is just as strict as it is for the rural areas. In fact, the national ministries often carry on local functions on the assumption that local units cannot function properly, either from lack of finances or from incompetent staff. Extreme centralization is the chief characteristic of local government in these four states.

This was also true in the *United Arab Republic* (Egypt) before 1960, when a new system of local government was adopted. Three types of local units were established: governorates, towns, and villages, each governed by a council. The councils are composed of three types of members: (1)

[13] W. Hardy Wickwar, "Note on Local Administrative Areas and Local Government Units in the Middle East," *International Review of Administrative Sciences,* no. 2, 1958, pp. 148–151.

those elected as members of the executive committees of the National Union (the political organ of the state taking the place of political parties) at the respective levels; (2) those selected by the competent minister from among the active members of the National Union; and (3) ex officio members representing the various national ministries within the district. The law states that the elective members shall constitute a majority. The powers of these councils are broad and inclusive, even extending to economic enterprises. Their financial resources, while not equal to their range of functions, include taxes on real estate, both buildings and land; license fees, some nationally collected and locally shared; profits and earnings from locally owned utilities and commercial activities; national subsidies; and loans. The governorate is the dominating unit with important powers over the town and rural councils. But the chief figure in local government is the governor of the governorate, who not only is the chief officer of the state in his district, enforcing all national laws and regulations, but is the executive of the governorate council and the chief administrator of the entire district with supervisory power over the town and village personnel. He, like the presidents of the town and rural councils, is appointed by central authority. Within the governorate are technical staffs of the various national ministries whose activities are being deconcentrated to the governorates. They are administratively under the governor but technically directed by the various ministries. The five largest cities of the United Arab Republic, including Cairo and Alexandria, are provinces and combine in one government both national and municipal functions.

While the objective of this reorganization is decentralization of governmental functions from the national ministries to the local units within five years, there remains at present substantial central guidance and control mostly concentrated in the Ministry of Local Government.

In the *Sudan* also, new local institutions have been established in order to achieve decentralization. The province has been given broad powers of its own and over subordinate local units. Governing the province are the provincial representative of the central government; the province council, some members of which are elected from lower-level councils and others ex officio members of the national government ministries in the provinces; and the province authority, an executive body consisting of national ministry representatives in the province. Local municipal and rural councils are established by the Ministry of Local Government in five stages depending upon their readiness and financial sufficiency. The main objectives are to decentralize administration but to subject it to rigid central control.[14]

In *Saudi Arabia,* the King is the source of all authority, subject only to the Holy Sharia. He has a Council of Ministers accountable to him through the Prime Minister. The amirs are the governors of the five provinces with financial, judicial, and administrative powers, subject to central authority. They are the final resort of all villages and tribes within their jurisdiction. They are assisted by an elected administrative council, no members of which should be department heads within the province. For each of larger cities and towns there is a *qaimaqam,* an appointee of the King, who is the administrative head. Only a few of the 40 larger cities and towns are municipalities which have municipal councils elected by electors who belong to the propertied classes. The president of the council is elected by and from the membership but must be approved by the Minister of Interior, who supervises the work of the municipalities. There is also an administrative council made up of officials. Outside of the cities and towns are the nomadic tribes headed by their chiefs or sheikhs. Assistance of a financial nature is given to them by the King or his representatives when they are paying the usual annual visits. This is customary, known as desert assistance.

[14] The following references have been used for material in the sections relating to the Arab states: Harold F. Alderfer, Annex to Paper on *Public Administration and Finance Problems Associated with Rapid Urban Growth in the Arab States and Measures and Machinery Required to Cope with Them at Different Levels of Administration,* United Nations, Jan. 15, 1963; Mohamed Tewfik Ramzi, "Municipal Institutions in the Arab World Today," in the proceedings of an International Seminar sponsored by the Egyptian Society of Engineers and the Congress for Cultural Freedom, Cairo, 1960; Abdul-Hussein R. al-Ameri, *Local Government in Iraq: Comparative Study with the French Local System,* master's degree thesis, New York University, New York, 1961; Bernard Lewis, "Municipal Reform in the Ottoman Empire," International Seminar, *op. cit.;* Harold F. Alderfer, Mohamed F. El Khatib, and Moustafa Ahmed Fahmy, *Local Government in the United Arab Republic—1963,* Institute of Public Administration, United Arab Republic, Cairo, 1963; Hubert Morsink, *Rapid Urban Growth in the Arab States,* Beirut, Lebanon, 1963; Ali Hassan Abdulla, "Local Government in the Sudan," in United Nations Technical Assistance Programme, *Decentralization for National and Local Development,* New York, 1962, pp. 179–187; A. A. G. Wallis, "Local Administration in the Sudan," *Journal of African Administration,* July, 1961; and Mohamed Abdullah El Araby, *Local Government in the United Arab Republic,* Cairo, 1961.

In *Yemen* there are seven provinces (*liwas*) headed by amirs, districts (*qadas*) headed by *amels*, and *nahiyahs*, headed also by *amels*. These represent the national government. There are no local councils, and the central government exercises strict control.

Bahrein, Kuwait, Muscat, Oman, Qatar, and Aden are, like Yemen, located along the southwestern shore of the Persian Gulf. They are small, independent nations, or are sultanates bound to Great Britain by treaties.

GREECE

Greek local government has deep roots in the past. From time immemorial, the basic geographic unit and the unbreakable social atom of Greek life has been the settlement. This consists of a number of families living in a group of houses built close together in a compact physical unity. To earn a living, the inhabitants till the soil or tend flocks outside the physical confines of the settlement on land which either belongs to them privately or to the community and which is an integral part of the settlement. Even when large landholders had superimposed themselves, as was the case when powerful families and monasteries held vast tracts of land during the Byzantine period or during the four centuries of Turkish occupation, and even after independence during the nineteenth and early twentieth centuries, the settlement continued as the foundation of existence. Its people were the hewers of wood and the drawers of water no matter what the overall political and economic structure happened to be.

During the period of classical Greece the world-renowned city-state (polis) was the political entity. It usually consisted of a number of settlements geographically contiguous. *Metrokomia* was the ancient name given the mother community, which was usually the largest and exercised governmental leadership over the others. The city of Athens, as early as the fifth century B.C., was such a one, containing all present Attica within its jurisdiction. In the city-state, each settlement had representation on the central council but retained certain administrative independence.

During the Byzantine millennium (A.D. 330–1453) the Greco-Roman pattern of local government changed. Christian Orthodox dogma and organization altered the complexion of the Greek community. Instead of being organized on the basis of individuals living in a geographical area as was the classical mode, it became a body of believers, invisible and incorporeal, united in common purpose that included spiritual as well as material objectives. Within this framework, new concepts of local government grew. One was the council as a vehicle for the consensus of the community as a whole; another, the assembly of all members of the Christian community to give assent to major decisions; still another, the leadership of the clergy in community affairs. These ideas were indigenous to Byzantine culture. They continued during the Turkish occupation and are still a part, even if not immediately visible under the veneer of Western institutions, of present-day local government in Greece.

It was the Greek community which carried Byzantine culture through the Turkish occupation and kept alive Greek Orthodox religion, the Greek language, and Greek learning. The Turks allowed the communities a great deal of independence as long as they kept the peace and contributed taxes for the upkeep of the Ottoman Empire and its functionaries. They even devolved upon them functions such as care of the indigent and sick. During this period there were many economically successful, self-governing communities as well as confederations of communities in Greece and the islands. Some of them carried on extensive economic activities on a cooperative basis under which individuals contributed their land and wealth to a communal fund and their work to communal direction. After Turkish taxes and local expenses were paid, profits were distributed between owners of land, investors, and workers. The commune during this period was called *politia* (state), *kinotis* (commune), and *kinon* (common); the communal assembly, *synodos* (synod); the communal leadership, *gerontes, protevon,* and *arhontes,* meaning generally old, first, and noble, as the case might be. The foundation of the community was the assembly, which included "all the people and officials" including "the most reverend clergy." The *megisti synodos,* or greatest council, was the synod assembled by settlements and communes in the regional capital. The synod agreed upon communal officials. Three classes had to approve: the clergy, the nobility, and the people. The powers of the communal authorities included the administration of community property, the collection of taxes, the appointment of communal employees, the administration of schools and churches, transportation facilities, and the calling together of the assembly of the commune in case of emergency. They administered justice, communal and civil, on "ancient Greek principles" and were accepted as representatives of the communes by the Turkish authorities, even often as administrative advisors.

The war for independence began in 1821 and resulted in the establishment of the modern Greek state in 1833 under the sponsorship of the Western powers. The constituted government was Western in character with a written constitution, a king without decisive powers yet a symbol of national solidarity, an elective parliament, a ministry, and a permanent civil service. As for local government, the commune disappeared as a political entity although it continued as a vital social organism. Greece was divided into *nomoi,* eparchies, and demes without regard for economic, social, and governmental facts. These were counterparts to the prefectures, *arrondissements,* and communes of the French local system after which they were modeled. The deme was the most local unit of the hierarchy but contained many communes. It had an elective council but with little power. Functions that before had been carried on by the communes were taken over by national ministries, and rigid controls were placed upon all provincial and local units. Throughout the nineteenth and early twentieth centuries, this system continued to operate with only minor variations, although there was rising dissent against what was described as "apoplexy of the center and paralysis of the limbs" in Greek government. The law DNZ of 1912, fashioned under the republican leadership of Venizelos, then prime minister, broke up the demes which since liberation numbered no more than five hundred, and established demes and communes as local units, the former being the more urban towns and the latter the rural communities. But in neither case was there any growth of self-government. In fact, until 1951, local powers, revenues, and freedom actually decreased. The establishment in 1912 of thousands of small communes from single settlements proved a tragic and profound mistake. These communes were too small to function with any degree of effectiveness, thus paving the way for ever-increasing national centralization and depriving the Greek people not only of free government but of the services which strong local government could render and which could not be furnished by the national government. Thus the early nineteenth-century Western European system of national centralization, based as it was on Napoleonic legislation, was grafted upon the new nation without regard for the facts of Greek life and the capacities of the Greek people. It was sad to hear as late as 1950 the declarations of local government officials in northern Greece, which was liberated in 1912, that "local government was better under the Turks, we had more resources and more independence."[15]

World War II brought enemy occupation of Greece for four long years; this was followed by Communist-inspired revolution. Both were terrible in their consequences. The Greek nation was almost annihilated, its people decimated by violence and starvation. Ultimate survival as a free nation was due to the heroic efforts of the Greek people plus military and economic aid from Great Britain and the United States. Stimulated by the American mission, the Greek government undertook significant steps to improve local government and to deconcentrate the national administrative apparatus. In 1951, elections for local officers were held for the first time since 1934, legislation was enacted granting demes and communes 50 per cent of the nationally collected tobacco tax, and a community voluntary labor program was inaugurated. In 1954, a new and modern municipal and communal code, giving local units specific powers, was adopted. In 1955, in a move to deconcentrate national authority, *nomoi* or regional councils were established to deal with local problems not within the jurisdiction of demes and communes. Further, a *nomos* treasury was instituted, governed by a six-member board made up of representatives of official groups, national and local, in the *nomos*.[16] Both the *nomos* council and the *nomos* treasury are dominated by national ministry officials and personnel. They are neither elective, local, nor self-governing, illustrating deconcentration rather than decentralization of power, and in addition the intrusion of national administrative personnel in the local policy-making function.

The key official in Greek regional and local government is the nomarch, the appointed representative of the Minister of Interior in the *nomos*. He is responsible for the enforcement of law, the legality of all actions of

[15] Harold F. Alderfer, *Facts on Greek Local Government,* Economic Cooperation Administration, United States Government, Athens, 1950. Harold F. Alderfer, "Modern Greek Government, I. The Basic Framework, and II. The Realities," *Journal of Central European Affairs,* January, 1953, pp. 331–345, and April, 1953, pp. 28–46.

[16] Alex. Drakakis, *Local Government in Greece,* Ministry of Interior, Kingdom of Greece, 1958, pp. 11–13.

demes and communes, the police, the port authorities, and all governmental agencies except the judiciary, and has disciplinary power over all governmental employees except those of the Ministry of Justice. The nomarch, in short, has "the right to decide on all local matters." Besides the nomarchs, there are a Minister of Northern Greece and a subminister of Epirus who outrank the nomarchs in those areas.

The structure of demes and communes may be characterized in American terms as mayor-council with emphasis on the strong mayor. The mayor of the deme is elected as such by a vote of the electors; the president of the commune council is elected by the council from its own membership. Both are the executive and financial officer of their local units, and both are entrusted by the national government with various duties such as the keeping of vital statistics and military registrations. They are the chairmen of the boards of other local legal entities such as hospital, charitable, and welfare agencies. In demes, council membership ranges from 9 to 31, and in communes from 5 to 15 on the basis of population. By the terms of 1959 legislation, elections are held on the basis of "simple proportional representation," which is defined as "a majority system joined with representation of the minority." Terms are for four years. Demarchs, or mayors of demes, have no veto power, do not vote in council, and do not preside at council meetings. However, they are chairmen of the municipal committee of five, which is described by director Alex. Drakakis of the Greek Ministry of Interior as a "multi-member executive authority of the deme," and as "both a legislative and executive instrument." [17]

ISRAEL

The Jewish state of Israel was proclaimed on May 14, 1948. Previous to that there was fragmentary local government, first under the Ottoman Empire and then under the British mandate which followed the British conquest of Palestine in 1917. Under the Ottoman Empire, the only tasks the Turks allowed local authorities of the country's two or three cities were the removal of refuse and the illumination of a few main streets. At the end of the empire, 22 municipalities had been organized, most of

[17] Drakakis, *op. cit.,* pp. 14–15. Catherine D. Papastrathopoulos, *Local Government in Greece,* master's degree thesis, University of Minnesota, Minneapolis, 1962.

which were small and weak. Under the mandate a greater degree of local autonomy was granted, but this was still severely limited by strict control by district and central authorities. However, Jewish municipalities, especially Tel Aviv, went far beyond the legal limits set forth, and established local institutions which they regarded as being the foundations of the future state. Mandate ordinances still supply the legal foundations of local government in Israel, for they established three classes of local authorities: municipalities, local councils, and village councils for cities, towns, and rural settlements, respectively. At the end of the mandate there were 24 municipalities and 38 local councils. There was no central office for the control of local authorities, but supervisory power was vested in district commissioners or governors serving directly under the High Commissioner. As a result, local government was not encouraged to develop, and local frustration bred inaction, hostility, and indifference.[18]

In 1958, there were 21 municipalities, 87 local councils, and 50 regional councils, representing almost 2 million people living in 650 settlements, with 10 per cent of the population still unorganized. The last were largely new immigrant settlements and Arab villages for which future plans call for the establishment of local government. The regional councils are made up of representatives of committees of constituent cooperatives or other village entities in the council's area.

[18] Marver H. Bernstein, *The Politics of Israel: The First Decade of Statehood,* Princeton University Press, Princeton, N.J., 1957, pp. 285–286; M. Kalir, "Local Government in Israel, 1948–1958," *Israel Year Book,* 1958, Israel Publications, Ltd., Tel Aviv, 1958, pp. 275–282.

4 The Evolution of Form and Structure: The Communist Nations

YUGOSLAVIA

THE ORGANS of local government in Yugoslavia are called people's committees because they are derived from the struggle for liberation in the early days of the German invasion in 1941, when they were organized under the name of National Liberation Committees. They assumed power in areas freed by partisan forces and the national liberation army. These collegiate bodies were not only the political institution of the fighting forces but also the germ of the new government. They represented the working classes, the intelligentsia, some elements of the working middle class, and the peasantry, in contrast to the prewar bourgeois ruling class which controlled governmental institutions since liberation from the Turks in 1878, and the large landholding class during the Turkish occupation.

The Constitution of 1946, which established the People's Republic, legalized these people's committees as the basic governmental body of the new state. In effect, the state was built from the ground up in contrast to the prewar days when local government was part of a highly centralized system with limited administrative responsibilities. The struggle to eliminate the danger of state bureaucracy began in 1949 after the central executive committee of the Revolutionary National Assembly had taken plenary powers and enforced them through its local executive committees. This was comparable to the Soviet "classical" system of transforming the whole state into a central bureaucracy. The 1949 law tried to solve in a national and democratic manner, independent of Soviet theory, various relations between the higher and lower organs of government. The higher authorities were allowed only to annul "unlawful" acts of the people's committees, which were the final judges in local matters. Administrative functions were decentralized from the federal level to the republic, district, and commune levels. All state economic enterprises were freed from administrative control by the central bureaucracy. Since all property belonged to the people, the more direct social ownership of the means of production carried with it the right of local management. In other words, the basic principle in Yugoslavic government is that the state is a body of communes constituted into a single entity; it is not a federation of communes in the syndicalist sense. The reality of the people's sovereignty and the substance of socialist democracy is evidenced in the broad scope of local power exercised by the people of the communities through their committees. This is even considered as a step in the transition from capitalism to socialism, when according to Marxian theory the state itself must ultimately wither away.[1] While it is true that the national leadership is emphatic in its refusal to countenance the emergence of another party than the Communist in the political arena, nevertheless voters' meetings, which are the principal means for the nomination of candidates, are required to put forward at least two candidates for each committee seat. Thus, it would appear that elections are freer from party control than in the Soviet Union.[2]

Present-day local government in Yugoslavia, therefore, dates from January 31, 1946, when a constitution was promulgated by a constituent assembly in which the Communist-controlled People's Front had an overwhelming majority. By its provisions, Yugoslavia became a Federal People's Republic with a bicameral national assembly, with real power

[1] Jovan Djordjevic, "Local Self-government in Yugoslavia," *American Slavic and East European Review,* April, 1953, pp. 188–200.

[2] Derek J. R. Scott, "The Development of Local Government: Yugoslavia's Experience," *Journal of African Administration,* July, 1954, pp. 129–137.

in a supreme presidium of 39 members. On January 13, 1953, both houses of the national assembly adopted a new constitution, which it was claimed was based on a return to original Marxist teachings in order to avoid a reversion to state capitalism. This constitution sought to introduce a maximum of local self-government and economic self-management compatible with a centrally planned socialist economy. The national assembly remained bicameral, but the second house, instead of being organized on the basis of the six federated republics that compose the nation, was replaced by a producers' council elected by organizations of workers, artisans, and peasants. A federal executive council succeeded the presidium and was elected from the first house of the national assembly, whose members in turn were elected by secret, universal suffrage.[3]

Under the present local government law passed in 1955, each of the six republics is divided into districts, and the districts are composed of communes or municipalities (*opstinas*) which, regardless of size or urban-rural composition, have the same legal status. In 1961, there were 72 districts, and 725 communes, of which 30 were urban municipalities. The government of the commune follows the national pattern. There is a bicameral municipal council called the people's committee made up of a political chamber, which is the general political body elected by all adult citizens, and an economic chamber, composed of representatives of industry, commerce, and agriculture in ratio to each producer group's contributions to the total economy. Members of the political chamber are elected from settlements or villages, each having at least one representative, while members of the economic chamber are elected by organizations representing various branches of the economy. Both hold office for four years. Both chambers participate in separate meetings in drafting the economic plan for the commune, and in major decisions relating to finance, public works, and labor relations, and must pass identical texts of proposed laws if the laws are to be effective. At a joint meeting of both chambers, the members elect the chief municipal officers and employees, including municipal judges. All other business is discharged by the political chambers. This includes education, welfare, and public health services, as well as cultural matters and daily administration. Permanent

[3] *Encyclopaedia Britannica,* vol. 23, pp. 922–923.

joint committees prepare the details of proposals to be brought forward, and a large amount of the council's work is performed by functional committees concerned with such subjects as town planning, finance, and housing. Although each of these committees must have at least two members of the council, most of the members are drawn from the body of citizens representing various groups, interests, and competencies within the commune, so that the committees act as a link between the municipal administration and the independent organizations of the community. The chief administrative officer is the council president, who is analogous to the American "weak mayor." He presides over the council and has certain veto powers over acts of administrative departments. He is assisted by a municipal secretary, who acts as manager in the field of administrative routine operations and gives legal opinions on important matters that arise, and by a cashier who handles finances. In those communes that include several villages or settlements, local committees may be formed to discharge business of direct interest to the local population. Committee members include those elected to the municipal council and others elected at voter meetings. Finances and administrative assistance for projects and activities of these submunicipal units are often supplied by the municipal council. In 1958, there were more than 10,000 of these. In densely populated metropolitan areas, municipalities may be joined to carry on specific projects or functions in the district, or may organize intermediary councils. These agencies are not legally recognized organs of government, but they may make certain decisions of a general nature which are then binding upon the member councils.

Between the commune and the state is the district, with powers similar to those of the commune. It also has a bicameral council, but the members of the political chamber are elected from among members of the component municipal councils. The district is viewed as a coordinating and supervising agency, although it may carry out functions and projects covering the larger area it represents. National departments have certain limited supervisory powers over the districts, much the same as the district has over the communes.[4]

[4] Samuel Humes and Eileen M. Martin, *The Structure of Local Governments*, International Union of Local Authorities, Martinus Nijhoff, The Hague, 1961, pp. 302–308. *Local Government in the XXth Century*, International Union of Local Authorities, Martinus Nijhoff, The Hague, 1963, pp. 465–480.

POLAND

Polish government, national and local, after World War I was modeled along French unitary lines. There were provinces, large cities, counties, and communes. The executives of the first three were appointed by higher authority: the provincial governor by the President of Poland, the presidents or mayors of large cities and the county presidents by the Minister of Interior. The communal mayors were elected by the communal council or assembly. Each of the units had a legislative body, the first three elected by the next lower assemblies, and the communal assembly elected by popular vote.

After the conclusion of German occupation in 1944, reorganization proceeded along the Soviet pattern. The legislative bodies were turned into people's councils whose membership was based upon representation from selected groups such as political parties, trade unions, and social organizations, a resemblance to the corporate representation of fascism. The executive remained undisturbed. The law of 1950 brought back direct election of people's committees, did away with provincial and local executives, and greatly increased the powers of the people's committees. Thus "dualism" was eliminated and "democratization" established, but the people's committees of the smaller areas were made responsible to the next higher, and so on up to the Council of State which could dissolve a committee or annul its decisions. The local committees implemented the overall will of the Council of State and were given broad local powers to do so. The masses of citizens were encouraged to participate in meeting on the local level to discuss the reports of committees and officials. The executive organs of the people's committees were the presidium, a smaller executive committee made up of the membership, elected by them and recallable at any time, and other subject committees.[5] Poland is divided into 17 provinces plus 5 cities with provincial status, about 400 districts, of which 75 are both districts and municipalities, and approximately 8,100 rural municipalities.[6]

[5] Ralph A. Jones, "Polish Local Government Reorganized on Soviet Model," *The American Slavic and East European Review,* February, 1951, pp. 56–58.

[6] Humes and Martin, *op. cit.,* pp. 293–298. See also George Ginsburgs, "Local Government and Administration in the Bulgarian Peoples' Republic: 1951–1956," *Journal of Central European Affairs,* April, 1963, pp. 23–51.

COMMUNIST CHINA

Local government organization in the People's Republic of China was fixed by the Constitution of 1954. The country is divided into provinces, cities of central subordination, and autonomous regions. Provinces and autonomous regions are divided into autonomous districts, counties, autonomous counties, and cities. Cities of central subordination are divided into wards. The suburban districts of these cities and counties are divided into *volasts,* national *volasts,* and settlements.

In the provinces, cities of central subordination, counties, cities, wards, *volasts,* and settlements, assemblies of people's representatives are convoked and people's committees are established as their executive organs. The people's committees are responsible to the assemblies and to the higher-ranking state administrative organs, and are accountable to them. Final responsibility in the administrative hierarchy rests with the State Council. The courts and the prosecutors' offices are not under the people's committee.

These people's committees carry out state administrative directions in their districts, hold elections for the people's assemblies at the lower levels, maintain law and order, and carry on economic activities. They may suspend decisions of the assemblies. The chairman of the committee is looked upon as the chief executive officer of the state in his district. The people's committees carry on their manifold duties through departments, agencies, and commissions for specific functions under their jurisdiction. In the province, for example, these functions include civil administration, public security, justice, control, finance, enlightenment, public health, trade, industry, communications, agriculture, water and food supply, purchase of agricultural equipment, labor, statistics, culture, building, trade-industrial organization, handicrafts, material supply, meterological services, posts and telegraph, cadres for religious affairs, nationality affairs, physical culture and sport, and radio. In the cities, counties, and lower districts, the span is more restricted but still broad enough to include general needs of the population that are not served by other levels. In the *volast,* there are commissions directed by the people's committee on production, public order, civil administration, people's militia, finance and food, culture and public health.[7]

NORTH VIETNAM

North Vietnam's present system of local government grew out of the revolutionary movement first arising in Japanese-occupied French Indochina with the establishment of people's committees in areas secured by the armed forces of Vietminh. In 1945, following a nationwide directive, committees of liberation were organized in factories, mines, barracks, and government offices in regions, districts, towns, provinces, and villages. The dominant influence in these committees was that of the League of Vietminh. The committees were viewed not only as organs of insurrection but as provisional organs of state power. In the same year, a basic statute of local organization was promulgated by the president of the provisional government of the Democratic Republic of Vietnam. Four levels of local government were envisaged: village, district, province, and region. In each there were two organs of authority: people's councils, elected by the people at large through direct and universal suffrage; and administrative committees, directly chosen by the councils and functioning as elective bodies. At the two levels of province and village, both jointly exercised public authority. In the district and region only the administrative committees were formed, and these were elected by village and provincial councils. Each village elected its own council consisting of 15 to 25 members and 5 to 7 alternates. Provincial councils were comprised of 20 to 30 members with each electoral unit (district or municipality) sending one alternate in addition. Suffrage and the right to be a candidate for council, with few exceptions, were extended to all Vietnam citizens eighteen years of age or over. Urban areas were organized along the same general lines. Both councils and administrative committees were strictly controlled by central authorities through various means. Village constituencies were allowed to vote on the question of confidence in the council; and in the event there was no absolute majority of registered

[7] United States Joint Publications Research Service, *Local Organs of State Authority of the People's Republic of China,* no date.

voters for the council, the provincial administrative committee could dissolve it. All council decisions and administrative actions were reviewed by higher authority. With the outbreak of hostilities between the French army and Vietminh in 1946, the government was placed on a war footing. The people's councils and administrative committees were replaced by new committees of resistance and administration on a zone basis which were appointed by the higher echelons of authority.[8]

The Geneva agreements of 1954 brought some measure of peace to Indochina, and the Vietminh regime found itself in legal possession of the country which lay north of the 17th parallel and which is officially known as the Democratic Republic of Vietnam. Since then there have been some changes in local government structure, mainly in a special effort to satisfy aspirations for national autonomy in the regions inhabited by ethnic minorities. While the creation of autonomous zones by special decrees setting up local government enabled national minorities to be "masters at home," this not only created a separate state but constituted the zone as an integral part of the central government. By and large, the same kind of local organization was used in these autonomous zones, but several had three tiers instead of four. Likewise in the election process, large enterprises had representatives to the communal convocations and congresses, who were elected at general meetings of the workers and employees. Generally speaking, this period saw further centralization of governmental authority.[9]

MONGOLIA

The Constitution of the Mongolian People's Republic of June 3, 1940, established three levels of local government: regions (*aimaks*), districts (*somons*), and rural communities (*bags*); with the capital, Ulan-Bator, with special status as an *aimak,* subdivided into *khorons* and *khorins,* districts and subdistricts, the latter comprising 20-household blocks. The highest organ in each of these three levels of government was the *khural*

[8] George Ginsburgs, "Local Government and Administration in North Vietnam, 1945–1954," *The China Quarterly,* April–June, 1962, pp. 174–204.

[9] George Ginsburgs, "Local Government and Administration in the Democratic Republic of Vietnam" (part 1), *The China Quarterly,* October-December, 1962, pp. 211–230; (part 2), April–June, 1963, pp. 195–211.

of *arat* workers, a convention of delegates. In the *khorin* and *bag* these were elected by assemblies of all adult members, in the higher echelons by lower *khurals*. The *khurals* received reports of administrative departments in their areas, elected members of the organ of administration, and selected members of the next higher *khurals*. Each of the *khurals* had a little *khural* which acted as an executive committee, and in turn selected a still smaller presidium from its own membership which ostensibly provided the governmental leadership for the particular jurisdiction. The little *khurals* had broad economic and administrative powers, and were responsible both to the *khural* that elected them and to the next higher *khural* in the hierarchy.

Since 1940, there have been some changes in local government which are now reflected in the new Constitution of 1960. These include the abolition of popular assemblies in *bags* and *khorins* and the establishment in their place of regular *khurals* as in other levels; the abolition of indirect elections of deputies to *khurals* and the substitution of direct elections by the voters at large; the liquidation of little *khurals* on the *aimak* level; the invitation to ordinary citizens to participate in the work of permanent commissions established by the *khurals* as auxiliary agencies; the encouragement of open discussions in meetings of adult members of *bags;* the abolition of all *khurals* in *bags* and *khorins* except in the capital because the establishment of rural cooperatives made them superfluous; the later abolition of all *khorins;* and the recognition of urban municipalities in the governmental system as having the right to enjoy separate administrative status not yet defined except in the capital.

All these developments, according to Dr. George Ginsburgs, indicate a desire on the part of the leadership of Outer Mongolia to make rapid modernization of administrative techniques; the increase of administrative control and the concurrent reduction of local self-government and democratic representation; the increase of Communist party influence at all levels, not only at the center; and a general all-around adaptation to the administrative structure of the Soviet Union.[10]

[10] George Ginsburgs, "Local Government in the Mongolian People's Republic, 1940–1960," *The Journal of Asian Studies,* August, 1961, pp. 489–508.

5 The Evolution of Form and Structure: The Asian Subcontinent and the Far East

INDIA

FOR THOUSANDS of years, the way of life in India was agricultural; its social center, the village; and its dominant political institution, the village panchayat. Empires might rise and fall, invaders come and go, but the village lived on and exists today in much the same form as it did in the past. History, what there is of it, records the ups and downs of the state vis-à-vis the village; sometimes dominant, other times cooperative, and sometimes even dependent. Villages in ancient India were similar in structure and composition to those in rural areas in other parts of the world. Population tended to be from five hundred to a thousand, houses built close together, isolation from the outside world almost complete, village affairs governed by custom, community leadership in the hands of a council of elders and perhaps a headman. Cultivated land was worked by individual families, but there were common forests and pastures.

Jawaharlal Nehru describes the villages as almost independent and governed by their elected panchayats. At times a number of villages or small towns were joined together under a raja or chief who was sometimes elected and sometimes hereditary. Different village groups might cooperate with one another to build community facilities. The raja, who was the chief man, could not just do what he liked; he himself was subject to Aryan laws and customs, and he could be deposed and fined by his people.[1]

One important characteristic of Indian village society, however, differentiated it from the rest of the world. This was the age-old system of castes and communalism, which continues to influence politics and government even though its excesses such as untouchability are now legally abolished or frowned upon by progressive leadership. But even today there are 50 million "untouchables" who live segregated lives and do menial tasks, although they now have more opportunities than ever before, a few even occupying high positions in government and the professions. Nehru himself, following the general tone of Mahatma Gandhi, stated that the aristocratic approach based on traditionalism was wholly opposed to modern conditions and the democratic ideal.[2]

The village panchayat in ancient India was an elected council with both executive and judicial powers, and its membership was respected by king's officers, according to the *Shukra-Nitisai,* a description of the Indian village written about 800 A.D. Land was distributed by the panchayat, taxes were collected by it and paid to the central government for the village as a whole. The panchayat settled disputes between inhabitants and groups within the village, and appointed financial, educational, management, and protective officers and employees. The state officials, the king's men, were interested primarily in keeping law and order, and in collecting revenue for the central government. Otherwise, villages were able to operate on their own, and through the centuries they evolved a complex but workable and indigenous system of agriculture, commerce, crafts, land use, family relations, and protection based substantially upon mutual aid.[3]

[1] Jawaharlal Nehru, *Glimpses of World History,* Lindsay Drummond, Ltd., London, 1945, p. 24.

[2] Norman D. Palmer, *The Indian Political System,* Houghton Mifflin Company, Boston, 1961, p. 23.

[3] H. D. Malaviya, *Village Panchayats in India,* All India Congress Committee, New Delhi, 1956, pp. 66–91.

Hugh Tinker tries to disentangle legend from historical evidence regarding the panchayat. He notes that while there is clear evidence of its existence in ancient India, it appears to have virtually disappeared in medieval times under the Moghuls, and there is no mention of it by Moslem historians. It was, however, brought to light by the English, who perhaps saw in it a reflection of their own ancient self-governing institutions. According to Tinker, the word *panchayat* suggests form, not purpose:

> a technique of seeking agreement through consultation, hallowed, according to tradition, by divine sanction: *panch men parameswar.* This technique was mainly employed in social or economic organisms (the closest Western parallels are the medieval trade guild or the Victorian friendly society) but it was also extensively used for the arbitration of both caste and village disputes. With possible reservations regarding south India, the panchayat was not an administrative body in the usually accepted sense, although it was sometimes employed to apportion the village land revenue assessment and may have had a role in regulating the duties of the village servants.[4]

British rule in India covered 182 years ending with the attainment of national independence on August 15, 1947. During this period a strong central government was developed, mainly concerned with the collection of revenue, the protection of life and property, and the development of Western services of government such as communications, public health, public works, and education. Furthermore, beginning in 1861, urban municipalities with elected councils were formed in a number of the larger cities.

Rural government reform stemmed from the ideas of Lord Ripon, who as Viceroy of India declared in the famous resolution of 1882 that local government in India must be revived "as an instrument of political and popular education," and as an outlet for the ambitions and aspirations engendered by Western ideas. Accordingly the government of India allowed provinces to set up rural district boards composed of official and elected members, and encouraged the establishment of elective village panchayats. The venture did not pan out very well. The boards quickly

[4] Hugh Tinker, "Authority and Community in Village India," *Journal of African Administration,* October, 1960, pp. 195–196. Jayaprakash Narayan, "Decentralized Democracy: Theory and Practice," *The Indian Journal of Public Administration,* July–September, 1961, pp. 271–286.

came under the control of the district officers of the provinces, and the panchayats received only lukewarm support from the Indians themselves. The villagers had so long been separated from and antagonistic to the government that, as Tinker says: "Any attempt to revive the traditional institutions of village government was anyhow too late by the 1880's." For the local bosses were the agents of the landlords and other economic powers.[5]

The new Constitution of India went into effect January 26, 1950. It established a federal system consisting of the national and state governments. Presently, there are fifteen states, six territories, and one protectorate. The states are divided into provinces and the provinces into districts, which in turn in some states are divided into subdistricts called tahsils or *takukas*. In most states the district, an inheritance from British days, is the major political subdivision and the district officer the head of governmental affairs in his area. He is a member of the Indian Administrative Service and is described as the "bottleneck of the governmental process." His new duties make him comparable to the French prefect, yet he is still burdened with all his former responsibilities.[6] District boards are of declining importance in the new India and are likely to be abolished at some future date. The district subdivisions, the tahsils and *takukas,* while also presently declining in numbers and importance, were vital administrative units as far back as Moghul times. They include a group of villages under the administration of a tahsildar, who acts as collector of revenue for the central government and as a second-class magistrate responsible for the collection of testimony in court.[7] If these units survive in the future, they may be given responsibilities in the new community development program, perhaps integrated into the "community block" organization. Today, the main units of rural government are still the district and the village.

The new Constitution of India provides in Article 40 that "The State shall take steps to organize village panchayats and to endow them with such powers and authority as may be necessary to enable them to func-

[5] Hugh Tinker, *The Foundations of Local Self-government in India, Pakistan and Burma,* The Athlone Press, London, 1954, p. 55.

[6] Tinker, "Authority and Community in Village India," *op. cit.*, p. 201.

[7] Marian W. Smith, "The Misal: A Structural Village Group of India and Pakistan," *American Anthropologist,* January–March, 1952, pp. 41–56.

tion as units of self-government." Although this article is in the nature of a guiding principle, not legally enforceable, all the states have passed enabling acts giving legal status to panchayats and the central Parliament has enacted legislation to promote the system. Both the central government and the states have embarked on a policy of decentralization in which the aim is "to maximize the functions and importance of village governing bodies." [8]

The system of panchayats is in itself a complex institution. There are some that existed under British rule and continue to function; others have been set up after independence. In many villages they do not yet exist, although efforts are being made to cover the whole rural area of the nation with them. There are little panchayats in small villages, and large ones representing a number of villages. There are multipurpose panchayats, called *panchayats raj,* and panchayats which are primarily judicial. There are informal panchayats which perhaps have existed even before British rule and which have been lauded as being the great stabilizing factor in ancient days; these often still exist side by side with the more recent statutory panchayats. Sometimes these informal panchayats have greater local influence and prestige than those created by law.[9]

Internally, the village panchayat may consist of three bodies: the *gaon sabha,* consisting of all adult residents of the panchayat circle; the panchayat itself, with 30 to 50 members elected by adult suffrage by the *gaon sabha;* and an *adalati, gram,* or *nyaya panchayat* for judicial purposes, also elective.[10]

In spite of the push that Indian political leadership is giving the panchayat, its future is not clear at this time. To some, it represents old India. Said B. R. Ambedkar, chairman of the drafting committee of the new Constituiton: "What is the village but a sink of localism, a den of ignorance, narrow-mindedness and communalism. I am glad that the Draft Constitution has discarded the village and adopted the individual

[8] Morris E. Opler, "The Extensions of an Indian Village," *The Journal of Asian Studies,* November, 1956, p. 9.

[9] Palmer, *op. cit.,* p. 152. Henry Maddick, "Pan Chayati Raj—Rural Local Government in India," *Journal of Administration Overseas,* October, 1962, pp. 201–212.

[10] M. P. Sharma, *Local Self-government in India,* 3d ed., Hinds Kitabs, Ltd. Bombay, 1961. Kota Madhara Sastry, "The Executive in Village Panchayat," *The Journal of Social Sciences,* July, 1960, pp. 89–106.

as its unit." [11] Others have pointed out that the villages have not measured up to their possibilities, that at present the best-run political institution in India is the central government, and that the quality of administration deteriorates down the line through the states, the districts, the subdivisions, and the villages. The "village republics" on the lowest rung of the hierarchy, they claim, cannot do the required work of the twentieth century.

Hugh Tinker thinks that the free India panchayat experiment has yet to "get off the ground" and that conditions are about the same as before independence. An official report in 1957 indicated that not more than 10 per cent of the total number of panchayats were functioning effectively. Reasons for this include village factionalism, elections that foment local rivalry, separatism arising out of caste distinctions, conservatism of dominant landholders, and general apathy and poverty in the villages. Some authorities urge a return to the ancient Indian method of choosing leaders by general agreement. However, the determined drive for community development throughout India may alter this negative approach. A new complex of practices, organization, and attitudes is being formed. It stems from the "desire to live better." The village-level worker is taking the place of traditional officers concerned with law and order and the collection of revenues. He is "a multipurpose worker and friend of the village people." The development "block" is a new structural concept that is coming into rural local government; it consists of a number of villages in which projects and services are being planned and administered. It may well be that the panchayats, perhaps in three tiers, can be geared into the community development program. But many administrative problems remain unsolved. One of the most important is the relation of the central and state government ministries and their agents to community development. Are they going to take over, or can the villages and local panchayats raise themselves if they are stirred by the vision of a new India? Only time will tell. Meanwhile, local government in India is in ferment.

India is still a nation of villages. Five out of every six persons live in them, and four out of every five live by agriculture. According to the 1951 census, there is the amazing number of 558,089 villages in which

[11] M. V. Pylee, *Constitutional Government in India,* Asia Publishing House, London, 1960, pp. 15–16.

357 million persons live. But there are also many towns and cities—more than 3,000—in which about 62 million persons live. There are 72 cities with more than 100,000 population, and 5 have more than a million. There are 5 metropolitan areas of 2 to 5 million people. The local governments in urban areas are corporations, municipalities, notified areas, or town areas, according to population. They are under the supervision of state government but have a considerable degree of local autonomy. Each has an elective council which chooses a president or mayor, and a municipal commissioner appointed by the state is the executive officer in the larger places. According to Professor Palmer, Indian cities are overburdened with functions and poorly equipped to perform them. With greater urbanization and increased population, they must develop into stronger vehicles of local services than they are at present. In 1961, there were 21 municipal corporations, 3,014 municipal boards, 201 district boards, and 179,906 panchayats, a total of 183,142 local units.[12]

PAKISTAN

On August 15, 1947, Pakistan became a new state, separating itself both from British rule and from India. Before that date, its local government had practically the same history as that of India. After independence, however, Pakistan went in a different direction. By decree in 1959, after the Constitution of 1956 was abrogated, the Pakistani system of "basic democracies" was established. It differs from a full-fledged parliamentary system in that political parties are banned but "political participation at a limited local level has been made possible to the people." [13]

Organization under the national government is in the form of a five-tier hierarchy: (1) provincial development councils (one for East Pakistan and one for West Pakistan with the governor of the province as chairman); (2) divisional councils (15 in number with divisional commissioners as chairmen); (3) district councils (76 in number with deputy commissioners or district magistrates as chairmen); (4) *tehsil* or thana

[12] Palmer, *op. cit.*, pp. 153–155. N. Srinivasan, "Village Government in India," *Far Eastern Quarterly*, pp. 201–213. *Local Government in the XXth Century, op. cit.*, pp. 189–193.

[13] Khahid B. Sayeed, "Pakistan's Basic Democracy," *Middle East Journal*, Summer, 1961, pp. 249–263.

councils (599 in number with subdivisional officials as chairmen); (5) union councils (7,117 in number, for rural areas, with chairmen elected by the membership). In addition, there are 108 municipal committees, 62 cantonment boards, 219 town committees, and 880 union committees. The membership of the councils above the union level comes predominantly from the officials of national government operating within the areas, and from chairmen of boards on the level below.

The union councils, the lowest level, are composed of two-thirds (about ten) elected members and one-third appointed by government officials in the area. Each elected member represents 1,000 to 1,500 people, while those nominated are usually representatives of occupational and social groups in the area. One union council represents between 4,000 and 10,000 persons. The town committees are all elected. Of the five tiers, the district and union councils have most of the substantive powers of local government, while the divisional and the *tehsil* or thana councils are largely coordinators of union council activity in their areas.[14]

Under the Pakistani system, the principle of nomination rather than election has diluted democracy as elections have been abandoned in all but the union and town councils. Furthermore, government officials on the regional level may suspend any action of the union council and may disband the council itself. Appointive members may be removed by the government official who appointed them, while elected members may be removed by the next higher council. The general attitude of those in power has been that Western democracy is not suited to Islamic thought and practice, that government should be free from party disruptions, and that the union councils should not be influenced by former politicians.[15]

BURMA AND CEYLON

Burma became a sovereign state on January 4, 1948. The Union of Burma is made up of Burma proper and five special territorial jurisdic-

[14] Harry J. Friedman, "Pakistan's Experiment in Basic Democracies," *Pacific Affairs,* June, 1960, pp. 107–125. *Local Government in the XXth Century, op. cit.,* pp. 307–318.

[15] Habib-Ur-Rahman, "Basic Democracies as Institutions of Local Government," parts 1 and 2, *Journal of Local Administration Overseas,* October, 1962, pp. 239–256.

tions, each of which has its own government. In the latter no local units exist. Burma proper is divided into seven provinces with 34 districts which are made up of village groups and villages. Densely populated areas are organized into urban municipalities composed of wards.

The central government controls the various levels within the hierarchy, the Minister of Home Affairs making all the appointments. The district is the most important subordinate unit and is headed by the district officer. Village groups in 10 pilot districts have a council elected from individual village councils. The central official of the village group serves as executive officer for this council. The basic rural unit is supervised by a headman elected by the people, although if he proves unsuitable he can be replaced by higher authority. Each rural unit in these pilot districts has an elected council headed by a chairman and an appointed village clerk who acts as the executive. It has limited administrative duties and the judicial functions formerly exercised by the headman. The council is composed of five to seven members, eighteen years of age or more, and of either sex. Voting in villages is compulsory.[16]

Municipal committees were first established in Burma in the 1870s, and there are now 60 municipalities with very limited powers. Municipal councils are now selected by committees in each ward, which in turn are elected by the people. Following the English plan, most of the work is done through the committee system. Under each committee is an appropriate technical official who, with the municipal secretary, is appointed by higher authority. The Ministry of Democratization of Local Administration and Local Bodies must approve all local ordinances before final approval of parliament, and central assembly may legislate on all local matters.[17]

The Constitution of 1931 made Ceylon the first Asian country to enjoy universal suffrage. On February 4, 1948, the Ceylon Independence Act granted Ceylon full dominion status in the British Commonwealth. There are nine provinces, and the villages in them have elective councils as do

[16] Hugh Tinker, *The Union of Burma,* Oxford University Press, Fair Lawn, N.J., 1959.

[17] Samuel Humes and Eileen M. Martin, *The Structure of Local Governments,* International Union of Local Authorities, Martinus Nijhoff, The Hague, 1961.

the cities and towns. As subunits of the province, there are 20 revenue districts composed of 108 divisions, each headed by a divisional revenue agent in charge of a group of villages.[18]

SOUTHEAST ASIA

Since World War II, all the countries in Southeast Asia except Thailand, which was never a colony, have attained national independence. This includes Burma, Laos, Cambodia, Vietnam, Malaya, Indonesia, and the Philippines—all former Western dependencies. Professor Virgil B. Zimmerman sees in them a fundamental unity. He says:

> Beneath a colorful variety of costume and custom, the countries of Southeast Asia, from the Philippines in the east to Burma in the west, have much in common. Throughout the region tropical and sub-tropical climatic conditions and rugged topography have nurtured village economies in which rice is the staple food and for which the water buffalo is a well-nigh universal symbol. In such seemingly diverse people as the Tagelogs and the Sundanese run racial, religious and cultural strains which speak of common origins. By impeding transportation and communications, rivers, mountains, jungles and seas have bred varieties of language and custom and have held back the growth of national loyalty and union. Nearly all of these lands have also recently emerged from a colonial status which left indelible imprints upon institutions, attitudes, and ways of life.[19]

In precolonial days, before Western political domination had reached its height, the theoretical absolutism of the rulers was diluted by the general inaccessibility of the villages and the difficulty of imposing central authority on outlying regions. As long as local entities paid taxes, supplied conscripts to the armies, and kept the peace, all went well. Rulers came and went, but the villages remained intact for century after century.

But when the Western powers came in, they did not understand the local institutions. Many attempts were made to recognize, reorganize, and integrate them into the Western pattern of administration, but they were all more or less unsuccessful. Western authorities worked through the practices of direct rule and indirect rule, they strove to revive the ancient institutions that they had first spurned, but to no avail. Virginia Thompson

[18] *Ibid.*, pp. 386–390.

[19] Virgil B. Zimmerman, "Philippine Clues to the Future of Local Government in South-East Asia," *Journal of African Administration*, January, 1960, p. 34.

notes that contact with the West undermined or largely destroyed existing institutions at the village, town, and provincial levels.[20]

Practices which Western colonizers thought were desirable and administratively sound missed the mark. The colonizers standardized administrative units, marked out geographic boundaries, delegated specific duties to local officials, separated judicial from executive function, made local leaders minor officials of the central government, brought into areas trained personnel, European and native, and allowed elections to be held. All this might have added up to efficiency, but it destroyed the indigenous institutions of democracy, or at least localism, in Southeast Asia. But, Miss Thompson warns, the democracy of native institutions should not be exaggerated—for the elite controlled the villages. The superiority of the old regime was derived from sanction, custom, centuries of knowledge, concentration of powers, and permanency. The new officials were alien, were frequently changed, and impinged on traditional authority.[21] Colonial rural local government, she concludes, as it developed for seventy-five years before World War II, was a failure in Southeast Asia. However, municipal government in cities and towns had better success. Urbanization itself was a Western development, and town councils were run by Europeans. The government had strict control over them, for a majority of officials dominated the councils, and other members were nominated by the government to represent special groups. Moreover, there were no indigenous institutions to supplant when independence was achieved; little was changed. The governments were largely in control of native personnel already trained in Western administrative practices. However, the urge toward national freedom in these countries was strong and was derived from Western liberal and democratic philosophy, still flowering throughout the world as a result of the earlier English, American, and French Revolutions. So the twin concepts of national control and democracy existed side by side in the new nations and influenced the behavior of their top leaders, often on conflicting terms. Local units were given broader powers, but they were more rigidly con-

[20] Virginia Thompson, "Rural and Urban Self-government in Southeast Asia," in Rupert Emerson, *Representative Government in Southeast Asia,* Harvard University Press, Cambridge, Mass., 1955, p. 118.

[21] *Ibid.,* pp. 121–123.

trolled from above; villagers were offered elections, but those elected might be removed by higher authority. When the trained European civil servants left the scene, an administrative void was created that led to confusion. Chain of command often broke down because of political pressure. Furthermore, the ideals of democracy were extended to the desire to improve living standards on the part of the masses, and additional burdens were placed on governments poor in financial and administrative resources. The older order had already gone under the hammer of modern realities, but the new one had not yet been formed. Today national and local government in Southeast Asia is still in transition.[22]

Laos

In Laos, the basic pattern of government from time immemorial was absolute royalty with three levels of administration under the king: the "second king," the council of ministers, and the high officials who were of the mandarin type. In local government, the heads of families chose the village chief, delegates from the villages chose the canton chief, delegates from cantons chose the next higher chief, and the procedure reached as high as the provincial chief unless he was a member of the royal family. French occupation toward the end of the nineteenth century brought an overlay of French residents, the emperor lost absolute power, but the administration, national and local, went on at about the same pace.

Under the new constitution which established constitutional monarchy and which was proclaimed by the king on May 11, 1947, the government continues to be highly centralized, although the constitution provides that provincial governors may be assisted by provincial councils. The province is divided into districts, the districts into cantons which are groups of villages. Individual towns and small villages have a headman. The several larger towns have a district officer in charge, who is assisted by an elective council, while many of the remote and tribal areas are virtually self-governed. All national administrative appointments are made by the Minister of Interior or others in the hierarchy.[23]

[22] Robert E. Ward, "Village Government in Eastern and Southeastern Asia," *The Far Eastern Quarterly*, February, 1956, pp. 175–183. Rupert Emerson, Lennox A. Mills, and Virginia Thompson, *Government and Nationalism in Southeast Asia*, Institute of Pacific Relations, New York, 1942.

[23] Frank M. LeBar and Adrienne Suddard, *Laos, Its People, Its Society, Its Culture*, Hraf Press, New Haven, Conn., 1960, pp. 114–129.

Vietnam

Vietnam, before French occupation at the close of the nineteenth century, was an absolute monarchy. The civil servants under the Vietnamese emperor were mandarins modeled after the traditional Chinese official. In China, the only possible ambition for the intelligent man was to become a mandarin and thus fulfill his duties toward society. He was a man steeped in the literature and philosophy of Chinese civilization. Not only a member of the literati, he was distinguished on the basis of merit, which was indicated by the passing of rigid competitive examinations and accomplishments in the field of government administration. The power structure of Chinese civilization was not a concentration of religious officials nor yet a hereditary nobility. The mandarins came from the people and were in constant contact with their families and villages. In royalist Vietnam, the lowest mandarin was the district chief appointed and directly responsible to the emperor. Under him were the canton and village chiefs, who were outside the hierarchy and were representatives of the people.

At the village level, there were representative bodies and councils of notables. The latter consisted of persons in the village of high rank who were members automatically because of status. They directed the minor village officials who, like the headman, were elected by the people. Notables administered village affairs under customary law and were not harried by the emperor's men unless revenue for imperial use was not forthcoming, the peace was broken, or the recruits for the army could not be obtained. The monarchy dealt with the collective representatives of the villages rather than with individuals.

Under French occupation, little change was made in the government. The French residency supervised the national administration, keeping the mandarins and the councils of notables. The newer generation of administrators was educated at French schools in Vietnam or in France. National and provincial councils were established, their ranks filled by appointed notables. Most village officers were appointed by the next higher level of authority. During Japanese occupation the French administrative system broke down, and all responsibility went back to the Vietnamese emperor. In 1945 the Vietminh revolution proclaimed the Democratic Republic of Vietnam, and in the area of North Vietnam set up an entirely new administration patterned after the early Soviet system. All aspects of Vietnamese administration were done away with.[24]

In the Republic of Vietnam (South Vietnam), there is little change from the days of French occupation. Provinces are divided into districts. However, former small villages and hamlets which existed as independent units before 1956 have been consolidated into village groups (*lien-xa*) for administrative purposes under the control of a district officer. The enlarged village has a council composed of a village chief, a police officer, a finance officer, a youth representative, and a political officer, all of whom are salaried and appointed by the district officer. The village chief, assisted by the councilors, gives the national government instructions, decrees, and other communications directly to the hamlet (former village) chiefs. Each hamlet has a chief, appointed by the district chief upon recommendation of the village chief. Each hamlet chief appoints, with the consent of the village council, a number of *khom* (25 to 30 households) chiefs, who in turn appoint the chief of interfamily groups (*lien-gia*) within the *khom*.[25]

Malaya

The Federation of Malaya, a member of the British Commonwealth, is divided into nine quasi-sovereign states headed by hereditary rulers, and two former British settlements headed by appointed governors. The Federation as a whole is headed by a paramount ruler elected by the hereditary rulers of the states. The states are divided into districts which contain urban and rural municipalities. The districts are administrative units of the states; the chief officer of a district is centrally appointed, and he is the chief administrator with supervisory powers over the villages. The villages have elected councils which have some statutory powers but are under the control of the district officer.[26] The organized local authori-

[24] Luther A. Allen and Pham Ngog An, *A Vietnamese District Chief in Action,* Michigan State University Advisory Group, Saigon, National Institute of Administration, the Republic of Vietnam, Report no. 5, Provincial-Local Administration Series, May, 1961.

[25] John D. Donoghue and Vo-Hong-Phuc, *My-Thuan: The Study of a Delta Village in South Viet-Nam,* Michigan State University Advisory Group, Saigon, Report no. 1, Provincial-Local Government Series, May, 1961. *Local Government in the XXth Century, op. cit.,* pp. 457–464.

[26] Humes and Martin, *op. cit.,* pp. 395–397.

ties of the Federation are divided into five classes: municipalities, town boards, rural boards, town councils, and local councils. Municipalities are governed by ordinance and have councils, the majority of which are elected. There are 78 towns with town boards, the members of which are appointed by higher authority or are ex officio. There are three rural boards which include both urban and rural land in their jurisdiction. Their members are all appointive. Town councils and local councils, a majority of whose members must be elected, mark progress toward more democratic local government; they may be utilized by villages and rural areas on a decree from state or national authority.[27] The chief executive of these local units is a mayor, usually a member of the Malayan civil service, who is appointed by the state. He is a strong mayor with supervisory powers over the council and acts as chief administrator.[28]

Indonesia

Indonesia, formerly known as the Dutch East Indies, achieved independence from the Netherlands on December 27, 1949, and the next year became a federated republic of 10 provinces. Federalism gave way to a unitary structure, but with regional governments endowed with a measure of autonomy called "decentralization" which was justified by the demand for democracy in the new republic. Three levels of government are envisaged as being autonomous: the province, the regency, and ultimately the village. Each region, as it is granted autonomy, is given a regional elective council, a regional executive board, and a chief executive (*kepala daerah*). Regions are to govern their own affairs with minimum central control since a decentralization victory in 1958.[29]

Local government is carried on in the *desa,* an administrative unit containing two to eight villages and headed by a *lurah,* who is the contact man with the central government officials. Personnel attached to him include the secretary, the Islamic official (*modin*), and an irrigation repair

[27] Harold Bedale, *Establishment, Organization and Supervision of Local Authorities in the Federation of Malaya,* Government Press, Kuala Lampur, 1953.

[28] Humes and Martin, *op. cit.,* p. 397.

[29] Gerald Seymour Maryanov, *The Establishment of Regional Government in the Republic of Indonesia,* abstract of doctoral dissertation, Indiana University, Bloomington, Ind., 1959.

man. Below the *desa* is the village itself (*dukuhan*), whose headman (*kamitua*) is assisted by a security police officer and a herald.[30]

A specific study of a village in eastern Indonesia revealed the typical power structure of an Islamic village. Authority was divided between two groups of leaders: the *adat* or civil group, and the *hukum* in charge of mosque affairs or religious group. Each is headed by a paramount leader, the headman and the *lebe* respectively. A recent innovation, the village union, occurring in 1952, established another level of local government. At the head of village union is the village union head, and in each of the villages within the union is a resident deputy assistant who is assisted by a foreman and an inspector of community lands.[31]

Thailand

Thailand, known as Siam until 1939, was never colonized by Western powers and had uninterrupted independent existence since 575 A.D. Literally Thailand means "land of the free." An absolute monarchy since 1257, it became constitutional as a result of a *coup d'état* in 1932, and from that time efforts have been made to decentralize national government and democratize local government.

The country is divided into 71 provinces, which have 445 districts. Within the districts are about 4,000 rural municipalities with almost 40,000 submunicipal units. Provinces and districts are units of "local state government" administered by officials of the Ministry of Interior, and they include technicians under the supervision of appropriate line ministries of the national government. Central government officers and personnel supervise and administer their areas of jurisdiction in an ascending, tightly controlled hierarchy, which begins in the hamlet and village with the elected headmen, and ends with the Minister of Interior. In 1933, provincial councils were established as advisory bodies to the provincial governors, but the governors and the Ministry of Interior effectively control them through supervision and approval of their actions.

[30] Robert R. Jay, "Local Government in Rural Central Java," *The Far Eastern Quarterly,* February, 1956, pp. 215-227.

[31] Peter R. Goethals, *Aspects of Local Government in a Sumbawan Village,* Department of Far Eastern Studies, Cornell University, Ithaca, N.Y., 1961.

Districts have no representative body, the district officer being the chief administrator.[32]

Before the change to constitutional monarchy in 1932, two local government institutions had been established. Sanitation boards were first used in 1905. These bodies might be established by the king in provinces, cities, or villages and were governed by a board of ex officio members: governors, district officers, health officers, engineers, and commune headmen, as the case might be. In 1933, these entities were made municipal corporations. They had some financial resources and were administered jointly by central and local officials. A second innovation occurred in 1914, when a local government enactment provided for village and commune elections of a headman who was given certain basic local administrative powers.

With these exceptions, a strong system of centralization prevailed before 1932. Since that year, important changes in local government have been made. Provincial councils, first made up of appointive central government officers, became elective after 1956. In 1952, the old sanitation district was revived, administered by central government officials and elected local members. The commune council was created in 1956. As a result, there are three municipal-type local governments: city, town, and commune, each governed by an elected council and an appointed executive committee, dividing legislative and administrative functions. As of 1963, there were 3 cities, 82 towns, and 35 municipal communes. But there are 4,700 traditional communes (*tambons*) each with a headman, and almost 50,000 individual villages (*muban*), also with a headman popularly elected. Likewise, the office of municipal adviser was attached to the provincial governor's office, and the office of chief administrator of municipal government, patterned after the American city manager, was created by ministerial decree.

Here again bureaucratic central control vies with democratic local bodies, with the former in a position of dominance. Dr. Choop Karnjanaprakorn describes the situation in the following words:

> At present, whether it wants to be or not, it is clear that from its very inception the Thai municipal government has become part of the hierarchy of the Ministry of Interior. Therefore, it seems true to say that although the

[32] Humes and Martin, *op. cit.*, pp. 411–419.

> municipal government in Thailand has been purposely created for the Thai people to practice self-government for their own welfare and as a process of political democratization for a further step towards parliamentary government at the national level, municipal government has not yet freed itself from the bondage of old traditional and cultural circumstances. The more the municipal law is revised, the stronger becomes the control.[33]

THE PHILIPPINES

The Philippine Islands, discovered by Magellan in 1520, conquered by Spain in 1565, and ceded to the United States in 1898, became an independent sovereign republic in 1946. The republic has 53 provinces, each with an elected governor and a small provincial board composed of the governor and two elected members. Neither governor nor board has much power. Line department heads of the province are responsible to their own central ministries. So the governor and the board members are neither administrators, legislators, nor judges; their main activity seems to be political. Central departments are usually staffed on a provincial basis in such fields as public works, education, health, and finance.

Provinces are divided into municipalities like those of Latin America in that they contain both semiurban and rural areas. They have corporate legal status and are creatures of the national government, their powers being severely limited and their activities closely supervised. The provincial governor exercises general supervisory power over them, and central government ministries direct or control line functions undertaken in the municipality. The chief executive of the municipality is the elected mayor; he appoints subordinate officers and employees of the municipality and is assisted by a municipal secretary. The municipal council is composed of the mayor, vice-mayor, and elected councilors. Each of the councilors "looks after" a number of barrios in the municipality. The municipality has a Spanish-period history, but only in the twentieth century did it ob-

[33] Choop Karnjanaprakorn, *Municipal Government in Thailand as an Institution and Process of Self-government,* doctoral dissertation, Indiana University, Bloomington, Ind., 1959, pp. 37, 188. John William Ryan, *Bangkok Government and Administration: Appearance and Reality,* doctoral dissertation, Indiana University, Bloomington, Ind., 1959. Frederick James Horrigan, *Local Government and Administration in Thailand: A Study of Institutions and Their Cultural Setting,* doctoral dissertation, Indiana University, Bloomington, Ind., 1959. *Local Government in the XXth Century, op. cit.,* pp. 373–378.

tain substantive functions. Even now it is greatly understaffed, underfinanced, and underprivileged. It has the form to do the functions that an American municipality carries on, but it has only the pale shadow of power beside it.

The barrio dates back before Spanish times; it is the historical survivor of the barangay, a village institution brought to the islands by Malay immigrants in some distant past. Early barangays were little more than extended families in a village setting. The headman, called raja, sultan, or *datu,* was absolute ruler although he was advised by a council of elders. The barangays were independently sovereign, although they sometimes formed loose confederations with neighbors for defense purposes. During Spanish times, the headman was stripped of his power and became an appointee of the governor; the barangays were consolidated into pueblos although they remained administrative units, and the name was changed to barrio.

The barrio today is a subdivision of the municipality, and it in turn is often made up of more than one settlement called a sitio. Barrios may be created or consolidated by higher authority. Within chartered cities there may be barrios which have not corporate standing but are neighborhood subdivisions. Each barrio has a barrio lieutenant who works with the municipal councilor to whom he reports.

A new law granting autonomy to barrios was made effective on January 1, 1960. They were established as quasi-municipal corporations and endowed with specific powers. The law sets up a barrio assembly to consist of all qualified electors and those who have resided in the barrio for six months. The barrio assembly shall meet at least once a year to hear the annual report of the barrio council, and when members of the barrio council are to be elected. In each barrio there shall be a council with the following members: a barrio lieutenant, a barrio treasurer, four council members, and vice-lieutenants, one from each sitio in the barrio, or one for each 200 inhabitants of the barrio. The election of barrio council members shall be held at a meeting of the barrio assembly. Terms of office shall be for two years. The mayor of the municipality "shall exercise the power of supervision over barrio officials." The barrio lieutenant is the executive officer of the barrio with power to maintain public order, to preside over meetings of the barrio assembly and barrio council, to organize a fire brigade, to approve vouchers for the disbursement of funds, to enforce laws and ordinances operative within the barrio, and to enter contracts with the approval of the barrio council. One interesting feature in the law is that barrio lieutenants, if they have a good record, shall "have preference" in appointments in government agencies and in purchasing public lands. Also incumbent barrio lieutenants receive free hospitalization and exemption from tuition fees for their children in elementary and intermediate public schools. Barrio councils are given a broad scope of powers to exercise with a minimum supervision by higher authorities, and power to tax within prescribed limits. Thus the local units of the Philippine Republic for the first time in their history are now armed with the necessary powers to conduct an active and constructive administration at the local level.

There are 28 chartered cities in the Philippines, each city having a charter of its own granted by the national Congress. These cities are not under provincial government as are the municipalities. In actuality, however, cities were less independent before 1960 than municipalities, for many of their mayors and other officials were appointed by the President of the republic. In 1960 legislation provided for the election of mayors, vice-mayors and councilors by the people. While the mayor may exercise the power of a strong mayor if he is on the same political team as the president, many of the city departments are under the wing of their counterparts of the national government, and the national government often intervenes in city affairs, even appointing heads of city departments. Each city has a vice-mayor who takes the place of the mayor in his absence and is often a member of council, and a secretary to the mayor who carries out his political wishes and does a number of routine tasks. The city council, now elective, has broad powers which are administratively limited by national supervision, especially in the financial field. Each councilman is assigned to supervise one or more submunicipal units (barrios) which are local neighborhood units with only advisory functions in cities. There is a barrio lieutenant and an advisory council with which he works.[34]

[34] John H. Romani and M. Ladd Thomas, *A Survey of Local Government in the Philippines,* Institute of Public Administration, University of the Philippines, Manila, 1954, pp. 76–118. Humes and Martin, *op. cit.*, pp. 420–422.

JAPAN

Before the new Constitution of 1947, local government in Japan was modeled on Western lines which provided for a highly centralized system. The present prefectures were created after 1867, which marks the emergence of Japan as a modern nation state. Before that, Japan was a feudal nation with ever-increasing power struggles between the fief lords and the imperial government. By imperial rescript of 1871, the feudatories were converted into prefectures so that the government of the country could be centered in a single authority. Then prefectures were consolidated, until of the original 302 only 43 remained by 1890. These were, like the French department, artificial entities. Most of the Japanese cities, towns, and villages also came into existence by imperial decree when the natural settlements proved too small as units of government. Thus centralization was made possible. Democratic reaction led to the establishment of local assemblies for these units, but assemblies were rigidly controlled by local executives who were under central control. Local government was structured with the Home Minister on top, the prefectures as the intermediate layer, and the municipalities at the base. During World War II nine regions directly under the central government controlled prefectures and all subordinate levels in a totalitarian system of centralized control.[35]

The Constitution of Japan, adopted May 3, 1947, and the new Local Autonomy Law, which became effective on the same date, were both fashioned by American occupation authorities. By their provisions, the governmental system was decentralized and local government units became virtually autonomous. The Constitution declares that the regulations concerning the operation of public entities shall be fixed by law in accordance with the principle of local autonomy; that the chief executives and the assemblies of all local entities shall be directly elected; that local entities shall have the right to manage their property, affairs, and administration; and that legislation enacted in the Diet applicable to only one entity must be submitted to a plebiscite in the locality concerned.[36]

[35] Kurt Steiner, *The Japanese Prefecture: A Pivot of Centralization,* a paper given at the annual meeting of the American Political Science Association, September 6–8, 1956, Washington, D.C.

[36] *The Constitution of Japan,* Chap. 8, "Local Self-government," Articles 92–95.

Other measures affecting local government enacted during the American occupation were the abolition of the Home Ministry, the decentralization of police and education, the reform of local finance and taxation, and the separation of national and local civil service. However, as Kurt Steiner observes: "In actuality the central government exercises general 'guidance' over the local entities and uses the prefecture, as before, for the guidance of the municipalities within its area. This guidance extends over the entire range of functions, and, indeed, the distinction between local functions and assigned national functions has little practical effect." [37]

Japan is divided into 46 provinces, which have popularly elected councils and council-elected chairmen, all serving four-year terms. The chief executive is the governor, elected also for a four-year term. He is both the executive for the provincial council and the provincial agent for the central government. The Local Autonomy Law of 1956 increased the responsibilities of the province as the arm of the national government.

The municipalities of Japan include cities (*shi*), towns (*machi*) and rural municipalities (*mura*). In 1962, there were 556 cities, 1,974 towns, and 930 villages. All have the same legal status and structure which are outlined in the 1947 Local Autonomy Law. They act as a local unit of self-government and also as an administrative organ of the national government. Each has a popularly elected council ranging from 12 to 120 members. The mayor is also popularly elected. However, council has authority to pass a no-confidence vote, in which case he must either resign or dissolve the council and call for a new election.[38]

Within the rural municipality, the villages that are recognized by law, are a number of scattered settlements, each one a cluster of houses surrounded by fields, called *buraku*. A century ago, each of these constituted a legal village, both a unit of government and an "association for cooperative living." More than 60,000 of these were abolished as legal entities during the last half of the nineteenth century, and some thousands more since then. But to think of these *buraku* as local self-government would, according to Kurt Steiner, be misleading; they actually functioned in a "vacuum of government" harassed only by the lowest rung of imperial

[37] Steiner, *op. cit.*, pp. 4–6.

[38] Humes and Martin, *op. cit.*, pp. 424–427. *Local Government in the XXth Century, op. cit.*, pp. 231–232.

functionaries. In other words, like "premodern" villages the world over, they were sociological but not political units, and they carried on according to local tradition and custom without much interference. Even today, although the *buraku* organization is extralegal, it is not illegal because the government recognizes that in their local collectivity the *buraku* do many things that are useful and cannot be performed by higher echelons of government.[39]

TAIWAN

In the Republic of China, Taiwan, the local government system, established by the executive board of the national government, provides for a provincial government with a council, a governor appointed by the executive board, and an elected assembly. Under it are sixteen county and five municipal governments whose officials are elected by popular vote. On the lower level are wards and neighborhoods in the municipalities, and townships and villages in the counties. In rural Taiwan, the township is the most important administrative unit. It is governed by a township representative assembly and a chief officer or head, both elected. The township has a full line of functions including education, health, social welfare, communications, and police. Within the township, each village has an assembly and a village head, also elected, and has limited local powers.[40]

[39] Kurt Steiner, "The Japanese Village and Its Government," *The Far Eastern Quarterly,* February, 1956, pp. 185–199. Robert E. Ward, "The Socio-political Role of the Buraku (Hamlet) in Japan," *The American Political Science Review,* December, 1951, p. 1025.

[40] E. Stuart Kirby, *Rural Progress in Taiwan,* Republic of China, Taiwan, 1960, pp. 87–110. *Local Government in the XXth Century, op. cit.,* pp. 93–96.

6 Local Government in the National System

THE PRECISE PLACE of local government in the national system varies with time, place, and circumstance. It is not found definitively in constitutions, laws, or regulations, although these documents can usually furnish the general pattern. But what is legal is not always real; the actual facts may be bound up in personalities, social organizations, economic conditions, and political movements.

In the modern sovereign national state, there is nothing like complete autonomy for local units of government, although that word is seen and heard in many places: smugly written into the laws of the land, beaten out on the drums of party propaganda, and spun into the web of political theories. Yet there is value in the concept of autonomy. It is an integral part of man's aspirations for freedom, basic in his quest for democracy, essential for internal stability, and a strong defense against outside enemies. Local autonomy, in one form or another, in some relative degree, is a fundamental ingredient of a successful nation.

It may be surprising to those steeped in the liberal philosophies of government that nurtured and rationalized the English, American, and French Revolutions to know that Western penetration into other parts of the world did not usually foster local autonomy. The fact is that it destroyed the traditional village autonomy and broke down the delicate balance of native politics in many places. Western forms of government were superimposed upon native institutions for purposes of commercial gain or political control, and even for the more laudable motive of improving standards of living. But they did not always work.

As with any such massive movement covering a period of almost four centuries, the effects of westernization were good and bad, depending upon where one stood. Western forms of government were part and parcel of Western culture, of a piece with the things that were going on in the West itself at the time of penetration: democratization, nationalization, industrialization, urbanization—a whole array of "izations," all of which meant westernization. For in this period, Western culture was the only one still developing and extending itself not only in a geographic sense but in the unfolding of ultimate possibilities. The end had long before come for all the earlier civilizations, the remnants of which were still visible to the eye and biologically viable as the West enveloped the world.

This is not to say that there was unity within the West itself. Democracy vied with nationalism, localism with centralization; nations fought against nations; feudal, bourgeois, and proletarian segments strove for supremacy. Much of this conflict spread throughout the world, so it may be said that problems still unresolved in the West are found also in all the places where the West has come. World wars and social strife originating in the West become worldwide as do Western inventions, economic practices, and governmental institutions.

It is in such frame of reference that the problem of local autonomy may be best understood. The four basic patterns of local government—the French, the English, the Soviet, and the traditional—are different in their approach to this problem. The French stress the unitary organization with a hierarchy of provinces, districts, subdistricts, and communes in a strict chain of executive command from top to bottom, making limited concessions to representative councils and local democracy. The English, after a period of colonial experimentation, emphasize the elected council as the dominant local institution, limit the executive, and view the central government and its hierarchy as an advisory agency. The Soviet gives local units broad, almost inclusive powers, and establishes elective councils with subordinate committees, but with strict party supervision and control. The traditional in its original and typical form is a semiautonomous village government dominated by the elite groups with minimum day-to-day contact with overlords.

The measure of local autonomy in any nation may be gauged by two criteria: the allocation of governmental powers between national and local units, and the control of the national administration over the subordinate entities. The first is mainly legislative in character, the second, administrative.

THE ALLOCATION OF POWERS

The allocation of governmental powers to local units is made in several ways: (1) by constitutional provision; (2) by national or state statute; and (3) by central ministry orders, decrees, charters, or warrants. Some allocations are of a general or blanket nature, others are specific; some are conditional, others are without strings; some require concurrent local action, others are gilded with financial assistance; some are mandatory, others are optional; some are meaningless, others are not implemented with enabling legislation. There are all kinds both as to substance and procedure.

The allocation of powers by constitution, statute, and decree is often illusory. In most developing nations, the central government makes the final decisions regarding the actual functioning of local government. It has two standard methods by which this can be done: (1) by the approval of local government resolutions and decisions; and (2) by the approval of the annual local budgets. But, in developing countries, it must not be thought that the central government is always concerned with restricting the activity of local units. In fact, the reverse is more often true. The central government may have a five-year plan to promote, or it may have made promises to the people to improve their standard of living. It wants a constructive, ongoing program that can show visible results. So it may often prod its local units into action rather than attempt to restrain them. Many times its inspection services are for the purpose of stimulating new projects such as those for education and general community development, and in many countries central governments take on functions in areas in which local government is moribund or lethargic. For often local authorities represent the conservative elements of society, while the national government is dominated by the new elite, the educated, and those who have opted for progress.

Constitutional provisions

Most of the states that emerged since the French and American Revolutions have written constitutions or fundamental laws that outline the basis of their government. Many of them, but by no means all, specifically provide for local government. A few examples will suffice.

The 1946 Constitution of the United States of *Brazil* assures the autonomy of the municipality "by the election of the prefect and of the aldermen" and "by self-administration in all matters concerning its own interest," especially the collection of taxes "within its competence," the application of its revenues, and the organization of local public services. However, prefects of capitals and other federally important cities may be appointed by the governor of the state in which they are located. Also the Federal government is given the right to intervene in states to assure municipal autonomy.[1] The Constitution also provides that 20 per cent of the municipal income from taxes be used for education, and allows states to inspect local financial administration.

The Political Constitution of the Republic of *Ecuador,* adopted in 1946, "guarantees the relative autonomy of the Provinces, in accordance with the law." Likewise "municipal governments are autonomous and independent of other public offices" in conformity with the Constitution and the laws, and they are given the right to the revenues from the tax on urban property.[2]

The 1940 Constitution of the Republic of *Cuba* declares that "the municipality is autonomous," grants it powers "necessary for freely disposing

[1] Russell H. Fitzgibbon, *The Constitutions of the Americas,* The University of Chicago Press, Chicago, 1948, p. 66. Samuel Humes and Eileen M. Martin, *The Structure of Local Governments,* International Union of Local Authorities, Martinus Nijhoff, The Hague, 1961, p. 345.

[2] *The Political Constitution of the Republic of Ecuador,* Articles 124–130, in Fitzgibbon, *op. cit.,* pp. 347–348.

of the business of the local community," but states that the powers with which the municipality is not invested by the Constitution are reserved to the national government. It authorizes home-rule charters.[3]

The Fundamental Principles of Government of *Afghanistan*, dated 1931, proclaims that the administration of the provinces is based on "three fundamental rules, i.e., delegation of authority, allotment of duties and fixation of responsibility," and the formation of municipalities and their duties by means of a special code.[4]

The Constitution of the Kingdom of *Hejaz*, adopted in 1926, provides for a council in Mecca, Medina, and Jedda appointed by the King, and gives this council "full right to examine everything in connection with the municipalities and to pass resolutions to ensure their good administration and order." [5]

The 1952 Constitution of the Kingdom of *Greece* declares: "The administrative organization of the state is based on decentralization and local government as determined by law. The election of municipal and communal authorities shall be effected by universal suffrage." [6]

The 1947 Constitution of *Japan* enunciates the principle of local autonomy for local public entities, provides for elections of local officers, gives local governments the right to manage their own affairs, and stipulates that special laws passed by the Japanese Diet affecting only one local unit have to be approved by a referendum of the majority of voters of the local area.[7]

The 1950 Constitution of *India* gives the responsibility of local government to the states but directs them to organize village panchayats and endow them "with such powers and authority as may be necessary to enable them to function as units of self-government." [8]

[3] *The Constitution of the Government of Cuba*, Title 15, *ibid.*, pp. 274–282.

[4] *The Fundamental Principles of Government of Afghanistan*, Articles 102–105, in Helen Miller Davis, *Constitutions, Electoral Laws, Treaties of States in the Near and Middle East*, rev. ed., The Duke University Press, Durham, N.C., 1953, p. 16.

[5] *Constitution of the Kingdom of the Hejaz*, Articles 62–75; *ibid.*, pp. 381–383.

[6] *The Constitution of Greece*, Article 99. Royal Greek Embassy Information Service, 1957, p. 22.

[7] George McTurnan Kahin (ed.), *Major Governments of Asia*, Cornell University Press, Ithaca, N.Y., 1958, p. 184.

[8] Harold Zink, Arne Wahlstrand, Feliciana Benvenuti, and R. Bhaskaran, *Rural Local Government in Sweden, Italy and India*, Frederick A. Praeger, Inc., New York, 1958, p.23.

Statutory enactments

The detailed allocation of powers to local governments is usually made in national or state laws. The form of such delegation is often a local government code, sometimes covering all subdivisions and sometimes only one level or entity. It is a general procedure in unitary governments to grant broad powers to subdivisions in general terms, allowing the Ministry of Interior and other appropriate national agencies to make detailed regulations regarding their administration. Sometimes cities come under separate municipal codes, while village and rural government is integrated into the hierarchical framework of province, district, and subdistrict organization. Often the lowest level of local government, for example, the municipality in Latin American nations, contains both rural and urban population, and its sphere of powers, identical in law, actually depends on factors of population, need, and resources. Education and police are in many countries strictly national functions, although local units sometimes are expected to supplement them in minor ways. Some functions are almost always handled at the local level, i.e., water supply or sewage disposal, while in others, such as health and highways, national ministries take the lead and direct the work of the subdivisions, either directly or through regional administrative units.

Again, a few examples. In *Brazil,* the municipal council may legislate on all matters of purely local interest such as city planning, zoning, building regulations, streets, parks, water, sewage, garbage, markets, slaughterhouses, hours of business, public health, social services, public utilities, and even some aspects of education. In rural areas, agricultural assistance such as distribution of seeds and other help to farmers is made available. An elected mayor acts as administrator.[9] However, in Brazil every municipality has the same form of government, the same constitutional powers, and the same statutory powers within the same state. The legal powers and functions of the most remote local authority in the Brazilian jungle are identical with those of the capital municipality. But regardless of what the Constitution and laws may say about local functions, the higher governments, both federal and state, may take over local functions without any objections if the municipality asks for help or shows its consent in one

[9] Humes and Martin, *op. cit.,* pp. 342–346.

way or another. It appears to some observers that the indifference of the citizens as to which level of government provides services, and the absence of interest in local government and democratic control, have led to federal and state activity at the expense of the local units. However, since 1946, when the new constitution vested more power in them, municipalities have expanded their activities and increased in personnel. The changing conditions of life have demanded new and expanded services.[10]

In *Ecuador,* municipalities have the same general scope of powers as in Brazil, but in addition they administer schools and colleges under national standards, have a police force for the local enforcement of health, building and rent control ordinances, and volunteer fire companies, although fire protection is a national function.[11]

In *El Salvador,* a high degree of centralization exists for all governmental functions, but municipalities supply such supplementary services as their resources will permit. Municipalities are primarily responsible for the maintenance and operation of municipal utilities and other such local services.[12]

Urban and rural municipalities in *Turkey* have broad power to render local public services, while the province carries on functions in the fields of education, public utilities, roads, drainage, agriculture, and social welfare.[13]

In *Lebanon,* the province maintains law and order, works to improve education, health, and the general welfare of the area, while the district head grants powers to the local units as need and conditions dictate.[14]

Municipalities in *Iran* have certain local responsibilities; the administration of some they share with central ministries, while rural local units are served almost entirely by the personnel from the central departments.[15]

The Local Government Law of the *United Arab Republic,* enacted in 1960, delegates to its local units (provinces, towns, and villages) almost

[10] W. Hoven and A. van den Elshout, *Central Services to Local Authorities,* International Union of Local Authorities, prepared for the United Nations, parts 1–3, The Hague, 1962, pp. 34–35. *Local Government in the XXth Century,* International Union of Local Authorities, Martinus Nijhoff, The Hague, 1963, pp. 66–67.

[11] Humes and Martin, *op. cit.,* pp. 346–351.

[12] *Ibid.,* pp. 356–361.

[13] *Ibid.,* pp. 370–378.

[14] *Ibid.,* pp. 368–370.

[15] *Ibid.,* pp. 366–368.

full power to legislate for any "felt need." Practically, however, they are restricted, as in other nations, by budget limitations and central government approvals. Their powers, moreover, are expressed in general rather than specific terms, and being more or less "all-purpose," overlap with the other councils. The Executive Regulations of 1961, however, have broken down the major local functions and allocated various parts of them to the three types of councils. For example, in the field of education, the rural councils administer primary schools; the town councils administer primary and preparatory schools; and the governorate council administers secondary schools, teachers' colleges, and schools in towns and villages where there are no councils. The same general partition is done for health, agriculture, public works, housing, and other fields. However, all councils have responsibilities for the encouragement of the cooperative movement, the promotion of local industry, and the development of the national five-year plan in their districts.[16]

In *Yugoslavia,* the basic local government unit is the *opstina* (municipality) and its governing body is the municipal assembly, which is bicameral. Its powers are determined by law, but are broad and inclusive, including the adoption of all municipal laws and local regulations; the preparation and adoption of programs of development; the adoption of a budget and the levying of local taxes and other forms of income; the selection and dismissal of the president of the municipal assembly and of municipal judges, inspectors, and senior civil servants; the setting up of new factories and other economic enterprises; the extending of loans and guarantees for bank loans to enterprises and other institutions; the participation in selecting directors of economic enterprises and other institutions; and the supervision of and assistance to all subordinate bodies of the council.[17]

In *Poland,* all local entities, provinces, districts, urban and rural local units exercise only such powers as are given them by the state; and these,

[16] United Arab Republic, *Law No. 124 of 1960 Concerning the Local Administrative System,* English translation, Government Printing Office, Cairo, 1960. Also the 1961 Amendments to the Local Administration in Law No. 124 of 1960, and the Executive Regulations relative to Law No. 124 in Presidential Decision No. 1513 for 1960.

[17] United Nations Technical Assistance Programme, *Decentralization for National and Local Development,* New York, 1962, pp. 234–235. Hoven and Elshout, *op. cit.,* part 4, pp. Y-1 to Y-14. Humes and Martin, *op. cit.,* pp. 302–308.

unlike those in Yugoslavia, come under strict control by higher authority. Under the present system established in 1950, all municipalities, whether large or small, have broad powers in education, public health, agriculture, public order and security including maintenance of a militia, regulation of commerce and artisans, transportation, street cleaning, water supply, and cultural activities.[18]

In *India,* local government responsibilities are allocated by special and general state laws. In urban municipalities, obligatory functions include roads, conservancy, street lighting, regulation of trades, abatement of nuisances, markets, primary education, hospitals, sanitation, and water supply; while optional functions are city planning, reclamation, mental hospitals, municipal utilities, and other such activities and enterprises. The rural municipalities, which are the villages or groups of villages, and are governed by panchayats, also have broad powers including sanitation, lighting, education, agricultural assistance, markets, fire protection, and social services. Here the district, the level above the villages, also has functions such as the construction and maintenance of markets, rest houses, roads, and bridges, and medical and health activities not rendered by the villages. The Indian government has great hopes that it can establish panchayats throughout India and make them the main agencies for rural administration and cooperation in the community development program. In fact, these panchayats, especially those that comprise a number of villages (*panchayats raj*) would take over the services now rendered by district boards, which would then operate only in a supervisory capacity. As stated in a resolution of the Village Panchayat Committee of the Congress Party: "For the achievement of the objectives laid down in the Constitution, the village panchayats should serve not only as units of Local Self-Government but also as effective institutions for securing social justice and fostering corporate life resulting in fuller employment." [19]

Pakistan also has taken steps to decentralize government functions and to revitalize local entities by the establishment of basic democracies. The drafters of Pakistan's First Five-Year Plan called attention to the high degree of centralization which tended to thwart local initiative and sap

[18] Humes and Martin, *op. cit.,* pp. 293–298.

[19] Norman D. Palmer, *The Indian Political System,* Houghton Mifflin Company, Boston, 1961, pp. 151, 154.

the energies of the people who suffered from frustration and apathy. They felt strongly that the need for developing local self-government institutions should be recognized by the federal and provincial governments in clear and unequivocal terms. The tendency, which was all too apparent, of curtailing the scope of the functions of local bodies should be effectively checked. The new political system in Pakistan establishes local government bodies in both East and West Pakistan with power to carry out local functions under their own steam. The first tier of basic democracies is the union councils, which are responsible for agricultural, industrial, and community development within their areas. Each council has its own funds and budget. It has authority to levy taxes, and it carries the brunt of local administration for any projects and services undertaken. The next higher councils are largely coordinating, research, and advisory agencies. In urban areas, municipal councils have powers similar to those of the union councils. The responsibility for law and order, however, has been transferred to provincial levels, while the emphasis of local government is on economic and community development.[20]

The recent trend toward granting grass-roots local units more power is exemplified in the *Philippines* by the 1960 legislation relative to barrios. These village-level units are given authority, clearly specified in the law, to construct and maintain public works, facilities, and services; to undertake cooperative enterprises and industries; to improve the economic well-being of the barrio residents; to employ community development workers trained by the national government; to organize citizen committees to work in certain fields of activity such as cultural affairs, juvenile delinquency, and adult education; and to levy taxes and funds for the operation of the barrio government.[21]

The municipal and communal code of *Greece,* adopted in 1954, grants demes and communes specific powers such as construction and maintenance of waterworks, irrigation and reclamation projects, sewage disposal, bridges, roads and streets, playgrounds, cemeteries, slaughterhouses, cattle markets, public baths, pastures, electricity projects, street cleaning, and garbage collections. However, municipal police, fire protection, and pub-

[20] Stanley Maron, "Basic Democracies in Pakistan," *Foreign Policy Bulletin,* Feb. 1, 1960. *Local Government in the XX Century, op. cit.,* pp. 307–318.

[21] Fourth Congress of the Republic of the Philippines, *An Act Granting Autonomy to Barrios of the Philippines,* Sections 5 and 10, approved June 20, 1959.

lic school education remain functions of the national government, and all actions of local councils and officials are strictly supervised and controlled. Also the nomarchy (province) has recently been endowed with a council with power to undertake regional public works and projects under the direction of the nomarch (prefect). This council is made up largely of personnel of the national government in the province. It has been strengthened by the establishment of a district fund to provide fiscal support, and it can be considered as an attempt to deconcentrate, but not necessarily to decentralize, the authority of the national government.[22]

In *Japan,* the Local Autonomy Law, fashioned under American occupation auspices, granted all local entities a wide range of functions which may be exercised. It even decentralized police protection and education. Legally, local units have a dual character—they are "autonomous local entities" of their own, but they also administer many national laws and directives. In reality, local officials work more to carry out functions of the national government than they do in their own "autonomous" field. In fact, the central government still exercises a general "guidance" over all local units. As Professor Steiner describes it: "There exists thus a hypertrophy of nationally assigned functions which is accompanied by an atrophy of proper local functions." [23]

The Local Autonomy Law actually restricts the power of the national government to functions that are of a supralocal nature. But there are areas of national administration that cannot be transferred to local units. These include judicial administration, disciplinary steps taken by the national government, national transportation and communication, postal services, and national welfare and educational institutions. Between the national and local government stands the prefecture, which handles such matters as comprehensive economic planning, maintenance of prefecture roads and bridges, compulsory education, coordination of local services with one another and with national objectives, and functions deemed unsuitable for smaller subdivisions. Cities, towns, and villages handle a wide range of affairs which affect the daily life of the people, such as health, roads, public utilities, schools, hospitals, markets, housing, and other local

[22] Alex. Drakakis, *Local Government in Greece,* Ministry of Interior, Kingdom of Greece, 1958, pp. 10–15.

[23] Kurt Steiner, "The Japanese Village and Its Government," *The Far Eastern Quarterly,* February, 1956, pp. 190–191.

facilities. However, the revision of the Local Autonomy Law in 1956 strengthened the prefectures as national agencies and reduced correspondingly the independence of local organs. Likewise, police and education have reverted to the control of the national and prefectural authorities. In addition, central ministries and prefectures hold powers of supervision and control over local government by virtue of the granting of subsidies.[24]

The powers and duties of the three classes of municipalities in *Thailand* are specified in the Municipal Act of 1953. The compulsory ones include the maintenance of public peace, roads and waterways, garbage and trash removal, suppression of infectious diseases, fire protection, local education and training, water supply, abattoirs, medical service, drainage, public lavatories, electric utilities, child and welfare services, and public health. In addition, municipalities may provide public utilities, markets, parks, sports, public gardens, ferries, and burial facilities; promote occupations for local inhabitants; maintain welfare services and vocational schools; and develop municipal trade enterprises.[25]

Allocation by central administration

The *Sudan* offers an example of ministerial allocation of power. By terms of the Provincial Act of 1960, its nine provinces are governed by provincial representatives, provincial councils, and provincial authorities. The provincial councils are multipurpose and have a wide range of powers granted to them by the Minister of the Interior. Although their powers are parallel to those of local councils, they may step in to carry out their purposes if the local council fails to do so, but only with the consent of the local council.

Local government councils are established on the basis of need for administration and financial self-sufficiency rather than population and area. The Ministry of Local Government may establish local governments in five stages, depending on their capabilities for government, as follows: (1) where a local government inspector exercises local government powers without an independent budget; (2) where a local government inspector

[24] Hoven and Elshout, *op. cit.*, part 4, pp. J-11 to J-14. *Local Government in the XXth Century, op. cit.*, pp. 233–234.

[25] Frederick James Horrigan, *Local Government and Administration in Thailand: A Study of Institutions and Their Cultural Setting,* doctoral dissertation, Indiana University, Bloomington, Ind., 1959, pp. 263–264.

operates with an independent budget and appoints an advisory council; (3) where a local government inspector delegates his powers to a council with the consent of the Minister of Local Government but may veto any decision of the council; (4) where a local government council with full powers has been established by warrant of the Council of Ministers but with an appointed chairman; and (5) where there is a council with full powers which can elect its own chairman. These stages are a distinctive feature of the local government system in the Sudan. Full local powers are granted only when the area is ripe for full local government.[26]

CENTRAL CONTROL OF AND ASSISTANCE TO LOCAL UNITS

There are many degrees of reality between complete central control of local units and complete local autonomy. In fact, the ultimate extremes do not exist; all nations have some combination of authority and freedom in national-local relations. The field is most complex and cannot be described in general terms without danger of oversimplification. For example, the generalization of innate conflict between the higher and lower levels of government, while perhaps applying to specific situations in older nations, has little validity in newly developing countries where the leadership of an active central government is imperative until the government becomes stabilized and the correct allocation of functions is found. Central agencies not only control but assist local units, so there is need to understand the relationships in terms of mutual interest rather than antagonism. Furthermore, there is an urgent necessity in each new nation to arrive at a rational division of powers and responsibilities in order that the maximum effectiveness of the governmental system may be directed to the solution of pressing problems and to the rendering of needed services to the people.

In a United Nations study, the role of the central government in a developing country in efforts to accelerate social and economic development was described as follows: (1) formulating plans for the allocation of resources on a geographic and functional basis; (2) providing for the legislative framework and funds for programs to carry out such plans;

[26] *Decentralization for National and Local Development, op. cit.*, pp. 180–181. Hoven and Elshout, *op. cit.*, p. 35. *Local Government in the XXth Century, op. cit.*, pp. 339–349.

(3) providing leadership, stimulation, policies, and technical standards for services on a national basis; (4) creating administrative machinery and training technical personnel; (5) conducting research; (6) introducing new ideas to the people; (7) supervising and supporting local and decentralized units; and (8) executing overall measures not within the possibilities of the smaller units. In newer countries, many of these responsibilities must initially be centralized, and once on their way may be devolved to lower levels where possible. The danger of overcentralization is, however, always present. Functions once administered by central ministries and agencies are difficult to deconcentrate or decentralize—there are hundreds of horrible examples where central authorities undertake control over minor actions of local units, seriously impairing efficiency, competence, and morale. On the other hand, there are examples of decentralization where ignorance, inefficiency, and lethargy are just as serious. The correct solution must constantly be sought not in static regulations but in workable solutions to actual problems.[27]

In most nations, whether federal or unitary, a central ministry or department is the apex of national-local or state-local relationships. This is usually the Ministry of Interior or of Local Government. The main functions of such an agency may be enumerated as follows:

1. Drafting legislation and regulations relating to local government and administration
2. Recommending or effecting, as provided by law, the establishment, alteration of boundaries, and dissolution of local government and administrative units
3. Coordinating national interest and activities that relate to local government and administration
4. Acting as a clearinghouse for information on local government
5. Providing technical and administrative consultation to local units of government upon request
6. Drafting model procedures of administrative practice
7. Carrying on research on local government problems
8. Promoting and assisting in-service training activities of local government officials and employees

[27] *Decentralization for National and Local Development, op. cit.*, pp. 5–14.

9. Approving decisions of local councils as to legality
10. Approving local budgets as to form and content
11. Coordinating physical planning activities of local units with national planning
12. Inspecting local administration [28]

However, there are other national or state ministries or departments involved in the administration of local units. First among these is the Ministry of Finance, State Audit Department, or a comparable agency which is concerned with the finances of local units, especially with the audit of annual financial accounts. Sometimes this financial supervision extends to approval of the annual budget, regulation of financial reporting, inspection of accounts, approval of expenditures and loans, approval of tax levies and rates of taxation, allocation of grants-in-aid and other financial assistance, and even assessment and collection of taxes for local units. These central functions may not all be concentrated in one ministry but are often diffused among several agencies, and their efforts are sometimes duplicated and uncoordinated.

A United Nations study suggests six types of central agencies that perform functions which can contribute "toward rational decentralization": a central organization and methods office, a central personnel office, a central budget office, a central planning agency, a community development agency, and a headquarters office to provide generalist field administrators.[29]

In developing countries, the service and technical ministries and departments of the national and state governments are vitally concerned with local government administration. Frequently these agencies maintain personnel in the provinces and municipalities to carry out their particular functions. Sometimes this personnel is under the administrative supervision of province or district, sometimes it works directly under the min-

[28] *Decentralization for National and Local Development*, *op. cit.*, pp. 72–73. See Humes and Martin, *op. cit.*, pp. 31–50, for an excellent analysis of such functions. Also see Hoven and Elshout, *op. cit.*, pp. 50–63. The foregoing list does not exhaust the functions that are carried on by such ministries and departments in developing countries, neither does it necessarily follow that all such functions should be carried on in each country. Rather the list provides a general outline of the scope of such agencies, but there are few that would be found administering all the enumerated functions.

[29] *Decentralization for National and Local Development*, *op. cit.*, p. 67.

istry independently of either province or municipal government. Such functions as education, public works, police, health, labor, agriculture, and community development are usually undertaken either in cooperation with established local administrative units or directly by the national and state agencies themselves. The problem of coordination of such services is one of the thorny problems of central-local relationships.

South America

In *Brazil,* control of local units by federal and state governments is primarily in the realm of financial affairs. In some of the states, municipal audits are made by the State Tribunal for Auditing. State limitations on local actions cover the granting of fiscal favors and exemptions by municipalities, the establishment of ceilings on the percentage of municipal income that can be used for local personnel purposes, the restriction on excessive taxation and borrowing, and the sale of municipal property. The courts have power to void municipal legislation on legal grounds, although the annulment of municipal ordinances except on financial subjects has been declared unconstitutional by the federal supreme court. Federal control of municipalities is found only in case of administration grants made to municipalities by the federal government.[30] However, many local functions are performed directly by the federal and state governments, and their field agencies are given power to render such services as well as to control the application of grants-in-aid and subsidies to local governing bodies. Relationships between the three levels of government, federal, state, and municipal, are carried out by agreements signed by the interested parties, each on an equal footing and not in any superior-subordinate relationship. An interesting governmental phenomenon in Brazil has been the rapid increase of municipalities during the last decade. The underlying reason for this is that both federal and state governments tend to organize their services on the basis of municipalities, so that being a municipality rather than an unincorporated district gives the area much better chance to get federal and state services and facilities such as schools, health centers, post offices, assistance to farmers, water

[30] Humes and Martin, *op. cit.,* pp. 345–346.

supply, sewers, electric power, and police, which the higher governments render directly.[31]

In *El Salvador,* central supervision over municipalities is almost complete. The Court of Accounts, an agency of the National Assembly, exercises pre-audit and post-audit review over municipal financial transactions, and prescribes in detail municipal accounting records and procedures. According to the constitution, local tax measures must pass the National Assembly, and laws provide that certain percentages of municipal income be used for specified purposes. Inspectors from the Ministry of Interior review all council minutes, make annual inspections, and audit all accounts. Besides, the provincial government also has broad supervisory powers over local units.[32]

In *Colombia,* the provincial governor may pass upon resolutions of municipal councils; he appoints and may dismiss the mayor, who is also the chief of police and immediately responsible to him. In fiscal matters, the municipalities are subordinate to provincial authorities and to the General Controller's Office of the national government. Special courts adjust differences in which the municipality is a party, and may declare unconstitutional an administrative act. The province acts as the link between local and central authorities.[33]

In *Ecuador,* the political chief of the municipality (*jefe político*) is the administrator. He is appointed by the central government on the recommendation of the provincial governor to whom he is responsible. He sanctions all municipal ordinances. Provincial councils and the central Ministry of Government and Municipalities are concerned with municipal action in a variety of ways: complaints about municipal government, tax ceilings, and procedures in meetings. Judicial control of municipal government is through the Supreme Court of Justice, to which any citizen may appeal.[34]

The Latin American municipality, says John J. Johnson, has been

[31] *Decentralization for National and Local Development, op. cit.,* pp. 140–143. Hoven and Elshout, *op. cit.,* part 4, pp. 20–25. *Local Government in the XXth Century, op. cit.,* pp. 68–73.

[32] Humes and Martin, *op. cit.,* pp. 356–361.

[33] *Ibid.,* pp. 351–355.

[34] *Ibid.,* pp. 356–361.

constantly dependent upon the whims of the chief executives and rubber-stamp congresses. "Municipalities are charged with education, education is taken away from them; they are given the right to tax, the right is removed; they may or may not elect their own officials, but always the chief executive of the nation exercises the right to intervene." The recent upsurge of "national planning" has also weakened the municipalities; their officials cannot resist national gratuities that come along with it.[35]

The Arab states

The most salient feature of local government in the *Arab states* is the extensive scope of national control in its affairs. This control covers administration, finance, planning, and projects. Moreover, national agencies actually perform many functions which are local in character. There is usually no definite statutory allocation of functions between national and local agencies. While supervisory control generally rests with the Ministry of Interior or of Local Government, other ministries such as those concerned with public works, health, education, social affairs, and agriculture operate directly in local areas to the point that most local governmental units, even the municipalities of large cities, must be considered of secondary importance at the local level. While cities and metropolitan areas are becoming larger and more complex, the municipalities as governmental entities are withering away, getting weaker and more ineffective. However, in recent years, there have been some movements toward deconcentration of central authority, at least to the provincial level.

In *Lebanon,* the Minister of Interior approves all major decisions of local units, including the budget and the annual financial report, the appointment of top officials, and the resolutions of local councils. The chief executives of the provinces and the districts, the *muhafiz* and the *qaimaqam,* are appointed by central authorities; in the city of Beirut, the *muhafiz* is also the prefect, or chief of administration.

In *Syria,* the Ministry of Municipalities and Rural Affairs, established in 1958, supervises and controls local government, inspecting local activities, approving budgets, distributing national subsidies, and actually executing local projects and services that local units cannot carry on.

[35] John J. Johnson, "The Latin American Municipality Deteriorates," *Inter-American Economic Affairs,* Summer, 1951, pp. 24–35.

(Only five municipalities outside of Damascus have their own service administration.) In the various provinces under the ministry, there is a local government section which carries on projects and services for the smaller units and helps to supervise them.

In *Iraq,* there is a Ministry of Municipalities and a Ministry of Interior, the former serving municipalities, the latter in charge of the administrative units of the national government: provinces, districts, and subdistricts. Central control is exercised directly or through the office of *mutasarrif* (governor) of the *liwa* (province) through which all local administrative decisions and actions must go.

In *Jordan,* the Department of Municipal and Rural Affairs is a branch of the Ministry of Interior, and this agency supervises the activities of local units and renders technical assistance.

In *Saudi Arabia,* five provinces are each headed by an emir, and the large cities and towns are under a *qaimaqam,* both appointed by the King. Under the *qaimaqam,* various municipal services are carried on, while in rural areas the national government renders direct services, and the King gives financial aid to the nomad chieftains. In the national government there is a Ministry of Interior, which supervises the work of the municipalities.

In the *Sudan,* the Ministry of Local Government is the central organ for the promotion and development of local government in the country. It may grant more powers to the local councils if it appears that such powers can be exercised in the public interest. Its advice is available to the councils through the specialized personnel in law, engineering, housing, community development, and planning. It also sees that national policy is followed by the local councils. At the provincial level, the Minister of Local Government is vested with general responsibility for regulating the affairs of the provincial governments and has at his command the powers of supervision and inspection. Every minister may appoint "fit persons" to inspect performances in their jurisdiction, and may suspend a decision of the province council, making a full report of the reasons to the Council of Ministers. Likewise, every minister is able to scrutinize the part of a provincial budget that covers his own sphere of administration, and the Minister of Local Government acts as the general coordinator. According to C. A. G. Wallis of the African Studies Branch of the Colonial Office of the United Kingdom: "The purpose of the new style provincial administration is three-fold, to decongest the centre, to take up the slack in local government and to allow for a measure of regional autonomy without undermining the unity of the nation." [36]

In the *United Arab Republic,* the local administration law of 1960 and its amendments in 1961 envisioned a program of decentralization from national ministries to the governorate and local council levels. Five years was the time given for the transformation of the old to the new and the transfer of ministry personnel and financial assistance to the governorate, and much progress was made in the first two years. Until complete transformation takes place, the national government will continue to exert more than advisory and technical assistance, which is to be its ultimate sphere of action. The changeover on the service side of local government involves the delegation to the governorate of responsibilities for services and projects within the area. However, while the personnel will be under the administrative control of the governor, the ministries will direct their technical activities. Likewise, the personnel will retain their place in the overall civil service system as members of their particular ministries. Under the new system, there are still many ways in which central authorities control local units. Officials who have some say in local activities include the President of the Republic, the Vice-President for Local Administration, the Minister of Interior, the Minister of Local Government, the various ministries representing technical services such as Social Welfare, Public Works, Education, Labor, and Agriculture, and the Ministry of the Treasury. The most important central authority in local affairs is the Ministry of Local Government, established in 1960, and destined to take over the central supervision and leadership in the field. It is mainly concerned with financial, administration, and planning supervision, and with inspection of local administration either directly or through the governorate.

The following are some important areas of central control as outlined in the new legislation: definition of extent of local boundaries, establishment of local units, appointment of the governor of the governorate and the chairmen of town and rural councils, appointment of selected mem-

[36] C. A. G. Wallis, "Local Administration in the Sudan," *Journal of African Administration,* July, 1961.

bers of the local councils, approval of local budgets and tax levies, approval of major local council decisions, approval of local government loans, inspection of local administration, assessment and collection of the tax on land used for local purposes, participation in local government projects, and dissolution of local councils.

In *Morocco,* the Ministry of Interior executes numerous and important functions as the overseer of local government, but other ministries are involved in local projects, so that final approval for a project may take from eighteen months to three years because of the number of agencies involved. In municipalities, the governor is the chief administrative official. The city of Casablanca, for example, is divided into 14 urban *arrondissements,* each under the authority of a khalifa, an official who reports to the governor and is on the staff of the Ministry of Interior.

Recent developments in *Libya,* provided by 1962 constitutional amendments, resulted in having most of the powers taken away from the three provinces and lodged with the national government.

In *Tunisia,* the Minister of the Interior, the Secretary of Finance, and the provincial governor exercise extensive control over local units. Local decisions are checked for merit as well as for legality. They may be declared null and void, and many of them must have prior approval before being enforced. Furthermore, national authorities may act locally if local authorities fail to do so. Councils and members of councils may be suspended and dismissed by higher authorities.[37]

Other nations of Southeastern Europe and the Near and Middle East

In *Yugoslavia,* the representative assemblies of the *opstinas* (municipalities) and the districts are the basic organs of local government. They are bicameral, both administrative and economic in character, and are governed under federal and republic laws. In the evolution of these bodies, there has been a continuous process of vertical decentralization

[37] Information relating to the Arab states was taken from a paper and annex prepared by Harold F. Alderfer, United Nations Consultant on Local Government, *Public Administration and Finance Problems Associated with Rapid Urban Growth in the Arab States and Measures and Machinery Required to Cope with Them at Different Levels of Administration,* for the Workshop on Administrative Problems of Rapid Urban Growth in Arab States, organized by the United Nations in cooperation with the Lebanese Government, Beirut, March 11–22, 1963.

which had for its purpose the reduction of the power of the central bodies and the increase of powers of the *opstinas* and districts. Concurrently with the increase of such power on the local level, *opstinas* and districts became subject to a process of vertical decentralization in which self-governing bodies within their jurisdiction came to have an administrative sphere of their own although they were subordinate to the local assemblies. The small self-governing bodies included the voters' meetings, housing committees, workers' councils, various public-service bodies such as health and medical institutions, and cultural and scientific organizations, which had their own organs of government, namely councils and committees. As it now stands, *opstinas* are more and more the reservoir of substantive local powers while the district is an organ for control, coordination, and technical assistance. There is, therefore, no central agency dealing with local government, nor is there any hierarchical subordination. But the higher administrative bodies of government are considered the technical helpers of the local units, preparing manuals, collecting and disseminating information, providing consultation and expert opinion, and pointing out weaknesses and illegalities in local administration.[38] The practical effects of the powers of decentralization are shown by the number of employees on the federal budget: 43,000 in 1948 and 8,060 in 1955.[39]

In *Greece,* local government is under the jurisdiction of the Ministry of Interior. According to legislation enacted in 1955, deconcentration of authority was provided through the establishment of provincial (nomarchy) councils to deal with matters not entrusted to the smaller demes and communes. The nomarch or prefect of the province is an agent of the central government, having the right to decide on almost all local matters, especially those requiring immediate action. He follows the orders of various ministers in matters relating to local government. Decisions of deme and communal councils are in force after ten days

[38] Hoven and Elshout, *op. cit.,* part 4, pp. Y-4 to Y-5, Y-12 to Y-23. *Decentralization for National and Local Development, op. cit.,* pp. 234–239. *Local Government in the XXth Century, op. cit.,* pp. 471–472.

[39] F. J. Tickner, "Public Administration in Jugoslavia," *The Indian Journal of Public Administration,* July–September, 1959, pp. 293–301. Jovan Djordjevic and Najdan Pășir, "The Communal Self-government System in Yugoslavia," *International Social Science Journal,* vol. 13, no. 3, 1961, pp. 389–407. Živorad Kovačević, *Communal System in Yugoslavia,* Belgrade, 1958.

from the day they are submitted to the nomarch, who may cancel them within that time. The Ministry of Interior has authority to give final approval to many important financial and personnel actions.[40]

In *Iran,* while the municipal law of 1955 ostensibly removed municipalities from control of the Minister of Interior, there is still a great deal of central control. Streets and roads are jointly constructed and maintained with the Minister of Roads and the State Police. Health and sanitation services and facilities are jointly administered with the Minister of Health. Authorization by central authorities of ordinances for city planning, social service, and fire protection must be obtained; 10 per cent of all municipal revenues must be spent on public health. The Minister of Interior may dissolve a municipal council or a municipality, and municipal budgets must be approved by him. In rural areas, the central government is supreme. There are no local councils; in some villages, however, there are councils for community development purposes. The heads of the provinces, districts, and subdistricts are directly responsible to the Minister of Interior, while other ministries such as those for health, education, social services, highways, and agriculture operate directly with their technical staffs in the local areas.[41]

Local government in *Turkey* is controlled extensively by central authority from the Ministry of the Interior through province and district. This control includes the prior approval of budgets, the closing of annual accounts, the making of loans, the annulment of council decisions, and the recommendation to the Council of Ministers for the dissolution of municipalities. The election of the president of the village must be approved by the district officer or provincial governor.[42]

In *Israel,* the main department dealing with local government is the Ministry of the Interior, established in 1948. The local government division of this ministry has the task of extending the scope and functions of local government, assuring the financial solvency of local units, and supervising activities. This division contains six units: budget, audit,

[40] Catherine D. Papastathopoulos, *Local Government in Greece,* master's thesis, University of Minnesota, Minneapolis, 1961, pp. 41–43; also Drakakis, *op. cit.,* pp. 19–21.

[41] Humes and Martin, *op. cit.,* pp. 366–368. *Local Government in the XXth Century, op. cit.,* pp. 203–206.

[42] *Ibid.,* pp. 370–378. *Local Government in the XXth Century, op. cit.,* p. 396.

regional settlements, minorities, general municipal affairs, and training for municipal government. In 1959, the Bureau for Municipal Research was set up to collect information and statistics. The Ministry of Local Government approves bylaws of local authorities, makes extensive financial grants and subsidies to local governments, issues loans for development, and approves local budgets. The State Comptroller is the supreme finance authority in Israel. He is responsible to the Knesset alone, controls the finances of the state and local units, and makes periodic financial inspections. Besides these officials, other national officers have relations with local government. These include the Prime Minister's Office, the Ministry of Agriculture, the Minister of Labour, the Ministry of Social Welfare, and the Ministry of Health, all of which have important contributions to make to local government.[43] The Local Government Advisory Council was established in 1956 in order to advise the Minister of Interior on local affairs. It is made up of fifty representatives of the ministry, local governments, and the public. Another hundred members belong to the four committees of the Council: legislation, control and guidance, finance, and organization of services. One of the responsibilities of this Council is to draft a new local government code.[44]

Africa

The development of democratic and representative institutions at the local level in British Africa beginning in 1947 increased the electoral elements on the council, developed local taxing power with central supervision, substituted some indirect for direct administrative controls, put greater emphasis on administrative services although discarding the function of control, and reduced the importance of the executive, making him subordinate to the elective council.[45]

In *Kenya,* the Ministry of Interior was employing 18 finance officers in 1960. Nearly all were professional accountants who received their training in the United Kingdom. Nine of them worked in the ministry and the other nine were "seconded" as financial advisers to district

[43] Hoven and Elshout, *op. cit.,* part 4, I-1 to I-23.

[44] The Israel Organizing Committee, *Union of Local Authorities in Israel,* Tel Aviv, Israel, 1960, p. 18. *Local Government in the XXth Century, op. cit.,* pp. 212–213.

[45] I. Woodroffe, "The Relationship between Central and Local Government in Africa," *Journal of African Affairs,* January, 1957, pp. 3–15.

councils. All were gazetted as government inspectors, and handled the audits for all local units: 7 county councils, 26 district councils, 6 townships, and 24 education boards. The finance officers in their capacities as auditors and inspectors reported also on general administrative conditions, and had full power to disallow expenditures and surcharge local officials for illegal spending. Also they sanctioned local government loans and exercised other financial powers.[46]

In *Ghana,* an independent nation since 1957, important changes in national-local relationships have been made. Traditional elements in local councils recognized by central authorities have been replaced by elective elements. District councils have been abolished, thus eliminating the two-tier structure of local government. Existing local units have been regrouped so as to be large enough and with sufficient resources to carry out all local functions. Government agents have been withdrawn from the field to regional headquarters under a regional commissioner with the rank of minister. Under him are district commissioners who supervise local government along with an inspection team consisting of one senior officer and one clerical officer, each team being responsible for three or four local authorities. They check finances, investigate performances, ensure the working order of the governmental machinery, and submit reports to the district commissioner. At the top of the hierarchy is a Minister of Local Government who is responsible to the President. In addition to the eight regions which have been established there are three Technical Advisory Centers which are prepared to furnish local government with technical assistance of all kinds. At present, the one-tier setup includes 4 municipal councils, 10 urban councils, and 55 local councils, each of which is established with an instrument outlining its powers, structure, and responsibilities.

In *Sierra Leone,* supervision of local units is exercised by a number of departments, the coordinating ministry being that of Internal Affairs. In *South Africa,* control over local government by the provinces is extensive, including the power to legislate on local government, the approval of

[46] A. Altorfer, "Financial Officers in the Ministry of Local Government, Kenya," *Journal of African Administration,* January, 1961, pp. 11–23. A. F. Greenwood, "Ten Years of Local Government in Ghana," *Journal of Local Administration Overseas,* January, 1962, pp. 23–28.

bylaws and municipal regulations, the approval of municipal projects, and financial control in assessment, levying, and collection of taxes, and local borrowing.[47]

In *Western Nigeria,* the main link between the central government and the local authorities is the Ministry of Local Government, which has a field staff of local government advisers. Their main duty is to see that councils carry out their responsibilities according to local government law, which is in detailed outline form covering all aspects of the work of the local councils. Local councils may be dissolved if they fail to function properly, budgets are approved by the Ministry except for those councils adjudged capable of making their own budgets, and staff regulations are prepared. Other ministries are free to approach local units on matters relating to their own specific functions, many of them having their own field staff which works in conjunction with local councils.[48]

Asia and the Far East

One of the most difficult problems in making available central services is that of *integration at the top level.* For the most part, the technical ministries handling such functions as health, welfare, education, and highways operate directly in the local areas with their own regional staffs. In some countries, there is a central agency, usually the Ministry of Interior, which has the overall responsibility for administrative subdivisions of the national government such as provinces and districts, as well as for local units such as municipalities and villages, but its administrative competence does not extend to the technical services. Thus there are often a number of national agencies working in the same geographical areas, and this results in administrative confusion.

In the *Republic of China* (Taiwan), there is no central agency to provide services to local government. Each ministry goes its own way. The provincial government, however, exercises supervision over the county and municipal governments which, in turn, exercise supervision over the villages, townships, wards, and neighborhoods in their jurisdictions.

In *India,* local government institutions come within the purview of

[47] *Local Government in the XXth Century, op. cit.,* pp. 322, 413.

[48] *Decentralization for National and Local Development, op. cit.,* p. 223.

the states of the Indian Union and not the central government, although the Union Ministry of Health deals with standard setting and coordination of local government programs and policies, and the Union Minister of Community Development has been established for the democratic decentralization of local government and the promotion of different types of rural cooperatives. In the various states of the Union, the separate technical departments work through their own inspection and field officers. The control of residuary powers, however, falls to the Local Government Department, which works through the district commissioners and collectors, who are the revenue and general administrative officers of the state governments. The state governments exercise many controls over local units—almost every local division and activity must have their approval.

In the *Republic of Indonesia,* the Minister of Interior and Local Autonomy works generally with local units, while technical agencies assist directly in the field.

In the *Republic of Korea,* the Minister of Home Affairs has jurisdiction over local units. Here, it was reported, a lengthy procedure is involved in obtaining central service. Forms must be filled out and a number of officials must pass upon any request.

In the *Philippine Republic,* there is no central agency whose major function is the provision of technical and other services to local governments. There is a high degree of centralization with local units basically dependent upon technical ministries for assistance. The Office of Local Government in the President's office assumes the burden of attending to such requests and all other forms of aid, but it was stated that local units could get quicker and more effective service by working through their local political leaders and legislators than by going through regular channels.

In *Japan,* the Autonomy Ministry provides the planning, drafting, and implementation of various programs dealing with local government, the local bodies defraying part of the expenses. Petitions for assistance go from the local units through the prefectures to the top ministries. There is no top coordination.

In *Thailand,* the Minister of Interior is at the apex of the hierarchy of subordinate units. Since 1958, many local self-government provisions have been suspended, and this makes the Ministry most powerful in local areas. Incidentally, the Department of Internal Revenue collects taxes "additional" to the national taxes which are levied for local purposes and charges a 5 per cent commission. Requests for central services are channeled through the Bureau of Local Government in the Ministry of Interior.

In *Vietnam,* there is no central agency for local units. In each province, there is a technical officer representing each central ministry. Requests for service channel through the provincial chief to the central agency.

Numerous *personnel services* are made available to local units from central agencies. In the *Republic of China,* personnel administration is centralized in the Examination Yuan. Local units choose personnel from those who have passed civil service examinations. Medical insurance and retirement benefits are also furnished by the central government. A national in-service training program with provincial and country training corps aids in recruiting mid-level civil servants for local units.

In *India,* state governments "second" personnel to local units when necessary.

In *Pakistan,* the Local Councils Service of the central government appoints the principal officers for town, union, and municipal committees. These and career employees carry out the policies developed by local boards representing the people.

In *Korea,* all local officials are integrated into the national pension system, while training institutes for local personnel are held by the National Official Training and Public Administration School of Seoul National University.

In the *Philippines,* training institutes in community development and finance administration are given for local personnel, including elected officials, by the Institute of Public Administration of the University of the Philippines and the Civil Service Commission. A national pension plan is available to local units who desire to join.

In *Japan,* the Autonomy Ministry established an Autonomy University to train local officials, while other ministries have similar institutes. The Autonomy Ministry carries out interchange programs between the central and local governments.

In *Thailand,* the Ministry of Interior conducts training programs, administers medical and pension plans, and pays local salaries.

In *Vietnam,* permanent civil service personnel of the central and provincial levels receive medical care, retirement pensions, and other benefits. They pay 6 per cent of their salary toward the cost, while the governments pay 10 per cent. The national government pays most of the local salaries and holds training programs for local officials.

In the field of *local finance,* central governments not only have many controls over local units but render substantial financial assistance and services. An interesting feature in the *Republic of China* is the law of Delineating Revenues and Expenditures, which empowers the higher governments to derive subsidies from prosperous local governments and distribute them to poorer units. All taxes are collected by the provincial tax collectors, with branches in all the counties. Audits are done by the Ministry of Auditing, the Control Yuan, which has branches in each province.

In *India,* grants-in-aid are given to local units by the state and national governments, while the state constructs supplementary public works and provides supplementary health and education facilities.

In *Indonesia,* the central government assists local units in borrowing money for major construction projects by designing plans and specifications which need prior approval by the Ministry of Interior and Local Autonomy before being submitted to a credit agency. It alone assists in the preparation of local operating and capital budgets.

In *Korea,* central authorities guarantee bonds for local construction, give grants-in-aid, administer a uniform accounting system, assist in making budgets, and audit accounts.

In the *Philippines,* the national government grants loans for major local projects, gives community development grants-in-aid, installs uniform accounting systems, supervises local treasurers in the collection of taxes, reviews budgets, and audits accounts.

In *Japan,* technical and financial assistance includes tax collection, budget review, subsidies, and grants-in-aid. Local units receive 28 per cent of national taxes.

In *Thailand,* the center controls local borrowing, budgeting, accounting, tax collecting, and auditing.

In *Vietnam,* villages with surplus funds must contribute to a communal assistance fund for projects of intermunicipal character. Provincial and local budgets and large expenditures are reviewed by the General Directorate of Budget. The provincial service of the national treasury controls provincial expenditures, receives cash raised in the province for national and provincial budgets, and serves as the bank for village funds. The Directorate General of Taxes supervises the assessments established by local units, which collect taxes for the central government for a percentage surcharge for their services.

Local planning is a relatively new function and therefore central stimulation and assistance are normal. While local governments have full power to plan in the *Republic of China,* counties must get provincial approval of their plans. In *Indonesia,* the central ministries do the local planning. In *Korea,* the Ministry of Home Affairs assists planning for urban growth and for irrigation and soil conservation in rural areas. In the *Philippines,* the National Planning Commission is consulted in town plans, zoning, subdivision control, and building codes. In *Japan,* the central ministries provide technical and financial assistance, while in plans involving national interest, approval of the Prime Minister must be obtained. In *Thailand,* planning is carried on by the central ministries, and in *Vietnam,* jointly by central and provincial governments.

Few examples of *centralized purchasing* are found in the Asian nations. In the *Republic of China,* uniform regulations are supplied from the center, but localities do their own purchasing. In *Indonesia,* each local unit has a Commission on Purchasing, but the Central Purchasing Agent deals with prices. In *Korea,* each local unit goes it alone, but the central government gives advice. In the *Philippines,* the Central Bureau of Supply Coordination in the Department of Central Services takes charge of all central and local purchasing. However, local governments may make direct purchases if products do not exceed standard prices, are pre-tested, and are made at public bidding. This bureau stores common-use articles, while the General Audit Office checks on quality. In *Japan,* local units do their own purchasing without national assistance. In *Thailand,* the central government lays down general rules, but local units purchase without advice on prices. In *Vietnam,* there is no centralized purchasing, but both national and local government operate on the same general procedures.

Local program improvement gets the attention of central agencies in some countries. In the *Republic of China,* the provincial government of Taiwan introduced an "administrative process checking method," by which responsible persons trace official documents if overdue and then check the dilatory process. In *Japan,* Autonomy Ministry experts carry on research in administrative methods. In *Thailand,* the central government has a system of inspection for local units. In *Vietnam,* the National Institute of Administration, directly under the President, studies organization and methods, and makes recommendations for administrative improvement.

Coordination between local units, wherever found, is usually carried out by central agencies. In the *Republic of China,* the provincial governments coordinate county governments. In the *Philippines,* the Office of Local Government under the President has this responsibility, but individual ministries are powerful in their own rights. In *Japan,* the central government holds many conferences and meetings of local officials to achieve coordination. Legal advice is a central government function in all countries.

The functions of education, police, health, welfare, and highways are usually centrally dominated. In many cases, the functions are administered directly by central ministries through their own subordinate units stationed in provincial capitals. In some, they are administered through provincial governments and other subordinate units of the national government, wherein the administrative head is responsible to the central agency such as the Minister of Interior, while technical supervision is in the hands of the line ministries. In still others, local units with elected councils and elected or appointed executives have certain powers to carry on specific functions, to provide certain services, and to construct and maintain certain public facilities, but they receive central technical, administrative, and financial assistance. In all these nations, there appears to be a rising and earnest interest in exploring and implementing ways and means leading toward decentralization and greater local autonomy. This stems, in some nations, from the movement for independence, which was democratic and liberal in its outlook. Autonomy is a major administrative problem to be solved, and one which requires dedication to democratic principles, administrative imagination, and statesmanship of a high order.[49]

[49] Much information on central services to local units came from the Eastern Regional Organization for Public Administration (Eropa) held in Manila, December, 1960. The following nations were present: the Republic of China, India, Indonesia, Korea, the Philippines, Japan, Thailand, and Vietnam. Papers were prepared by the following agencies:

National Reports: Republic of China, prepared by the Ministry of Interior; *India,* prepared by the Indian Institute of Public Administration; *Indonesia,* prepared by the National Institute of Administration, Djakarta; *Korea,* prepared by the Republic of Korea; *The Philippines,* prepared by the Institute of Public Administration, University of the Philippines, Manila; *Japan,* prepared by the Ministry of Home Affairs; *Thailand,* prepared by the Institute of Public Administration, Thammasat University, Bangkok; and *Vietnam,* prepared by the National Institute of Administration. This material will be further cited as Eropa.

See also: *Decentralization for National and Local Develoment, op. cit.,* pp. 153–155, 169. M. P. Sharma, *Local Self-government in India,* Hinds Kitabs, Ltd., Bombay, 1961, pp. 83–95. Chetakar Jha, *Indian Local Self-government,* 3d ed., Novelty Company, Patna, pp. 198–199. Humes and Martin, *op. cit.,* pp. 379–427. Hoven and Elshout, *op. cit.,* part 4, pp. C–13 to C–24, J–18 to J–22. Eva Duka-Ventura, "The Failure of Local Self-government," *Sais Review,* Winter, 1960. Harold Bedale, *Establishment, Organization and Supervision of Local Authorities in the Federation of Malaya,* Government Press, Kuala Lumpur, 1953, p. 24. Choop Karnjanaprakorn, *Municipal Government in Thailand,* doctoral dissertation, Indiana University, Bloomington, Ind., 1959, pp. 74–125. A. C. Grant, "The Vietnam Constitution of 1956," *The American Political Science Review,* June, 1958, pp. 437–462. Lloyd W. Woodruff, *The Study of a Vietnamese Rural Community,* doctoral dissertation, Michigan State University, East Lansing, Mich., 1960, pp. 12–28. Ngugen Xuan Dao, *Village Government in Viet-Nam,* Saigon, 1958, pp. 37–38, in Woodruff, *op cit.* John D. Legge, *Problems of Regional Autonomy in Contemporary Indonesia,* Cornell University Press, Ithaca, N.Y., 1957. John H. Romani and M. Ladd Thomas, *A Survey of Local Government in the Philippines,* Institute of Public Administration, University of the Philippines, Manila, 1954, pp. 119–135. Kurt Steiner, *The Japanese Prefecture: A Pivot of Centralization,* American Political Science Association, Washington, D.C., 1956. *Local Government in the XXth Century, op. cit.,* pp. 97–98, 199, 311–312, 382–384.

7 Local Elections and Politics

JUDGING FROM the available literature, national elections and politics are of supreme importance in most of the new and emerging countries of the world today, while local elections, if they are held at all, have small nationwide interest or significance. This predominance of national politics and elections in the lives of the people points to the focus of political power in central governments and in national capitals. For national governments not only have the bulk of substantive governmental powers; they have decisive controls over the subordinate units.

Nevertheless, machinery for local elections does function even if under the thumb of central authorities, and people on the local level do exercise local suffrage in many countries. It would be difficult to say whether all such local elections were free or not. In Communist nations, the political party screens candidates and supervises elections; in highly centralized nations, the Minister of Interior and national executive leadership can exercise great influence in local elections. This also applies to nations trying out the new device of national monolithic, non-Communist party organization. Even in the nations of the original Western core that are built upon democratic dogma, no one can doubt that national politics influence state and local elections. All over the world today, in some relative degree, national politics dominate the scene.

In several countries which have elections, the village assembly provides the foundation for democratic government. These assemblies are usually informal institutions that were operating long before Western influences were felt. Usually they were not recognized in the newer legislation because national governments were anxious to establish local units of government larger than the sociological village. However, today the assembly is still a recognized part of government in many nations.

T. E. Smith, an experienced British observer of election administration, says: "The combined experience of Asia, Africa and the West Indies clearly demonstrates that widespread education and literacy are not essential conditions for the successful working of adult suffrage." But, he continues, different electoral methods which are adapted to local conditions are necessary.

The English electoral law was the model adopted in British colonial territories, but it had to be adjusted from place to place and from time to time. The French mode was the basis in French territories. How these will ultimately fare after a number of years of national independence remains to be seen, but it appears that widespread suffrage and elections are basic in most of the new states. If anything, there is likely to be an extension rather than a restriction where full adult suffrage has not yet been obtained. In British Commonwealth countries in Asia that have gained independence since World War II, universal adult suffrage has been generally established. In British Africa, however, voting is considered a privilege and not a right, and different qualifications for voting such as literacy, education, property, and income have been put into effect. In French Africa, universal suffrage has been introduced. In some Moslem nations, women are not enfranchised.

The administration of elections includes the registration of electors, the nomination of candidates, and the polling and counting of votes. First of all, election authority must be established. In most of the nations of Asia and Africa, the Minister of Interior or a top-level election commission or commissioner is charged with general responsibility for elections. National commissions are usually assisted by provincial, regional, district, and municipal government officials. In an alternative arrangement, election administration is a joint effort between the government and rival political parties at all levels. This method was used in the Indonesian elections of 1955, as it was generally in the French overseas territories. In the British territories, the government usually takes full charge.

The protection of minorities receives attention in a number of nations and self-governing colonies. In some, the franchise is limited to those with such qualifications as property, literacy, education, and tax payment. This has had the effect of disenfranchising large segments of the population and has given elite groups predominance in government. In other places, certain racial or communal groups have been guaranteed representation in councils. For instance, in India this is done to assure representation for officially scheduled castes and tribes. There is also the possibility of gerrymandering constituencies, which can be done by the governmental authorities. In many countries, some form of minority representation is sought through systems of proportional representation or limited voting when multimember constituencies are set up. In most places, however, the single-member district is used. In some parts of Africa, where equality of individuals is not officially accepted, franchise weighing gives certain classes of electors not one but two, three, or even four votes to the ordinary elector's single vote. Electors with weighted franchises must have one or more qualifications such as property, literacy, or military or governmental service that differentiate them from the mass of the electorate. This method is used in many African tribal elections.

Candidates for offices are officially registered through the use of uniform nomination papers signed by a certain number of electors, and sometimes deposits are required to show serious intent. There is usually no legislation relating to nomination by parties; that is carried on in any way the parties wish to proceed. Where a one-party system is in force, the party decides how nominations should be made. In local elections, nominations are often made through open village meetings or by informal groups carrying authority in the village. The use of electors elected from villages or districts allows nominations to be made by them at meetings where final votes for the office are cast. In areas of high illiteracy, candidates for office rely on symbols to designate their candidacy and often their parties to the voters. Symbols have been used in elections in India, Malaya, Ghana, Nigeria, Sierra Leone, Indonesia, and the French African territories. Often the ballots are marked with these symbols or are colored so as to permit simplified voting. It is believed that voting by acclamation is a thing of the past—except perhaps in a few local elections—and so is the "whispering vote" where voters whisper their choice to election officers at the polls, who cast the ballot. If direct elections requiring secrecy are used, there are three standard methods: (1) A separate ballot box is provided for each candidate. (2) The voter marks his paper ballot and then deposits it in a single ballot box. (3) The voter is issued an official envelope in which there is a separate paper ballot for each candidate or each party list of candidates. He selects the paper of the candidate or candidates for whom he wants to vote, recognizing it by color or by symbol if he is illiterate, and puts the envelope containing the ballot of his choice into the ballot box.[1]

The present writer suggested to an official committee of the Ministry of Interior of Iran the following method of holding elections for a proposed five-man village council in rural areas where illiteracy, according to a recent census, reached as high as 90 per cent. Voters (all adult residents, male and female) would hold an official meeting of the village or ward assembly. Nominations would be made from the floor. When all nominations were made, each eligible voter would be given five round white disks, about one inch or 2.5 centimeters in diameter. The names of nominees would be called in alphabetical order by the presiding officer. After each name was called out, the voters who wanted to vote for this person would file out to a secluded place in the back of the meeting and cast their disks in a receptacle placed in charge of tellers. A voter could cast one, two, three, four, or five disks for one name; one for each of five candidates; or two for one and three for another, and so on. In other words, each voter could use his five disks in any way he

[1] Most of the foregoing material on election administration is taken from T. E. Smith, *Elections in Developing Countries,* St Martin's Press, Inc., New York, 1960. This excellent treatise confines itself largely to practices in tropical Africa, Southeast Asia and the British Caribbean. The book is the result of extensive administrative experience in colonial elections, study of official reports, and firsthand observation. While it is definitive in nature, the author points out that studies of election procedure in the countries of South and Central America, Japan, Thailand, and the Near East are still lacking.

wished, but when he had cast the five disks he was through with voting. After each nominee was voted upon in this fashion, the tellers would make note of the number of disks cast for the name, and certify it immediately to the presiding officer on a sheet of paper. The voters would return to their places after each vote until all nominees were voted upon. Then the presiding officer would read the results and the council would be elected. The white disks would originally be furnished by the Ministry of Interior through its local agents. The disks, which would be stamped with the year, would be destroyed after the election, and new ones would be used for another year.

LATIN AMERICA

The four federal states of Latin America—Argentina, Brazil, Mexico, and Venezuela—have elected provincial (state) legislatures. Except in Venezuela, where the federal executive appoints him, the governor also is elected. There are no elected provincial officials in the unitary states of Bolivia, Costa Rica, Dominican Republic, El Salvador, Guatemala, Haiti, Honduras, Nicaragua, Panama, and Paraguay. In Cuba, before the recent revolution, there was an elected governor and a provincial council composed of elected municipal mayors. In Uruguay, an intendant is elected along with a department (provincial) board. In Chile, Colombia, Ecuador, and Peru, there is an elected provincial assembly or council and an appointed governor or prefect.

In the municipalities, the mayor or chief executive and the council are elected in Brazil, Chile, Costa Rica, Cuba, Ecuador (in provincial capitals), El Salvador, Guatemala, Honduras, Mexico, Nicaragua, Panama, and Venezuela. The council is elected but the executive appointed by higher authority in Argentina, Bolivia, Colombia, and Haiti. In the Dominican Republic and Uruguay, the communes are administered by a council elected by popular vote. In Paraguay, all local officials are appointed; and in Peru, the provision that municipal councils should be popularly elected was never put into effect.[2]

Suffrage qualifications as found in the constitutions and general laws

[2] Miguel Jorrin, *Governments of Latin America,* D. Van Nostrand Company, Inc., Princeton, N.J., 1953, pp. 139–162.

vary in detail but conform to the general pattern of inclusiveness. In *Mexico,* all male citizens over 18 years of age, if married, and over 21, if unmarried, may vote. Married women over 18 and unmarried women over 21 may vote only in municipal elections. In *Guatemala,* all male citizens over 18 years of age and literate women over 18 may vote. Males who can read and write are obliged to vote; male illiterates may vote six months after being registered. In *Honduras,* male citizens over 18 years of age may vote if they can read and write; illiterates may vote at 20 if married, and 21 if single. The same holds in *Nicaragua,* except that all illiterates over 21 may vote. In *El Salvador,* suffrage extends to all male citizens over 18 and those unmarried under 18 if high school graduates, to women high school graduates over 21, and other women over 21 if they can read and write. In *Costa Rica,* male citizens over 20 may vote, and those over 18 if they are married, or if they have a professional degree, own property, or have an honest trade; women do not have suffrage. In *Panama,* all citizens over 21 may vote. In *Cuba,* all over 21 may vote, and voting is considered to be an obligation, not only a right. In *Haiti,* all male citizens over 21 may vote. In the *Dominican Republic,* all citizens over 18, or of any age if married, may vote; suffrage is obligatory, and voting is done in the presence of an electoral official. In *Colombia,* all male citizens over 21 may vote. In *Venezuela,* all citizens over 18 may vote; aliens may be granted the right to vote in municipal elections if they have lived in the nation ten years. In *Chile,* all male citizens over 21 may vote; women and aliens over 21 may vote in municipal elections. In *Bolivia,* all literate male citizens over 21 may vote if duly registered; women over 21 may vote in municipal elections. In *Peru,* all literate males over 18 if married, and over 21 if unmarried, may vote; literate married women and mothers of any age may vote in municipal elections; voting is obligatory up to the age of 60, after that, voluntary. In *Ecuador,* all literate citizens may vote; voting is obligatory for men, voluntary for women. In *Argentina,* all citizens over 18 may vote if they have their civil rights. In *Uruguay,* all citizens over 18 have the obligation to vote and be registered; certain foreigners may also vote. In *Paraguay,* all male citizens over 18 may vote. In *Brazil,* males and literate women over 18 may vote.

In some nations, the clergy, members of the armed forces, and those who have lost their civil rights may not vote. In a few nations, the Australian ballot is used; but in most, parties are allowed to print and distribute their own ballots. Usually the Minister of Interior, but sometimes the judiciary or a special election commission, is in charge of elections. In some countries, there are direct elections, but in most others some form of limited voting or proportional representation obtains in municipal elections so as to admit participation of local civic groups as well as national parties. In some, the obligatory voting clause is not enforced, but in a few, failure to vote is penalized.[3]

AFRICA

The extension of democracy in Africa under European forms undoubtedly spurred the movement for independence. This is especially true for the British colonies which recently achieved national sovereignty. Whether or not the colonial half-century in Africa will have left any tradition of orderly, democratic government, time alone will tell. But it must be stated here that the British treatment of the problem represented a high level of local government statesmanship. The British not only foresaw that national independence would come to many African colonies; they nourished this dream with appropriate action. A uniform series of steps may be discerned in their treatment of African colonies. First, of course, was direct administration of local areas by British government agents without any native assistance. This was followed by the establishment of indirect administration, by which traditional native leaders acted as local government officials. Then local councils were set up with an elected element alongside of the traditional leaders, and with British government agents as executive officials and advisers. Gradually, traditional leadership was supplanted by the elected elements, and British agents were replaced with native civil service at the district and provincial levels. The same general path was taken by the British at the top level of colonial government in both legislative and executive councils: first, administrative control; then, councils with native leadership and

[3] Jorrin, *op. cit.*, pp. 243 *et seq.* Austin F. MacDonald, *Latin American Politics and Government*, Thomas Y. Crowell Company, New York, 1954. Harold Eugene Davis, *Government and Politics in Latin America*, The Ronald Press Company, New York, 1958, pp. 389–390.

administrative officials; then, elected, traditional, and administrative members together; then, gradual elimination of traditional and administrative elements with full responsibility to elected, native leadership.[4]

One close observer of African affairs, L. Gray Cowan, raises some doubts as to the validity of too hopeful expectations that the Western ideals of democracy will flourish under the new regimes. He asserts that the present governmental structure and organization bequeathed by the colonial powers bear only a superficial resemblance to their European counterparts. Many changes, he says, have been and will be made. One of the most significant changes is the turning away in the African states from a biparty or multiparty system to a one-party system peculiarly African in inspiration. With one major exception, that of Nigeria, the opposition parties either are too weak to be effective or have coalesced with the major party. Even in Nigeria, no true national party exists; only in the Eastern and Western regions are there substantial opposition parties. In Ghana and Guinea, there is only one party, as in many of the new French states. The reason for this is that parties came out of the struggle for independence militant and united; there was no room for a "loyal opposition." There was also an inclination for strong central government, and there was no time for debate and discussion. Because of the need to resolve the conflict between the traditional authorities and the new national governments, stress was placed on authoritative leadership and away from any separation of powers. Besides, Mr. Cowan sees a tendency toward socialistic and communistic political thinking.[5]

The recent introduction of voting in Africa has raised administrative problems that require continual attention and sometimes on-the-spot adjustments to make the election process smooth and to assure honest elections. Some examples indicate the range of such problems. For the election of 1953, the Sudan set up a special electoral commission with an Indian as neutral chairman. In many countries a senior administrative officer or high-level board is entrusted with election administration. Some find it difficult to get enough qualified persons to act as registration or election officers. Using local government employees involves some risk

[4] Sir Andrew Cohen, "The New Africa, the United States and the Western World," *British Affairs,* September, 1959, p. 129.

[5] L. Gray Cowan, "Democracy in West Africa," *International Journal,* Summer, 1960, pp. 173–184.

of getting biased administration, while unqualified and illiterate personnel are likely to make elections in their districts a shambles. A good deal of publicity is required to get eligibles to register and to vote. In Nigeria, administrative officers make tours to villages to educate the voters. In many places where registration of births is not universal and compulsory, age qualifications pose a problem, and so does the alien voter. Literacy qualifications must depend on the basis of judgment because of the multiplicity of languages used in particular districts. Systematic, full-time revision of voters' lists is adjudged impossible in most areas. The method of voting has raised unusual problems in Africa. In some places, the orthodox method of placing a ballot marked by the voter is modified by a "whispering vote" where the illiterate voter may whisper his choice in the ear of the presiding election officer. Symbols indicating either candidate or party are used in many places. The voter may stick a pin in the symbol of his choice, or he may be asked to deposit his ballot in the box which shows his symbol. Furthermore, correct identification of voters at the polls is not always easy, what with the similarity of African names and different ways of spelling them. The use of voters' cards to prove identity is cumbersome, expensive, and complicated. Order is not easy to keep in polling places, and the establishment of electoral districts must take into consideration the distances for voters to come.[6]

Elective local councils have been supplanting native authorities in Southern *Nigeria* since 1952, but in Northern Nigeria traditional authorities have been maintained. The new form in the southern region takes on the English system of three tiers—county, district, and local—with the members of council elected by the people on the local level, and by the members of the local councils on the district and county levels. The English local government system had remained generally free from party politics in Nigeria, but in the southern region party politics has recently tended to intrude. Party leadership has begun to realize that councils are the bulwark of grass-root organizations. Party labels have been used as a convenience to candidates rather than as a basis of convictions on principles, and the party has been utilized as a vehicle for acquiring

[6] O. M. Bird, "Administrative Problems of Elections in Developing Countries," *Journal of African Administration,* October, 1957, pp. 167–174. Material for this article was gleaned from a number of governmental reports on the general subject of election administration in British Africa.

power, political favors, and higher offices. Party commitments have become more rigid in urban areas where voters become party-conscious as literacy grows. In the conflict between traditional leaders and elected councils, parties have been a medium for the latter although the leaders curry favor with traditional chiefs in order to win elections. Parties, it has been maintained, may become a means of welding together mutually antagonistic tribal units within the same political jurisdiction.[7]

In discussing elections in Northern Nigeria, M. J. Dent, former district officer, compares the traditional selection process with the parliamentary elections. Their objective is the same, namely the provision of arbitrament of the rival claims, acceptable to the participants. While the electoral process, he states, does this by being patently free and fair, the traditional process achieves it by allowing an opportunity for the purging of emotion in the course of selection by following various well-defined conventions. These conventions include the seeking of balance between the various elements, the idea of rotation of office, the battle of argument as against the counting of heads, the attempt to produce agreement by the elimination of the weakest, the desire to operate with freedom from outside interference, and the primacy of the concept of the "mending of the land" which means that tensions are to be removed, emotions purged, and opposing elements reconciled. The way this is done involves the application of the wisdom of the elders who understand the psychology of their people.[8]

The Parliametary and Local Government Electoral Regulations of 1955 in the Western Region of Nigeria call for a common register of electors with nearly universal suffrage. In compiling the register each constituency is placed in charge of a registration officer. He is empowered to employ assistants to manage the many registration offices, for no person in a registration district is made to travel more than three miles to register and no registration district is to contain more than 500 voters. Supervision of the entire operation is by an electoral commissioner. Inasmuch as the literacy rate has been below 10 per cent, radio and other

[7] L. Gray Cowan, "Local Politics and Democracy in Nigeria," in Gwendolen M. Carter and William O. Brown (eds.), *Transition in Africa: Studies in Political Adaptation,* American Research Studies, no. 1, Boston University, Boston, 1958.

[8] M. J. Dent, "Elections in Northern Nigeria," *Journal of Local Administration Overseas,* October, 1962, pp. 213–224.

media have to be used to get interest stirred up. Candidates who want to be elected are the main activators for registration. Qualifications for voting are somewhat complex. Those who live in the division for two years and have paid direct taxes are eligible irrespective of age. But all over twenty-one years of age may register. Having registered, the voter is given a receipt card, but cards are not required in order to vote.[9]

In *Tanganyika,* the elections to rural councils held in 1956 were indirect. One elector was chosen for every fifty taxpayers. These electors were chosen at public meetings by popular acclaim. The election for councilors was held at the rural council building in each area and was supervised by two government officers. First, the names of the electors were called and checked against the official list. Second, the nomination of candidates was called for from the electors. As three classes of councilors were to be elected (representing the hereditary rulers, the great commoners, and the common people), the election had to be conducted in three parts, each group of seats being voted on in order of their class. In previous elections, voting was done by a show of hands, but this had proved confusing and inaccurate. In this one, the "whispered vote" was used. All the electors were seated in a roped-off area which spectators were forbidden to enter. The two officers conducting the election sat at a table in front of the electors. Each elector went in turn to the officers, whispered his choice, and then left the enclosure. When the electors had voted for one seat and the enclosure was empty, they returned and voted for the next seat. Each elector had as many votes as there were seats. It took a long time, but the method proved highly popular to electors, candidates, and spectators alike. In another area, more backward, each voter was given as many sticks as there were seats, surrendering one stick each time he cast a vote.[10]

In the first local government election in the North Mara district of Tanganyika under the new constitution of 1959, representatives were chosen from eight areas on the basis of one representative to 1,000 taxpayers. The earlier pyramidal system of councils and participation of

[9] Philip Whitaker, "The Preparation of the Register of Electors in the Western Region of Nigeria, 1955–1956," *Journal of African Administration,* January, 1957, pp. 23, 29.

[10] Keith G. Mather, "A Note on African Councils in the Rungwe District of Tanganyika and Their Election," *Journal of African Administration,* October, 1957, pp. 182–188.

clans, as such, in council or elections was supplanted by direct elections with adult suffrage for all citizens over twenty-one even though illiterate. The control of elections was by the district commissioner and his officers, and by chiefs and native authority officers in election districts. Representatives of political parties acted as observers in the various polling places. The secret ballot was used; votes were cast in the banda, a temporary building erected for voting purposes, in which there was a box for each candidate designated with his name and color.[11]

In *Sierra Leone*, by terms of a 1950 ordinance, district councils consisted of the paramount chief and one representative from each chiefdom in the district, and in those with larger populations an additional representative. The council itself elected three and the district commissioner was a member, until 1955 the chairman. The chiefdom's second representatives, chosen by the tribal authorities in each chiefdom, consisted largely of village headmen who were usually elected from the hereditary ruling classes. The election was by public acclamation and the nomination usually unopposed, but when contested, was decided by the counting of hands. The 1956 election ordinance keeps the paramount chief ex officio, but provides that additional chiefdom members be elected by secret ballot on a franchise including all persons liable to pay a local tax and women who are literate and own property.[12]

In elections to district councils in *Kenya,* several methods are used, but most voting is open and direct; candidates stand out in open *baraza* and their supporters line up in back of them for counting. In other places, secret ballots with colors or symbols are used, and in some constituencies, indirect elections are held in which voters vote for electors who finally make the choice for the council.[13]

South Africa is divided into four provinces. Each is controlled, subject to approval of the central government, by administrators, provincial executive committees, and provincial councils. The administrator is appointed by the government, the executive committee of four by the

[11] K. E. Shadbolt, "Local Government Elections in a Tanganyika District," *Journal of African Administration,* April, 1961, pp. 78–84.

[12] D. Kirby, "Ballots in the Bush," *Journal of African Administration,* October, 1957, pp. 174–182.

[13] M. N. Evans, "Local Government in the African Area of Kenya," *Journal of African Affairs,* July, 1955, pp. 125–127.

provincial council, and the provincial council by "parliamentary voters" who are as follows: (1) European citizens over eighteen years of age unless disqualified by insanity or criminality; (2) a limited number of colored males in Natal; (3) colored males in Cape Province who are twenty-one, literate, and occupy property worth a certain amount or earning a certain amount per year. In all local units of urban and rural areas from the township upward, the councils are always elected. In all provinces except Transvaal, there is a small property or occupation qualification for voting. In the Free State and Transvaal, all non-Europeans are excluded; in Natal, colored persons, but not Africans or Asians, have the same right to vote as Europeans. In the Cape, all races may qualify, but only a few Africans do because they may not own land in European areas. Colored persons and Asians not only have the right to vote, but they have held council positions. The government has announced its intention of instituting a separate council for colored people, who will then cease to be on the common roll or to be eligible for election to town council.[14]

THE ARAB STATES

In the *United Arab Republic,* the Local Administration Law of 1960 established three types of local councils: governorate, town, and rural. Each of these councils is composed of elected, selected, and ex officio members. The elected members are members of the executive committees of the National Union at the various levels: village, town, and district. The selected members are active members of the National Union appointed by the Minister of Local Government. The ex officio members are the representatives of the various ministries working in the governorate, town, and village administrations. The National Union, which takes the place of all former political parties, was established by the constitution of 1956 in the following terms: "A National Union will be established by the people to work for the realization of the aims of the Revolution and to muster all efforts for the sound building of the nation in the political, social and economic fields." All citizens of the nation,

[14] Leo Marquard, *The Peoples and Policies of South Africa,* 2d ed., Oxford University Press, Fair Lawn, N.J., 1960, pp. 82–87.

male and female, of sixteen years of age are ordinary members of the National Union. Those among them who have formally adhered to the principles of the National Union, and have paid an annual subscription of 25 piasters, are considered active members. All members, ordinary and active, are eligible to be members of National Union committees and assemblies, but active members alone may be selected members of councils appointed by the Minister of Local Government. The National Union executive committee forms the elective element in each council, and the elected members constitute the majority. These elected members supervise the activities of the local council and report back to the National Union organization in their area. The National Union committee also serves as the community development center and stimulates and undertakes activities outside the realm of the local council.[15]

In the *Sudan,* while parliamentary democracy came to an end in 1958, a Constitutional Development Commission was established to consider the structure of national and local government and make recommendations on elections in local government councils. The Commission made its report in 1962, and it is assumed that the recommendations will be adopted and have the force of law. The Local Government Ordinance of 1951 has been amended to provide that councils shall be made up of elected and appointed members, and that the appointed members shall not exceed one-third to one-half of the total number, depending on the stage that the council has reached in its powers of self-government. The chairman and vice-chairman of each council are to be elected by the council members. The term of councilmen is to be four years. Elections shall be direct, secret, and in a single stage. Qualifications for voting include: male sex, Sudanese nationality, twenty-five years of age, residence in the election ward for not less than six months, being a taxpayer or a tenant farmer but not a paid laborer. The executive officer of the council shall be the registration officer and shall draw up the electoral role. The province authority shall fix the date for elections, and there shall be an electoral committee of six, one of whom shall be the returning officer. Nominations of candidates shall be made in writing to the returning officer, with the signatures of five electors in the electoral ward from which

[15] Mohamed Abdullah El Araby, *Local Government in the United Arab Republic,* Cairo, 1961, pp. 12–24. Emil J. Sady, United Nations *Memorandum,* Feb. 20, 1961.

the nomination is being made. If there are more nominations than there are offices, the returning officer sets an election date. There shall be one polling station in each electoral ward in charge of a presiding officer. Voting shall be secret by means of ballot paper with symbols; the ballot shall be issued to the voter by the person in charge of the voting place. The voter votes in a screened place and returns his ballot to the person in charge, showing him the mark of authentication, and then drops it in the ballot box. The Minister of Local Government may allow voting by tokens instead of paper ballots when he deems it necessary.[16]

On May 29, 1960, *Morocco,* which had been independent since 1956, after a preparation of more than two years held its first nationwide elections for rural commune council members. In the approximately eight hundred rural communes, which are now the basic unit for local reform, these communal councils are to become Morocco's first experiment in self-government and the agency for a self-supported community development program. This, in an absolute monarchy that was evolving toward constitutional monarchy, is in itself of more than national interest, especially when in many of the newer and emerging nations there is a bias against political parties and elections along Western lines. At the central level, it was decided to have single electoral districts rather than some system of proportional representation on the basis of party strength with multiple-member districts. Thus party affiliations were not always clear and all concerned were trying, after the election, to unearth the politics of the successful candidates and to give the elections some national party significance.

Election preparation was under the supervision of the Minister of Interior, whose officials are barred from party activity. Local officials in charge did not appear to intervene in the election process. There were three major administrative tasks: the fixing of election districts, the registration of voters, and the registration of candidates. Both men and women twenty-one years of age and over could register and vote upon proof of residence and identification. Police, along with persons in certain other minor categories, were disqualified. It was estimated that 4,591,000 persons were eligible to vote, and figures indicate that 4,009,000, or 87 per

[16] *Report of the Constitutional Development Commission,* Government Printing Office, Republic of the Sudan, 1962.

cent, actually registered. Voters totaled 2,979,000, or 74 per cent of those registered.

Any Moroccan registered to vote and twenty-five years of age, with the exception of small cadres of judicial and rural administration officers, was eligible for office. Before the first election could be held, rural communes had to be established and tribal organizations had to be transformed into legal communes. This had been completed in 1958, when 798 rural communes were set up. Over 47,000 candidates were registered in more than 10,000 election districts, an average of almost 5 per district. The electoral law fixed the number of councilors per commune from 9 to 51, depending on population.

Under the law organizing these rural communes, they have not been given a broad range of powers. Their major function is to be the vehicle for local economic and social improvement under the close supervision of local agents of the central government. Likewise, the Minister of Interior has certain powers over the agendas and can make the influence of his department felt in many other ways.[17]

SOUTHEASTERN EUROPE AND THE NEAR EAST

Local elections in *Greece* had been held only four times between 1912 and 1951. Since then, they have been held every four years. The 1954 Municipal and Communal Code of Greece provides that deme and communal councils ranging from 5 to 31 members shall be elected by the people at large. All members of demes and communes of twenty-one years of age or over have the right to vote. Voters must be registered. The law of 1959 provides for a simple proportional representation system: the distribution of seats dependent upon the number of votes cast by each coalition. During the 1951 elections, women voted for the first time in Greece. In this election, the use of names and emblems of parties was forbidden by law, and candidates could not run as members of an established party. As a result, many independent candidates were elected. For many years after Greece became independent, local politics hardly existed; national politics influenced local leaders as it does today. Recently, how-

[17] William H. Lewis, "Rural Administration in Morocco," *The Middle East Journal,* Winter, 1960, pp. 45–60; and Douglas E. Ashford, "Elections in Morocco: Progress or Confusion," *The Middle East Journal,* Winter, 1961, pp. 1–15.

ever, a spirit of localism has been growing, particularly directed to the problems of community development.[18] One of the most important provisions of the 1954 code is that after the termination of the fiscal year, the mayor of the municipality or the president of the commune shall invite the citizens to a meeting at which he renders an accounting of his year of administration. Any citizen has a right to object to the mayor's or president's report, and to make a complaint to the nomarch, who must answer the complaint in writing. Council meetings are held in public. A majority of members may vote for an executive session, but decisions must be made public, and citizens may ask for a copy of the minutes of any meeting. Eligibility to hold local office requires both men and women to be twenty-five years or over. According to Alex. Drakakis, in the elections of 1955, one woman mayor was elected and 246 women councilors.

Associations of local officials are established by law in each of the 50 *nomoi* of the nation, along with a central conference of local authorities in Athens. Each council elects its representatives to the *nomos* association, the meetings of which are chaired by the nomarch, and each of these sends delegates to the national conference. The object is the exchange of information, the representation of local problems to the national authorities, and the development of favorable local legislation and regulations.[19]

In *Yugoslavia,* the municipal bicameral people's committees are composed of the municipal council and the council of the producers. The former is elected by adult citizens by direct, equal, and general ballot from single local electoral units. The electoral units of the council of producers are the organizations of workers in various branches of industry, business, and agriculture. Members of both councils are elected for four-year terms. Where the municipality is composed of more than one village, there can be village local committees, which may be requested by local residents when the distances are too great for administration by the overall municipality. Local committees are made up of municipal councilmen elected from the territory and a number of members elected by the voters at the village meeting. The upper tier of local government is the district, and here too are bicameral people's committees. However, the

[18] Catherine D. Papastathopoulos, *Local Government in Greece,* master's thesis, University of Minnesota, Minneapolis, 1961, pp. 60–63; Alex. Drakakis, *Local Government in Greece,* Ministry of Interior, Kingdom of Greece, 1958, p. 35.

[19] Drakakis, *op. cit.,* pp. 33–35.

district council is elected from among the components of the municipal councils.[20]

The new election law, which went into effect in 1953, made some important changes in procedure: nominations of candidates now can be made in open meetings or by petitions; and printed ballots are to be used. Being nominated in open meeting gives "organization" candidates a great advantage because party leaders are in charge of the meetings and can discourage opposition candidacies. Likewise, campaigning on a personal basis is now frowned upon, the emphasis being on loyalty to the party and its program. Plural candidacies, while relatively rare in federal elections, and somewhat more common on the republic level, are put forward in many town and district elections. But the party maintains a tight rein on elections throughout the nation.[21]

In *Israel,* the right to vote in any local election is granted to every person over eighteen years of age who has been a resident in the local area for six months. There are now 24 municipalities, 104 local councils, and 50 regional councils to which more than 1,500 persons have been elected as councilmen. All eligible voters over twenty years of age, including women, are eligible. Terms are for four years, and the elections are based on a system of proportional representation.[22]

All elections in *Turkey* are on a single-degree direct-vote system. All Turkish citizens, male and female, have the right to vote if they are eighteen years of age or over. Voters must have resided in their district at least six months, and must not have been convicted of crime. Each province is governed by a governor, a provincial assembly, and a provincial council. Provincial assembly elections are held every four years from single-member districts. The provincial council is composed of four members elected by the assembly from their own number, and the governor, who is also elected, as chairman. Municipalities in Turkey are governed by a mayor, a municipal advisory commission, and a municipal council, elected directly by the people for four-year terms. Municipalities

[20] Samuel Humes and Eileen M. Martin, *The Structure of Local Governments,* International Union of Local Authorities, Martinus Nijhoff, The Hague, 1961, pp. 302–308.

[21] Thomas H. Hammond, "Yugoslav Elections: Democracy in Small Doses," *Political Science Quarterly,* March, 1955, pp. 57–74.

[22] The Israel Organizing Committee, *Union of Local Authorities in Israel,* Tel Aviv, Israel, 1960, pp. 20–21.

are divided into districts, which have a council of elders and a headman. In villages, the assembly composed of all residents of the village elects a council of elders, a headman, and an imam (religious official). In municipal elections, the mayor authorizes the council of elders of his various districts to choose two voters by secret ballot. After a meeting in the town hall, the voters draw lots to make up observer committees of five to watch over the elections at all polling places in every part of the city. Polling places are set up on the basis of 500 votes per booth. Representatives of political parties may be stationed at the booths during polling, but they are to be invited in writing by the observation committees in charge. Registration and candidate lists are prepared before the election and posted in a public place. Voters write their choices on a ballot, place it in an envelope which is provided, and deposit it in the ballot box.[23]

ASIA AND THE FAR EAST

Local government in *India* consists of districts and villages. The system of direct elections for district boards or councils was introduced in 1931. Persons eligible for the franchise were property owners, taxpayers, literates, pensioned or discharged soldiers, and military pensioners. Candidates had to be registered as voters. Insolvents, tax delinquents, government employees except village officers, and those with interest in government contracts were ineligible to vote.[24]

In India, legislation provides for two types of village organization: (1) the *gaon sabla,* or assembly, which consists of all adult residents of villages, and elects the *gaon panchayat* or executive committee; and (2) the village panchayat, which is elected directly by the adult population. The panchayat consists of from 3 to 25 members, usually elected for a three-year term. Actually, the elders of the village, together with the younger leaders, determine the membership on the council which the formal election approves. In recent years, parties invaded the local scene, but they followed the traditional divisions of the community along factional and personal lines. Parties, as such, have developed no substantial program

[23] Turkish Information Office, *Self-government in Turkey.*

[24] V. Venkata Rao, *The Administration of District Boards in the Madras Presidency (1884–1945)*, The Local Self-government Institution, Bombay, 1953, pp. 63–94.

for villages.[25] All urban municipalities have elected councils composed of from 16 to 80 members, with three- to five-year terms. Elections are by universal or limited suffrage.[26]

The extension of political democracy in Indian villages through the election of a panchayat on the basis of adult universal suffrage has changed the character of village leadership and made the politically ambitious candidates seek support from existing caste groups. For example, the village of Bariapur had a statutory panchayat for fifty years. Before democratization in 1955, the members were nominated by the assistant collector from among the important families of the village. There were two ex officio members: the police patel, who served as chairman, and the village schoolteacher. Now, members are directly elected.

Prior to 1955, the panchayat was an organ of national and state government at the local level rather than an organ of local self-government. It was mainly concerned with maintenance of records and vital statistics, but also supervised local public works on behalf of the state. It had no development functions and was an institution of the status quo. The first three panchayat elections changed things considerably: lower castes received representation on the basis of population, members of the 18 caste groups worked together, and the individual political leaders emerged with fewer commitments to castes and groups and were able to pursue a relatively high degree of independent action.[27]

The Democratic Local Government Act was passed in *Burma* in 1953. Under this act, each village elected a council of five members; each ward in a town elected a ward committee of three to five members, which sent representatives to an urban council. The village and urban councils were brought together in a township council comprising one representative of each urban council. Each township council was represented by four to eight members on the district council. The township and district committees chose a small executive committee to carry on their work between the semiannual sessions of their councils. Authority flowed down from the Ministry of Interior to the district council, to the township councils,

[25] N. Srinivasan, "Village Government in India," *Far Eastern Quarterly,* February, 1956, pp. 206–211.

[26] Humes and Martin, *op. cit.,* pp. 379–386.

[27] A. H. Somjee, "Groups and Individuals in the Politics of an Indian Village," *Asian Survey,* June, 1962, pp. 13–18.

and thence to the urban and village councils. Each council was an agent of the central government and of the local district it represented.[28] In 1959, the government of Burma decided to abandon the large-scale democratization provided by the 1953 legislation on the ground that elected councilors were ignorant of their responsibilities. It returned to its ancient system of centralized command.[29]

In *Thailand,* local elections are under the supervision of the governor of the province, who acts in behalf of the Minister of Interior. If he approves of holding an election, he fixes a date for it and a date for filing the applications for candidacy; he also designates the location of polling places. Adults twenty years of age or over are eligible to vote, with a few exceptions. Candidates for office must meet residence and taxpaying qualifications and be Thai nationals. In municipalities, a council of between 12 and 24 members is elected. The municipality provides the facilities and the election officers, who are under the supervision of the governor. The central government prepares the ballots. Municipal campaigns are conducted mainly by person-to-person contacts; no political parties or pressure groups exist. Policies are developed after the election, not before. A study of the municipal elections of 1948, 1953, and 1958 showed that in the more than a hundred municipalities holding such elections, only about 40 per cent of the eligible electors cast their votes; of these, about 10 per cent spoiled their ballots so that their vote did not count. The study further showed that the largest group of elected members had a partial secondary school education, had completed the secondary school, or had passed the university preparatory school. More than half were small-business owners, and there was a substantial percentage of farmers and lawyers.[30]

Provinces and sanitary districts have councils with some elective and some selected members. In the politics of provincial towns of Thailand, there are no locally based organized political parties; until recently there was little or no identification of candidates with a national party. Candi-

[28] J. S. Furnivall, *The Governance of Modern Burma,* Institute of Pacific Relations, New York, 1960, pp. 82–83.

[29] Eva Duka-Ventura, "The Failure of Local Self-Government," *Sais Review,* Winter, 1960, pp. 16–20.

[30] Choop Karnjanaprakorn, *Municipal Government in Thailand,* doctoral dissertation, Indiana University, Bloomington, Ind., 1959, pp. 137–138.

dates campaign for offices and are elected on their popularity rather than on the basis of a set of principles.[31] In rural municipalities, a chief is elected by village chiefs, and a council is popularly elected for three-year terms from villages.[32]

The 1947 Local Autonomy Law of *Japan* provides that the mayor and the village assemblymen be elected by secret ballot with universal suffrage. It must be remembered that the 7,000 Japanese villages are in the main artificial units (*mura*), and that they are made up of "sociological" villages, 180,000 in number, called *buraku*. Kurt Steiner sees two patterns in local elections: the conservative and the progressive. The conservative views voting not as an individual right but as a duty owed to the *buraku,* called by some the "womb of the election." Close to 100 per cent voting is recorded where this pattern is found. Almost all the candidates run as independents; campaigning is deemed neither necessary nor desirable. Balloting is a formality; nomination is all-important, for candidates are chosen by the village leadership. In one-third of the villages, where only one candidate is nominated for mayor, no election is held. High value is given to harmony and to self-effacement. The progressive pattern follows the West: candidates run for office on issues, appeals are made to individual interests, elections are real contests. The number of assemblymen ranges from 12 to 30, depending on the population of the village. They have a four-year term. The assembly has the right to vote "no confidence" in the mayor, in which case he may dissolve the assembly and call for a new election. Another form of citizen participation in government is by means of making direct demands for the enactment of bylaws for the inspection of village management. These two modes of citizen action were brought into Japan as a result of American occupation influence. However, the typical Japanese way to resolve difficulties is to have the mayor or the assembly resign.[33]

In the *Philippines,* legislation promulgated in 1960 made elective all the offices of mayors, vice-mayors, and councilors in the chartered cities.

[31] Frederick James Horrigan, *Local Government and Administration in Thailand: A Study of Institutions and Their Cultural Setting,* doctoral dissertation, Indiana University, Bloomington, Ind., 1959, p. 242.

[32] Humes and Martin, *op. cit.,* p. 419.

[33] Kurt Steiner, "Local Government in Japan: Reform and Reaction," *Far Eastern Survey,* July, 1954, pp. 97–102.

Before this some were appointed by the President or other national officials. In 1954 barrio councils were made elective, and in 1960 they were given additional powers. In the municipalities, which are both urban and rural in character, mayors, vice-mayors, and councils are elected for four-year terms as they are in the provinces.

The barrio lieutenants and councilmen are elected at a meeting of the barrio assembly, which is held in the month of January every two years. According to the law, this meeting shall be called by the barrio lieutenant, who shall preside. The assembly shall elect three tellers, one of whom shall be a schoolteacher who shall act as chairman. Voting shall be by secret ballot, although open voting may be allowed if two-thirds of those present shall so decide. The limit of holding office shall be three consecutive two-year terms.[34]

The local assemblies of the people's representatives of the People's Republic of *China* were first elected in 1953 and 1954. The assemblies of the lower administrative districts are elected directly by the people, while on the higher levels they are elected by the deputies of the lower assemblies. Elections are open or secret, depending upon literacy in the lower levels. In the higher echelons they are secret. At the first elections, 86 per cent voted, and in the elections of 1956, there were 90 per cent at the polls. In the 1956 election the number of women deputies elected increased as did the number of nonparty deputies, and the number of persons deprived of the right to vote was reduced. Elections are held every two years, the term of all elected officials being two years. Sessions are two to four times a year, the people's committees carrying on the executive and administrative work on a regular full-time basis in most cases. The assemblies elect the people's committees from their own number. These committees appoint electoral commissions to hold elections for the assemblies. These commissions draw plans and administer elections, make up lists of voters, create electoral districts, print and distribute ballots, pay election expenses, and make a consolidated report on each election to the next higher level.[35]

[34] Fourth Congress of the Republic of the Philippines, Second Session, *An Act Granting Autonomy to Barrios of the Philippines,* Republic Act No. 2370, appr. June 20, 1959.

[35] L. M. Gudoshnikov, *Development of the Organs of Local Government and Administration in the People's Republic of China,* Moscow, October, 1957, United States Joint Publications Research Service, Washington, D.C., no date.

8 Local Government Finance

THE MAIN CHARACTERISTICS of local finance in developing countries are (1) the extremely small portion of the total public income that finds its way into local treasuries to be used for local public purposes; (2) the substantial share of local public revenue that comes from national grants-in-aid, national subsidies, and national loans; (3) the lack of a strong local tax and revenue-collecting system (many local taxes are actually collected by national agencies); and (4) the broad scope of national controls over each phase of local finance including budgeting, auditing, spending, allocation of grants, purchasing, tax levying, and tax collecting.

NATIONAL CONTROLS OVER LOCAL FINANCE

National dominance and control in the field of local government finance appear to be worldwide (Yugoslavia provides an exception). The trend is apparent not only in the newer nations but even in older ones that once had a more substantial measure of local autonomy in the field of finance than exists at present. This condition cannot be understood in terms of geography, education, colonial background, ideology, personality, political theory, or political party. It is the same in Asia, Africa, South America, North America, and Europe (again with Yugoslavia the exception). Naturally, national dominance and control in financial matters assumes national dominance and control in local government as a whole, for finances control what government will do and how it will be done. Not only does such dominance and control come from laws and decrees of the national government; it comes also from the power of the national government to grant subsidies to local units and to implement them with national regulations. Local governments cannot refuse to accept national financial assistance, no matter what are the conditions, but in accepting such aid their own financial potential is reduced and their indigenous resources become emasculated through disuse.

However, even where there is the possibility for decentralization (and there are indications of a countertendency in that direction in some nations), certain financial operations may well be centralized in order to carry out national or state programs and policies, and to secure honesty in the handling of funds. These include: (1) allocation of funds to local administrative units in accordance with national or state plans for development; (2) regulation of financial and accounting procedures, and auditing of financial transactions to ensure the proper handling of funds; (3) granting of tax and revenue powers to local authorities on a uniform and nationally consistent basis; (4) allocation and supervision of grants-in-aid and their integration with local budgets; and (5) financing of projects serving larger areas than single local units.[1]

National controls come mainly from Ministries or Departments of Interior or of Local Government. But there are others concerned, such as the Ministry of Finance and the Ministry of Treasury. These agencies may audit local accounts, and even approve budgets and expenditures; they may collect local taxes, grant national subsidies, and approve financial transactions of all kinds. Sometimes, when individual service ministries such as those concerned with education, health, and public works wish to finance certain local projects or services through provinces and districts, or through municipalities and villages, the Ministry of Local Government,

[1] United Nations Technical Assistance Programme, *Decentralization for National and Local Development,* New York, 1962, p. 55.

the Ministry of Finance, and the local governor or mayor get together and decide how things should be done. But too often fiscal coordination at the national level as well as in national-local relations is a chimera found only in the provisions of law and regulations. It is pretty rare in actual practice.

One of the main obstacles to fiscal unity on a local level is the presence of numerous *ad hoc* agencies operating in the local sphere but having national, not local sponsorship. Among these are the semiautonomous commissions for the supply of public utilities such as water, electricity, gas, and transport in metropolitan areas, and the agricultural cooperatives in rural areas. In many countries, these institutions are so numerous that local government unity is hopelessly fragmented and fiscal resources are dissipated.

SOURCES OF LOCAL REVENUE

Local revenues fall into several classes:

1. *Additional percentages of taxes levied by the national government.* These are mainly on customs, on corporate property and profits, on agricultural land, on money at interest, on sales and commercial turnover, and on subjects that provide substantial national revenues but cannot easily be taxed locally. Usually these percentages are very small. They must be approved by national authorities if levied in particular municipalities or provinces, and they may be withheld from local units if the money is needed by the national government. Also charges are sometimes made for the assessment and collection of such taxes, even further reducing the local "take."

2. *Local taxes on land and buildings, including agricultural land.* Such taxes account for an important share of local revenues in most developing countries, although full utilization of these sources is not often achieved. In urban areas, such taxes may be based upon the capital value or upon the rental value as determined by the assessing authorities. In most emerging nations, it is easier to tax rental values than market values because of the difficulty of finding market values. Qualified personnel to make valuations of real estate, both urban and rural, are few, so that if these taxes are used they are either administered by national agencies or,

in large cities, by urban governments. Taxes on agricultural land are often on the basis of a percentage of annual productivity, in some places still paid in kind in the same manner as in the Roman Empire in the reign of Diocletian. Productivity rates may be assessed by the acre, the feddan, the hectare, or some other land unit for particular regions every ten years, and taxes are based upon such formulas.

3. *Personal taxes.* These taxes are levied on persons, on adults, on classes of persons according to occupation, or on other bases. Taxes are levied to obtain revenue from those persons who do not pay the property or rental taxes and who should bear their just burden of local expenses.

4. *License fees and taxes.* These are levied generally as local taxes throughout the world, and may be placed on all manner of economic activities such as restaurants, hotels, abattoirs, stores, or places of entertainment; and on vehicles of transportation, especially motorcars. Some of them are for control purposes in order to apply standards of cleanliness and safety for the community.

5. *Earnings from public utilities and services.* In most countries, public utilities such as water supply, electricity, gas, and public transportation are administered on the theory that revenues will be able to pay the capital and operational expenses of the utilities. Sometimes they bring in profits which may accrue to the local government owning and operating the utilities. But often the utilities are in charge of semiautonomous boards or commissions under the national government, and the local governments receive no revenue from these sources in spite of the municipal and local ancillary expenses often involved in servicing them. When the utilities are privately operated under a franchise granted by the national or local government, the franchise tax or rental may accrue to the sponsoring government. However, profits generally are limited, and reduction of rates to the users and consumers or improvements in the utility services are made from excess funds. In this same category might be placed the revenues that come to a local government from the rental of its own property and the use of its equipment by private parties or public entities.

6. *Grants from the national government.* These are becoming the most important source of local revenue in most of the developing countries.

The reasons: (*a*) The national government has absorbed the best sources of public revenue, and is therefore obliged to assist local units. (*b*) The national government is saddling local governments with additional services for which no additional local revenue is forthcoming. (*c*) The national government is attempting to equalize governmental services between the richer and the poorer areas and is making national funds available on the basis of some formula such as wealth per capita. (*d*) The national government is trying to stimulate local units to undertake some new services or projects and is making national funds available on a matching basis of some sort. When national funds are thus made available, they should be put on a scheduled basis so that localities will be able to make proper adjustments in their annual budgets to include such grants; they should be rationally planned to ensure equity between areas of the country and classes of people benefitting therefrom, and they should be simple to administer.

7. *Revenue from commercial enterprises.* In some nations, local governments are given the power to undertake commercial enterprises, the net revenue of which is a resource of the local government. Such enterprises are undertaken mainly in socialistic and communistic nations, although most economic undertakings in such countries are administered by national ministries or by national semiautonomous boards of directors under national ministries. In Yugoslavia, however, the municipality may own and administer economic, communal, cultural, educational, health, and social institutions. Furthermore, it has powers of legal supervision over many economic organizations within its borders. The municipality, therefore, accumulates its budgetary revenues partly from the economy, actually from net profits of enterprises after costs and the turnover taxes are paid. In the United Arab Republic, local governments are allowed to undertake economic enterprises within their jurisdictions. The worldwide development of agricultural and consumer cooperatives is another feature which has significance for local government. While they are not generally a part of local government, being organized directly from national ministries, they overlap and cooperate with rural and urban local governments in many ways.

8. *Voluntary contributions and gifts.* In rural areas in many sections

of the world, especially in the Near and Middle East, revenues of agricultural villages and small towns often include voluntary contributions. Assuming that people do not like to be taxed, that many people cannot pay taxes, and that it is easier to raise money for community projects in an informal way, communal councils often make more or less firm financial assessments on heads of families and on commercial enterprises. Because of their communal value these voluntary contributions have almost the same sanctions as regular taxes, and sometimes more. Likewise, many communities receive gifts from former residents and members of the community who have achieved financial success in foreign countries. Money is sent home for schools, churches, mosques, water-supply installations, and the like. In many countries, rural communities are allowed by law to request every able-bodied adult male citizen to give a certain number of days (usually ten) of voluntary work on communal projects such as roads, bridges, and other public facilities.

9. *Loans.* Many large-scale, permanent installations and constructions of a community character such as schools, municipal buildings, modern roads and bridges, and water-supply facilities cannot be financed out of pocket. The annual revenues of an ordinary local government cannot finance such items in one year. Therefore, loans must be made. Local governments in developing countries generally have difficulty in floating loans for projects that require capital outlays. It is impossible for them to resort to direct public borrowing through the issue of bonds except in the larger cities; it is equally unsatisfactory to borrow from commercial banks because of the high rates of interest. Local authorities will not often be able to earmark proceeds from certain taxes or portions of current revenue, or reserves from local enterprises for such purposes, although such practices have been reported in Tanganyika, Uganda, Ghana, and Nigeria.[2] In many new and emerging nations, however, it would be helpful if the central government could establish a special agency to make loans to local governments. This would be especially practical for local revenue-producing projects such as water supply, irrigation works, electric

[2] Ursula K. Hicks, *Development from Below: Local Government and Finance in Developing Countries of the Commonwealth,* Oxford University Press, Fair Lawn, N.J., 1961, pp. 397–398.

plants, and transport facilities, which could be financed at low interest rates on a long- or short-time basis to be repaid in such a way as to make a rotating fund available for continued use. Along with the loans, the central government could furnish expert financial and technical advice on projects thus financed.

In *Kenya,* a Local Government Loans Authority was established in 1953 with power to make loans to local authorities for purposes for which they are authorized to borrow money. Loans have been made for housing projects and community facilities such as sewerage and drainage, water supply, roads, street lighting, markets and slaughterhouses, schools and health centers. Management of the Authority is in the hands of a board made up of ranking national officials dealing with local government, mostly from the Ministry of Local Government and Lands, the Minister of which is chairman.

Another such organization is the Institute for Development of Municipalities of *Guatemala,* established in 1957 as an autonomous public body with broad powers to promote the welfare of municipalities by affording them financial and technical assistance. The Institute receives the proceeds from a tax of 8 cents per liter on *aguardiente,* a Latin American alcoholic beverage, which totals about $600,000 annually. Its capital in 1962 came to more than $3 million. Municipalities are required to use the banking facilities of the Institute. The governing board consists of the chairman whom the President of the republic appoints, the vice-chairman who is appointed by the governing body of the National Association of Municipalities, and another member whom the National Monetary Board appoints. The manager of the Institute is appointed by the President on the nomination of the board. The Institute loans money to municipalities for community facilities and the purchase of machinery and equipment. It also provides technical assistance: preparing plans and specifications for projects, rendering advisory and administrative services, and supervising construction.

A credit institution for local governments was established in 1954 in *Israel* as a joint-stock company of municipalities and was used to channel loans from the national government to the localities. In 1960, the founders' shares were distributed between the local authorities, the Ministry of

Finance, and three large financial institutions. The bank makes loans to communities for facilities and commercial enterprises.[3]

FINANCIAL ADMINISTRATION

Included in financial administration are several important activities. First and foremost in the preparation of an *annual budget,* which includes the estimated receipts and expenditures of the local government for the fiscal year. This is prepared or approved by the finance officer of the local government, the finance committee of the local council, the various heads of departments of the local government, and finally the chief executive. In many countries, national or provincial authorities must approve the budget before it becomes enforceable.

Second, the *system of accounting* must reflect accurately the day-by-day financial transactions—the receipt of revenues, the payment of expenses, the changes in allotments and allocations in the budget, the contracting of liabilities, the custody of funds, the operation of bank accounts, the custody of stores, the payment of salaries and wages, and other such matters. In the larger local governments, there is usually a finance department manned by trained finance personnel; in the smaller and rural units, where the financial operations are simpler, the secretary or one finance official handles these matters. In both cases, accounting forms should be prescribed by the state so as to achieve uniformity of reporting, and central inspection of finances as well as annual audits of accounts should be made.

Third, there should be a *local system of administration of property taxes.* In many countries, the national finance ministries or departments actually assess and collect local taxes because local personnel is not sufficient or well enough trained to do this. However, every effort should be made to have local tax assessment and collection. Where villages are too small to do a good job, it should be done at the district or the provincial level. With local assessment and collection of taxes, there is a greater chance of developing a stable and ever-increasing volume of local revenue because local personnel can do a better job, and taxpayers will be more inclined to pay local taxes when they are admin-

[3] *Decentralization for National and Local Development, op. cit.,* pp. 64–65.

istered locally. It would be salutary, also, if national and local taxes could be entirely separated rather than intermingled.[4]

Some illustrations of problems in property taxation are found in the *Philippines* where since 1900 real property has been the principal source of tax revenue available to the provinces, the municipalities, the cities, and the barrios. While it produces only about 20 per cent of all local government revenues, it could produce a great deal more because present assessments are far below the legal standard, while procedures and practices in assessment and collection appear far from satisfactory. It was found that ratios of assessment to market value ranged from 21 per cent to 125 per cent, the median being 42 per cent; that the assessment level in cities was higher than in provinces by about 12 per cent; and that there were substantial inequalities in assessment levels within the same taxing jurisdiction. Substantial legal exemptions, including church and government property as well as landed estates acquired by the government for purposes of land distribution, substantially reduced the net assessment for tax purposes. The statutory tax limit in provinces is 1 per cent of the assessed valuation; the maximum rate for cities is set forth in their respective charters, but it is not to exceed 2 per cent.

Collection of property taxes left much to be desired. The survey showed that in 1956 only 54 per cent of the total collectible tax of provinces, municipalities, and municipal districts was collected. In cities, 81 per cent was collected. Land-tax delinquencies as of January 1, 1957, were about 40 per cent of the amount collectible for that year in cities, and about 160 per cent in the provinces. Assessment of property for all Philippine local government is done in the provinces and cities, but many of them do not have special assessment officers, the work being carried on in the offices of the provincial and city treasurers. The Department of Finance of the national government supervises local financial operations, and the President of the republic appoints the treasurers and assessors.[5] Professor Lloyd M. Short, a special consultant, recommended that the property tax

[4] A. H. Marshall, *Financial Aspects of Urban Local Government in English-speaking Africa, Excluding South Africa,* prepared for the United Nations Workshop on Urbanization in Africa, February, 1962. This monograph contains much excellent information and advice on local government practices in the field of finance.

[5] J. G. Castillo, *Property Tax Administration in the Philippines, 1956,* report to the Special Tax Revision Committee, Manila, 1957.

should be developed as a major source of increased revenue for local governments, and stated that such development would call for improved assessment and collection. He also advised raising the maximum rate at which local governments are permitted to tax property in their respective jurisdictions. Another authority, Melville Monk, said: "The failure of local governments to develop a higher degree of financial stability and civic responsibility springs directly from the limitations imposed on their taxing powers and the consequent reliance on allocations of national government revenues for financial support." Professor Short cited specific improvements that could be effected: technical assistance to and in-service training of provincial and city assessors; the increase of full-time assessing officers, with higher salaries for all; an informational tax education campaign; increased penalties for delinquent taxpayers; and modern records of property ownership.[6]

South America

Taxes in *Brazil* are imposed and collected by the federal, state, and municipal governments. In 1960, revenues of the federal government constituted 45 per cent of all public revenues; revenues of state governments 44 per cent; and revenues of municipal governments 11 per cent.[7] Since 1891, Brazilian local governments have witnessed inroads into their theoretical legal autonomy through the development of financial supremacy on the part of the federal and state governments, and the increasing dependence of local units upon federal and state authorities for fiscal survival. The 1946 Constitution increased this dependence. Furthermore, most of the local revenue is concentrated in the capital cities. Local revenue is of four kinds: (1) exclusive local imposts on urban land and buildings, on industries and professions, and for licenses of various kinds; and local taxes for social security and assistance, administration, and sanitation; (2) revenues returned to *municipios* from state taxes collected in municipalities whenever the state collections exceed "the total of local income of any nature," after which the state returns

[6] Lloyd M. Short, *The Relationship of Local and National Government in the Philippines,* Institute of Public Administration, University of the Philippines, 1955, pp. 24–28.

[7] Joseph P. Crokett, "Tax Pattern in Latin America," *National Tax Journal,* March, 1962, pp. 93–104.

30 per cent of the excess collected; (3) exclusive federal imposts returned to the states for local distribution, including mainly the tax on liquid and gaseous fuels, 40 per cent of which is kept by the national government, 48 per cent given to the states and federal districts, and 12 per cent left to the *municipios,* all of which must be spent for highway purposes in conformity to national plans and standards; (4) exclusive federal imposts distributed directly to localities, including one-sixth of the tax on electricity consumption, and 10 per cent of the revenues from the income tax, half of which must be spent for projects in rural areas. As each *municipio* gets an equal amount of the income tax despite population differences, there has been a rapid increase of new *municipios,* most of which exist almost entirely on this source of revenue.[8]

In *Venezuela* in 1958 and 1959, national government expenditures constituted about 88 per cent of total government spending, state government expenditures about 9 per cent, and local government expenditures about 3 per cent. Major local sources of revenue are taxes on business and industry, on motor vehicles, on real estate rentals, and on public spectacles; charges for local utilities and facilities; and state grants. The state grants to local units constitute about 10 per cent of the national grants made to the states, and they are unevenly administered by the states. Major local expenditures are for police, sanitation, public works, and education.[9]

In *San Salvador,* the national government collected 89 per cent of total public revenue, the lottery for welfare institutions 4 per cent, and municipal governments 7 per cent. The right of municipalities to levy taxes and to assess charges against property within their boundaries is severely limited, but the Municipal Rate Law of 1939 permits the municipalities to administer their own real estate, movable property, and income therefrom. They may also collect charges for public services such as light, water, and sanitation. Local taxes must not impede the free flow of commerce or be harmful to the economy of the country. Municipal authorities may establish taxes and fees, which must be approved by

[8] Carl L. Donald, "The Problems of Local Government Finance in Brazil," *Inter-American Economic Affairs,* Summer, 1959, pp. 21–38. *Local Government in the XXth Century,* International Union of Local Authorities, Martinus Nijhoff, The Hague, 1963, pp. 69–70.

[9] Carl S. Shoup et al., *The Fiscal System of Venezuela,* The Johns Hopkins Press, Baltimore, 1959, pp. 313–353.

the Ministry of Interior before their publication. The actual revenues of a municipality consist primarily of an assortment of fees and charges for local services.[10]

Africa

In *Africa,* there is a great gulf between the status, capacity, and financial resources of the central governments and those of local governments. African urban local governments are notoriously poor in comparison with the central government; in fact, they are often not as rich as some rural areas which are blessed with crops and cattle, sources of revenue more productive than the slum dwellings of an African town. For this reason, says Dr. A. H. Marshall, central governments are likely to retain in their own hands, or allot to special national agencies, duties and responsibilities that are in many countries strictly local functions. In practice, African central governments tend to keep to themselves such services as higher education, secondary public schools, hospitals, main roads, planning, housing, and piped water supply. The central government handles directly such functions as main roads, education, and hospitals, while it may delegate to special authorities, centrally financed, planning and housing.

The principal taxes of urban local governments in English-speaking Africa (except South Africa) are property taxes on land and buildings, and personal taxes. Property taxes provide the greater part of the tax revenue. Additional sources include charges for services, profits from commercial enterprises, license dues, rents of property, and grants from the central government. For capital outlays borrowing is done through the central government because very few African communities could borrow directly from the world's money markets. Central governments set aside funds which are advanced to their local governments for the acquisition of new assets. Local governments pay back into such revolving funds in a manner agreed to at the time of the loan. The funds are composed of surpluses, transfers from balances, and money borrowed by the central government for capital works.[11]

[10] Henry C. Wallich, John H. Adler, et al., *Public Finance in a Developing Country, El Salvador: A Case Study,* Harvard University Press, Cambridge, Mass., 1951, pp. 45, 56–57.

[11] Marshall, *op. cit.*

In *Western Nigeria,* local governments derive their revenues from three sources: (1) their own tax levies, including income taxes which they are allowed to levy; (2) license fees of all kinds; and (3) grants from the national government. The third category includes grants-in-aid for staff wages, education grants consisting mainly of 100 per cent of teachers' salaries, road grants, health grants, equalization grants, and police grants. The main sources of public revenue are in the hands of the national government, and grants are used to make governmental services possible in rural areas.[12]

Southeastern Europe and the Near East

In *Greece,* the main sources of local revenue are: a 3 per cent tax on the value of agricultural products sold wholesale by farmers and cooperatives (the most important source for agricultural communes); the nationally collected tobacco consumption tax, which was substituted for the old octroi taxes abolished in 1948; and an assortment of fees, dues, and excises from local utilities, services, and facilities. In communes and smaller demes, personal service not exceeding ten days may be imposed upon the population for local public works. Likewise the national government helps to finance a small common-utility projects program through the various *nomoi* by loans and grants-in-aid. Technical assistance and administrative services are also furnished by the *nomoi.* Other agencies, private and governmental, may make loans for the purpose of constructing public works such as water supply, land improvement, rural roads, and sanitation.[13]

In 1948, total governmental revenues in *Turkey* were divided as follows: national government, 84 per cent; provinces, 7 per cent; municipalities, 6 per cent; and villages, 3 per cent. The system of local government in Turkey is on a two-tier basis: the provinces and the local governments. The province is both a part of the system of national government and the first step under the Minister of Interior in the hierarchy; it is also a semi-autonomous, decentralized corporate local unit of government, representing regional interests. It has its own budget and it has taxing power, but

[12] *Decentralization for National and Local Development,* op. cit., p. 222.

[13] Alex. Drakakis, *Local Government in Greece,* Ministry of Interior, Kingdom of Greece, 1958, pp. 24–33.

a substantial part of its revenue comes from the central government. In 1946, for example, 51 per cent of provincial revenue came from building, land, and road taxes, while 37 per cent came from national grants, and the rest from miscellaneous sources. The main expenditures for provinces were, in the order named: education, administration including police, public works and roads, health and social welfare, and agriculture. In 1956, 18 per cent of all public expenditures was by local units and 20 per cent by provinces.[14]

The two classes of local authority, the municipalities and the villages, have different sources of revenue. The municipalities operate under an act of 1948 which provides direct and indirect taxes, contributions, and a charge for benefits accruing to real estate resulting from public works. Direct and indirect taxes include charges for public services, utilities, and facilities made available by the municipality. Contributions are for public works adjacent to real estate, and for fire-fighting services. In Turkey there are no additional percentages of national or provincial taxes for municipal government, but the municipalities receive from the national government 5 per cent of the income tax, 15 per cent of the import duties, 5 per cent of net profits from state monopolies, and 15 per cent of motor-fuel taxes. The taxation system of villages is built mainly upon the labor services the inhabitants are required to perform. This is supplemented by an "apportionment tax" levied on families according to ability to pay, and on others who have material interests in the village, not to exceed 20 Turkish pounds per annum, which can be paid in money or in kind. Additional taxes may be levied by municipalities and villages for the indigent. Communities also may float loans, but these must be approved by the central authority. Usually they borrow money from the departmental bank in which are deposited certain funds from the provinces and municipalities. In 1950, about 20 per cent of municipal revenue came from higher-authority grants and shared taxes, 40 per cent was from taxes, and the rest was from utilities and other commercial sources. Villages obtained about 40 per cent of their tax revenue in money and cereals, 30 per cent in labor services, and the rest in other taxes and yields.

[14] Orba F. Traylor, *Turkish Local Government and Methods of Financing,* Economic Cooperation Administration, Athens, Greece, memorandum of Sept. 12, 1951. *Local Government in the XXth Century, op. cit.,* pp. 392–393.

Both municipal and village budgets need approval from central authority, but only upon legal grounds; accounts are audited also by central agencies.[15]

In *Yugoslavia,* the national and state governments have restricted sources of revenue, while the local units governed by the people's committees have broad and residuary fiscal sources. For the federal republic the turnover tax, the tax on profits, and customs duties form the basis of financing; for the state, income taxes, rents, and a part of the total revenue of the people's committees on the local levels are made available. The remaining sources of revenue belong to the local units. They consist of the following: a part of the profits made by all economic enterprises in their territory; the land tax; an additional tax on agricultural, professional, and property income; a tax on the employment of hired labor; a death and gift duty; a local turnover tax; a local surtax; and revenues of state organs and institutions financed by local budget funds. In 1953, 70 per cent of the total revenue of towns and urban municipalities was derived from profits of economic enterprises. In prewar times, only 17 per cent was so derived; this indicates an about-face in the nation's public finance pattern. The profits of the economic enterprises remaining after the federal tax of 50 per cent are distributed to the states in the form of rent, to the enterprise itself, and to the local autonomous units of the district. Taxes on the population amounted in 1953 to only 19 per cent on all local revenues in towns and urban municipalities. In rural municipalities, revenue from the people assumed 71 per cent of the total. The federal and state governments do not subsidize local units systematically, but they allow grants to certain economic enterprises which are not profitable but are deemed to be in the public interest. Also subsidies are available for local budget deficits, especially in undeveloped areas. Local authorities may contract loans, but they do this only rarely on a short-term basis from the National Bank. Loans from private persons and the state are deemed inconsistent with the spirit of the Yugoslavian system of government.[16] In 1961, the budget resources of the nation were

[15] International Union of Local Authorities, *Local Government Finance and Its Importance for Local Autonomy,* reports prepared for the Rome Congress, Sept. 26–Oct. 1, 1955, The Hague, 1955, *Turkey,* pp. 329–346.

[16] International Union of Local Authorities, *op. cit., Yugoslavia,* pp. 366–377. W. Hoven and A. van den Elshout, *Central Services to Local Authorities,* International

divided as follows: 56 per cent to the Federation, 1 per cent to the Republics, 9 per cent to the districts, and 22 per cent to the municipalities.

In *Israel,* government revenues are derived from property taxes, license fees, charges for services, and grants-in-aid from the national government. A special lottery to raise money for local government purposes is held fortnightly, 50 per cent of the proceeds going to the winners and the rest for local loans and grants to local government, education, and hospital services. Short-term loans are made for capital purposes, and they have been consolidated through the issue of local government debentures.[17]

In the *United Arab Republic,* mandatory sources of local revenue include: (1) a land tax, assessed and collected by the central government and given to the local units, one-fourth to the provinces and three-fourths to the towns and villages; (2) a tax on buildings, levied only in towns; and (3) a tax on occupiers, not more than 4 per cent of the annual rental value. In addition, local units get certain additional taxes grafted on national taxes: 3 per cent on state customs taxes, the same on income tax on stocks and shares, from 5 to 15 per cent on the state income tax on industrial and commercial enterprises, the receipts of which are distributed to provincial councils who in turn distribute to the towns and villages. In addition, local units may levy a number of miscellaneous fees subject to central government approval. Town and village councils may levy a special assessment or a compulsory contribution to pay the costs of specific projects. Local units also receive substantial grants-in-aid because of their added responsibilities under the new regime. They get half of the rental or sale of state property in their area, and the net revenue from government markets, from the operation of public utilities, from loans, and from voluntary contributions. Many of these sources belonged to the central government before 1960; some of them are collected at the provincial level and divided with the towns and villages.[18]

In the *Sudan,* direct taxes have been assigned to local units. These in-

---

Union of Local Authorities (prepared for the United Nations), The Hague, 1962, pp. Y-8 to Y-9. Živorad Kovačević. *Communal System in Yugoslavia,* Belgrade, 1958, pp. 7–9. *Decentralization for National and Local Development, op. cit.,* p. 259.

[17] The Israel Organizing Committee, *Union of Local Authorities in Israel,* Tel Aviv, 1960, pp. 24–26.

[18] Mohamed Abdullah El Araby, *Local Government in the United Arab Republic,* Cairo, 1961, pp. 38–48.

clude house, land, animal, crop, and poll taxes; the last may include a fixed-sum tribal payment. The local governments collect the taxes for the national government; for this they receive a commission of from 5 to 10 per cent. There are also profits from local enterprises such as public utilities and facilities. The national government makes contributions to the local units in lieu of tax on government-owned property, deficit grants, cotton grants (a share of the national tax on cotton), grants for education, roads, tribal staffs, public health, and community projects. Rates on property are levied in the larger towns. Local units may contract loans but the state is the only source from which these can be obtained.[19]

Asia and the Far East

In *India,* the overall distribution of governmental revenues during the year 1946 was as follows: central government, 53 per cent; states, 34 per cent; local government (municipalities and district boards), 13 per cent. The major local government revenues consisted of the property tax in municipalities, the local fund cess (a percentage of land revenues) for district boards in rural areas, and government grants. Major expenditures of local units were for education, public health, medical services, drainage, roads, public safety, communications, and general administration. Education was by far the most important function for the district boards. The municipal corporations of the larger cities are more or less self-supporting and do not receive a great deal of national or state aid. They are empowered to raise money by loans in the open market and may issue debentures for financing municipal projects.[20]

Municipal revenues in India are illustrated by those of the state of Bihar. With the sanction of the state government, a municipality may impose a tax on holdings within the municipality assessed at their annual value, a tax on occupations, a water tax, a latrine tax, a tax on professions, a drainage tax, and a tax on vehicles. Municipalities receive nonstatutory grants for specific purposes from the state government. In a recent year, taxes on houses and land amounted to 25 per cent and grants-in-aid amounted to 30 per cent of the total income. Loans can be made from

[19] International Union of Local Authorities, *op. cit., Sudan,* pp. 293–301. *Local Government in the XXth Century, op. cit.,* p. 343.

[20] International Union of Local Authorities, *op. cit., India,* pp. 173–186.

revenue-producing projects, and they are used to give relief in time of famines, to prevent the spread of disease, and to repay borrowed money. Main items of expenditure for these municipalities were conservancy, education, water supply, drainage, roads, public welfare, and public health.[21] The district boards in the state of Bihar derive revenue from the "road cess" on the total rent payable for land or for quarries and mines. They also receive grants-in-aid from the state government for the improvement of communications, the maintenance of hospitals, dispensaries, and schools, and the repair of roads. Grants-in-aid come from state motor vehicle and gasoline taxes.[22] In village panchayats in the state of Bihar, two compulsory taxes are levied: labor from all able-bodied males, eighteen to fifty years of age; and a tax on persons owning immovable property. Other levies that may be made include professional license fees, tax on vehicles, market fees, utility fees, and pilgrim taxes. Another source of revenue is the grant-in-aid from the state government, which accounts for more than one-half of the total income of the panchayats of Bihar.[23]

In *Ceylon,* local authorities are empowered to levy taxes on real estate. For town councils the rate must not exceed 9 per cent of the annual value. Village committees may levy on buildings and land, but such actions must have the sanction of the responsible minister. In addition, local units levy a number of license fees. Financial assistance from the central government comes in the form of block grants, but these grants will be reduced if the local unit does not raise a stipulated amount by means of its own tax levies. Likewise the central government makes some payments on account of living expenses for local government personnel. There are also specific grants for child welfare, housing, recreation, and rural community development. National grants make up 30 per cent of municipal budgets, 54 per cent of urban council budgets, 50 per cent of town council budgets, and 61 per cent of village budgets. Local government loans are made by the Local Loans and Development Fund. They may not exceed ten times the annual revenue, but actually they are for much smaller amounts. Budgets need not have approval of higher authorities but are submitted to the Commissioner of Local Government. He may

[21] Chetakar Jha, *Indian Local Self-government,* Novelty Company, Patna, 1958, pp. 88–100.

[22] *Ibid.,* pp. 118–121.

[23] *Ibid.,* pp. 142–146.

control, however, urban and town council budgets if the responsible minister deems it necessary. Auditing is done by the local units themselves and by the Auditor General of the central government.[24]

The Municipal Revenue Act of 1954 of *Thailand* grants municipalities the following revenues: (1) direct taxes, collected by the municipalities, including a real estate tax, duties on animal slaughter, and taxes on signboards; (2) shared national taxes, namely, 50 per cent of the national vehicle tax; (3) surtaxes levied on national taxes, including a 10 per cent "municipal development" surtax on businesses and rice exports, and .05 baht (20 baht = $1) per liter gasoline tax; (4) grants-in-aid from the national government (more than 3 million baht in 1957); (5) income from municipal utilities and enterprises; and (6) loans from a municipal development fund which is capitalized from the deposits of the municipalities in provincial treasuries (in 1955, 18 million baht in loans to 50 municipalities) and used for capital outlay.[25]

The income from 120 municipal corporations in 1962 totaled 300 million baht, of which 48 per cent came from taxes, 4 per cent from fees, 21 per cent from grants-in-aid from the central government, and 27 per cent from other sources.[26] About one-third of this amount was used for salaries and living costs. It is pointed out that without national grants-in-aid, municipal budgets would generally be out of balance, and that these grants-in-aid are used only indirectly to control local government, the Ministry of Interior allocating them automatically, for the most part for salary purposes. However, it is stated that because of limited financial resources, municipalities do not carry out services required of them by law. For example, only 65 out of 114 own and operate electric plants, and only 34 provide municipal water supply. On the other hand, 86 own and operate markets because of the greater profit derived from them. It is further stated that the municipal collection of land and building taxes is not efficient and that the evasion is "enormous." The municipal treasurer simply assesses and collects these taxes from the rent reported by the owner, not from the real rental value. Furthermore, the sanitation district,

[24] Hoven and Elshout, *op. cit.*, part 4, pp. C–27 to C–32.

[25] Frederick James Horrigan, *Local Government and Administration in Thailand: A Study of Institutions and Their Cultural Setting*, doctoral dissertation, Indiana University, Bloomington, Ind., 1959, pp. 264–270.

[26] *Local Government in the XXth Century, op. cit.*, p. 208.

which is operated by government employees deriving their salaries entirely from the central government, is forging ahead of the municipality as the basic municipal unit of government. From 1933, the first year for municipal corporations, to 1956, only 120 municipal corporations were established. In contrast, from 1952, the first year of the revival of the sanitation district, to 1956, 404 were created and only three raised to the status of municipal corporations. This was done by the Ministry of Interior "in order to accelerate the system of local self-government according to the ideals of democracy for the local people as quickly as possible." [27]

In *Japan*, prefectural and metropolis (Tokyo) revenues include taxes on inhabitants, enterprises, acquisition of real property, consumption of tobacco, amusements, food and drinks, motorcars, mine lots, hunting, and water and land profits. Taxes levied by cities, towns, and villages are on residence, tobacco consumption, real property, bicycles and carts, electricity and gas, water and land profits, national health insurance, and mineral and timber products. No additional percentages of national taxes are levied for local purposes. Next there are profits from local utility and profit-making enterprises. A third local source of revenue, coming largely from national income, corporations, and wine taxes, is that of subsidies and grants-in-aid; and from taxes levied nationally and distributed locally, including the admission tax. Local bodies are also authorized to make loans. In 1960, total revenues of local bodies were raised as follows: 37 per cent from local taxes, 41 per cent from national sources, 22 per cent from loans and miscellaneous. National government expenditures were 33 per cent of the total, and expenditures of local bodies 77 per cent. Regular levies and loans need no prior approval from higher authority; there is no approval necessary for the budget or the accounts, but there is a regular audit by higher authority.[28]

In the post-World War II period, the public finances of Japan underwent a thorough survey by an American mission of experts headed by Dr. Carl Shoup. This group made important recommendations in the field of local finance and national-local relations. One overall objective

[27] *Ibid.*, pp. 210–215.

[28] International Union of Local Authorities, *op. cit.*, *Japan*, pp. 224–241. *Local Government in the XXth Century*, *op. cit.*, p. 233.

was to eliminate or reduce national taxes shared with local units in order to stimulate greater tax consciousness at the prefectural and municipal levels. To offset this reduction of shared taxes there would be an increase of national government grants on the basis of local need and resources, called the equalization grant. Sales taxation was to be taken from the national government and given to the prefectures, while the municipal property tax was given a broader base with rates subject to approval by the Local Autonomy Agency of the national government. These recommendations, if adopted, were to make prefectures and local units more or less financially independent of the national government. But the Japanese Diet either did not adopt these recommendations or, if it did, repealed them within four years, except in part. National shared taxes survived, the equalization grant was dropped. National grants to local units are now largely *ad hoc* with strings attached and are used as a control mechanism. They came to 15 per cent of all local revenue in 1953. Local units which were given education and police functions have been returning these to the national government because of insufficiency of funds. But local taxes increased from 16 per cent of the total in 1940 to 28 per cent in 1954. The property and inhabitant taxes were kept entirely municipal, while the amusement, admission, and enterprise taxes went to the prefecture.[29]

It appears that postwar Japanese local government is leaning on national financial assistance to an alarming degree. Local government personnel has increased and is overpaid, extravagant "vote-buying" projects are undertaken without much thought of financing. In 1953, it was reported that 35 out of the 46 prefectures, 4 out of 5 of the largest cities, 201 other cities, and 2,391 towns and villages failed to balance their budgets. The total deficit of all local bodies in 1955 had risen to 56 million yen. Part of the blame was placed on the inexperience of local electorates, supporting local bosses who "never vote for a tax or against an appropriation," and a great deal on the national government, which set unreasonably high standards of quality and quantity on rural education, health, and welfare agencies as conditions for the sharing of grants-in-aid, paying no attention to local financial conditions. As a result, 63 per cent

[29] M. Bronfenbrenner and Kiichiro Kogiku, "The Aftermath of the Shoup Tax Reforms," *National Tax Journal,* part 1, September, 1957, pp. 236–254.

of local expenditures were compulsory and 74 per cent were under some form of regulation from Tokyo.[30]

At the present time, local authorities receive subsidies if they exercise functions in which the national and local governments have a mutual interest, if they construct public works within national economic plans, if they are required to carry out national functions, if they are deemed to require national aid, or if a serious disaster occurs in the locality. During the fiscal year 1959, the national government and local units joined in financing compulsory education, livelihood protection, child welfare, local construction works, unemployment relief works, and certain wholly national functions. Subsidy payments are supervised by the prefect governor as well as by the competent minister, and the accounts are audited by the Board of Audits. In 1960, out of total revenues of 1,538 million yen, local taxes raised 40 per cent; local allocation taxes, from national taxes, 19 per cent; locally shared taxes 2 per cent; defrayments from the national treasury 26 per cent, and local bonds 5 per cent, while other revenues made up the remaining 8 per cent. National grants assumed more than half the total expenditures for a substantial number of local services, especially livelihood protection, child welfare, construction of new villages, improvement of farming, and most of the construction programs. Except in the case of subsidies, and where continual deficits are shown, there is no national control of budgets and audits.[31]

In the *Philippines,* local governments are dependent upon grants-in-aid and allocations of revenues from the national government for about 40 per cent of their receipts. Provinces have practically no independent taxing power apart from the property tax, and that is on a restricted base. Chartered cities have their taxing powers written into their individual charters; municipalities are authorized to impose occupational and business license taxes, to collect service charges, and to levy just and fair taxes for local purposes. The principal tax given to local units was the property tax, which amounted in 1951–1952 to only 34 million Philippine dollars out of total local revenue of 195 million. Of the total, 73 million dollars came from national sources, 28 million from other taxes, 26 million from operation of businesses and utilities, and 33 million from other sources. In fiscal

[30] *Ibid.,* part 2, December, 1957, pp. 345–360.
[31] Hoven and Elshout, *op. cit.,* part 4, pp. J–22 to J–28.

1955, real property taxes accounted for 16 per cent of provincial, 21 per cent of municipal, and 25 per cent of chartered city revenue. It has been suggested that real estate should pay more local taxes and that it does not because of the concentration of land ownership and the high incidence of absentee landlordism.[32] Legislation enacted in 1959 grants the barrio, the smallest political subdivision, revenue-raising powers including the power to collect an additional percentage, not exceeding one-fourth of 1 per cent of the assessed valuation of the property within the barrio. This is collected by the municipal treasurer along with the tax on real property levied for the municipality. Likewise, 10 per cent of all real estate taxes collected within the barrio limits accrues to the general barrio fund, which sum is then deducted in equal amounts from the shares of the municipality and the province. Other barrio sources include voluntary contributions, license fees, voluntary labor, national grants-in-aid, and private gifts. All revenue ordinances must be passed by both the barrio assembly and the barrio council.[33]

[32] Frank H. Golay, *The Philippines: Public Policy and National Economic Development,* Cornell University Press, Ithaca, N.Y., 1961, pp. 205–210.

[33] Fourth Congress of the Republic of the Philippines, Second Session, *An Act Granting Autonomy to Barrios of the Philippines,* Republic Act No. 2370, approved June 20, 1959.

9 Modern Administrative Problems

NEW AND EMERGING nations in the world today have certain characteristics that affect the role of their governments and the organization thereof. First, they are basically rural nations. Urban settlements and cities in many of the countries are relatively recent, developing after the introduction of the Western way of life. Second, the basic human needs of food, clothing, housing, and other items are far greater than the immediate resources available, and the demands upon government become greater in proportion to the knowledge of availability of such things and to the promises made to the people by their leadership. Third, there are such problems as widespread illiteracy, poor communications, geographic isolation, and cultural differences which make the job of government most difficult. Fourth, shortages of public revenues and trained personnel seriously handicap public administration.

Therefore, the leaders are confronted with the necessity of getting positive, sometimes immediate governmental action in many fields. They are obliged to protect the nation from external enemies and internal subversion; they must provide for the ever-increasing needs of the people.

They are committed to modernizing traditional institutions or to establishing new ones in order to achieve the goals they have set for themselves. It is not enough to make declarations of policy or even to pass statutory enactments, although these are fundamental. Nor is it enough to establish the form and structure of the governmental organization through which action must be channeled. The most important work of government is administrative in character: sufficient funds must be raised, competent personnel recruited and trained, projects completed, services rendered, and the people for whom all this is being done must be integrated into the governmental process.

It is clear that there is nothing like complete local autonomy in the nations of the world today. In fact, no matter what the democratic trappings of local government may be, there is substantial and in some cases overwhelming central or outside domination. What is happening in the nations that constitute the core of the West is happening in all other places. This is true whether the original pattern of local government was French, English, Soviet, or traditional. Nationalism and centralization are winning the day; local government is a creature, many times an abject one, of the state.

There are, of course, reasons for this condition. National survival calls for governmental unity not only for defense against outside enemies but as a protection against internal strife. These two dangers are omnipresent in all too many nations today. Those who are in command react by requiring uniformity and subservience at the local level. These qualities are more easily obtained by administrative controls than by education or the show of armed force.

Another reason is the worldwide aspiration for a better way of life. This means to millions of people more food, better housing, gainful employment, and some of the material products that can be made available by modern industry. These cannot come from a society organized on the basis of the traditional village polity and economy. They are possible only through large-scale operations either within or outside national jurisdictions, and in either case they require the ministrations of a nationwide government.

Then, too, there is the insistent demand for freedom and democracy. National leaders in most of the nations today are dedicated to these concepts, in one way or another. But almost to a man they turn to the national government as the vehicle through which the ideals can be obtained. Traditional institutions, whether they be village, town, or city, have been found wanting; they stand for the status quo; they are either too lifeless to cope with modern needs or in the hands of lethargic, privileged segments of society. National freedom, once purchased, can be kept only by national vigilance; democracy can be established only by national effort. Grass-roots democracy, popular as it is in print, simply does not exist or cannot be nurtured in the short time allotted for the achievement of national goals. At least, such is the argument of the centralist.

Another reason for national centralism is the quality of national leadership itself. In most of the newer emerging nations, it is the educated elite who have taken control after the withdrawal of colonial administrations. These are comparatively few in numbers, and have been educated and trained for the most part in Western ways of government and Western ways of life. Coming into control, they institute practices and procedures that they learned from their teachers or predecessors, and come out with a system of government very close to the dominant Western type, which in colonial areas tended to be highly centralized. In fact, there appears to be almost as much of a chasm of misunderstanding between this elite and the uneducated masses as there was between the Western administrators and the people as a whole. This is not at all to disparage the good will, enthusiasm, and abilities of either the new or the older type of administrator, but to point up the fact that more or less identical solutions to basic national problems appear to be the only ones at hand.

In spite of the strong national controls over local units throughout the world today, there are tendencies toward granting more local autonomy. Such is the case, for example, in Yugoslavia, the United Arab Republic, Pakistan, India, Japan, and the Philippines. In some countries, as we have seen, national agencies or party officials continue to supervise and control. The establishment of local units with full powers even with outside supervision is, however, significant and shows a trend in the direction of more local self-government.

Local government is one of the keys to sound administration. Local units must be strong enough to carry a substantial part of the total national load. The central government must organize them, grant them adequate financial resources, service them with administrative and technical assistance, stimulate and guide their activities in the direction of national goals. While it must exercise control to keep them within legal bounds, it should allow them as much freedom as possible so as to utilize the potentials of local leadership and democratic participation.

Major administrative problems exist in all countries, but absolute solutions applicable to all do not exist. Each nation must work out its own administrative salvation; this requires a high order of competence and statesmanship.

Three basic administrative problems are discussed in this chapter. The first involves the types of subdivisions and local units needed; the second, the development of competent personnel; and the third, internal administrative organization and structure.

TYPES OF ADMINISTRATIVE SUBDIVISIONS AND LOCAL UNITS

It is impossible to administer any nation entirely from the center. There must be some administrative subdivisions or local units through which governmental power may be deconcentrated or decentralized. On the other hand, if there is to be a nation in fact, it is just as impossible to administer everything locally. The problem, therefore, is to find the best working arrangement between extreme centralization and extreme decentralization.

There are two general principles upon which the center allocates power to its subdivisions. In *deconcentration,* it merely sets up administrative units or field stations, singly or in a hierarchy, separately or jointly, with orders as to what they should do and how they should do it. No major matters of policy are decided locally, no fundamental decisions taken. The central agency reserves all basic powers to itself. Local officials are strictly subordinate; they carry out orders. In *decentralization,* local units are established with certain powers of their own and certain fields of action in which they may exercise their own judgment, initiative, and administration. In actual practice, most systems combine elements of both in some relative degree.

We are, therefore, confronted immediately by two major configurations: one, where subordinate governmental units are created, staffed, and controlled by the central government and responsible solely to it; the other, where they are established to be governed by freely elected, representative bodies, or by traditional or hereditary officials who do not owe their position to appointment by central or centrally appointed authorities. However, no clear line of demarcation can be drawn between these two sets of units because many local entities have elements of both types. For example, freely elected councils are sometimes at the mercy of the central government as to the actual holding of elections, for the central ministry decrees when elections are to be held. Furthermore, in many countries freely elected councilors may be removed by higher authority; in still others their decisions may be nullified by arbitrary decision at an upper level. Likewise, traditional officials may be ousted when they do not measure up to standards imposed from above. On the other hand, centrally appointed local officials (for example, traditional chiefs in Africa), because of the depth of their local roots and their knowledge of local conditions, are often the decision makers and the dominant segments of the local power structure. They can flaunt the dictates of central ministries, and often they do. Then again, there are many instances where provincial, district, and communal councils are made up partly of elected officials and partly of those who are either national officials operating in local areas or are appointed by central authorities. To which class does a local unit belong when its council is elected and its executive is appointed by the central government? It is not profitable to examine local government with too great dependence upon logical classification. Having in mind that the two general patterns of local government are basic, nevertheless they should not be considered as definitive. Nor can the terms "local self-government" vis-à-vis "local state government," and "local representative government" vis-à-vis "local nonrepresentative government," and "general-purpose local government" vis-à-vis "special-purpose local government" be utilized too freely. Most actual units of local government are configurations of elements of one, two, or more such types.[1]

[1] See the excellent description of these classifications in Samuel Humes and Eileen Martin, *The Structure of Local Governments,* International Union of Local Authorities, Martinus Nijhoff, The Hague, 1961, pp. 1–6. G. Montagu Harris, *Comparative Local Government,* Longmans, Green & Co., Inc., New York, 1948, p. 9.

The definition for local government as developed by the United Nations is as follows: "The term local government refers to a political subdivision of a nation or (in a federal system) state which is constituted by law and has substantial control of local affairs, including the power to impose taxes or exact labor for prescribed purposes. The governing body of such an entity is elected or otherwise locally selected." [2] While this definition is logical enough from the purist standpoint, it would be difficult to give a true picture of local government in any one nation if it were followed. Many local units, legally constituted, may have one of these qualifications but not all of them. To describe the local government picture without mentioning such agencies would give an incomplete description of the process of government in local areas.

A United Nations classification of systems of field administration and local government is helpful in making a comparative study and in clarifying the relationships between central and local agencies. There are four general systems: (1) the *comprehensive local government system,* in which local government units are multipurpose and carry on local as well as nationally directed functions; (2) the *partnership system,* in which some services are rendered by field units of the national government and others by local authorities; (3) the *dual system,* in which central ministries administer technical services directly, while local units have legal authority to perform services but generally do not do so because they cannot compete with the central agencies in finance, personnel, or competence; and (4) the *integrated administrative system,* in which the central government administers all technical services directly and where local authorities have little or no power to act.[3]

One of the problems that must be resolved in a nation establishing its local government machinery or substantially altering it to meet modern needs is the number of tiers or levels of local government desired. First of all, the need for division of the nation or state into provinces is obvious. At this level the central agencies and ministries can deconcentrate their administration, and the various central services can be coordinated under one administrator. However, the "dual responsibility" bugaboo presents

[2] Emil J. Sady, "Improvement of Local Government and Administration for Development Purposes," *Journal of Local Administration Overseas,* July, 1962, pp. 135–148.

[3] *Ibid.,* pp. 138–140.

itself with technical supervision by the ministry from which the technicians come and administrative responsibility given to the provincial governor. When central ministries set up separate field units outside the provincial organization and without coordination, as they do in many nations, confusion is inevitable.

Complete solution of the vexing problem of coordination is rarely found. There are many complex problems. National agency programs must be coordinated; national ministry activities must be coordinated with local activities of the same kind; local activities must be coordinated in the same areas.

A number of methods have been tried with some success. One is for the central Council of Ministers to develop overall national-local policy and to direct its enforcement through one ministry, usually the Ministry of Interior, under whose direction are the provincial and district offices of the central government. But the Minister of Interior is of the same rank as other ministers and cannot always exercise the necessary leadership. In some countries a second method has been used; the task of coordination has been given to the President or Prime Minister. Still another method is to have top national ministry personnel in the various provinces form an advisory or administrative council or committee under the chairmanship of the governor, who will take on the responsibilities of overall coordination in his jurisdiction. This is also difficult if the ministerial personnel looks to its individual ministries for technical direction and for employee status and benefits. In some countries, the provincial governor is also responsible for coordination of all local activities in his area. In larger cities, the nationally appointed executive or the elected mayor is theoretically responsible for coordination. However, in many cases coordination does not exist. Each ministry, each department, each local unit renders services to the people, going its own way, oblivious to what other units or agencies are doing in the same functions and the same geographic areas.

Many countries follow the French pattern by having districts and subdistricts corresponding to the French *arrondissements* and cantons between the province and the communes, municipalities, and villages. These act mainly as coordinators of local administrative efforts, but also they may be involved in line functions such as tax collection, election administration, and the maintenance of law and order through centrally responsible police organization. Such echelons increase the amount of bureaucratic friction and delay. In some of the newer reorganizations, functions once at these levels are being transferred either to the provincial level or to subordinate local units, which are being reconstituted so that they are large enough and financially competent to carry on an ongoing administration that will promote national and community development on the lower levels.

It has been suggested by the Working Group on Decentralization of the United Nations, convened in October, 1961, that two levels of rural local government make the ideal arrangement. The lower level should be the largest area in which a sense of community exists and direct participation in making local decisions is possible. The higher level should be the largest area from which technical services may be efficiently provided, but not so large that elected councilors cannot easily meet with regularity. Urban and rural populations should be included in the larger unit and headquarters for it should be stationed in a town or city centrally located.[4]

The sociological village, however, should be the foundation of a democratic system of government, for it is here and only here that direct participation of the people is possible. Each of the smallest local units should have an assembly of all adult citizens where problems could be freely discussed, and village officials, such as a headman and a council, could be elected. This council, in turn, could elect a representative or representatives to the council of the larger rural local unit, or the people of the lower unit could do this by direct election. The higher level of the two should be multipurpose, and a trained administrator elected by its council but approved by the provincial governor should be established wherever possible.

In a survey looking toward the reorganization of subordinate districts and local units in Vietnam, the issue at stake was the number of levels of administration. At that time, there were regions, provinces, districts, cantons, and villages standing between the central government and the people. This constituted too many levels; they slowed up unification of the nation by their divisive tendencies, and there was too much delay of

[4] United Nations Technical Assistance Programme, *Decentralization for National and Local Development*, New York, 1962, pp. 21–22.

action because of "red tape" involved. The recommendation was to abolish the regions, and to reduce the number of provinces calling them areas. Each area should have a chief and a representative from each national technical ministry. There should be an area elective council with single-member districts, each representing 50,000 people. Below the areas would be the municipalities and villages, which would be given broad substantive powers including the police function.[5]

The United Arab Republic has set up in Egypt "combined centers" of local administration for the provision of agricultural services, primary education, and health and welfare services on the basis of 15,000 people per center. This has been, since 1955, the UAR approach to the problem of field coordination of technical services in rural areas. Technical personnel were assigned to head various divisions—health, agriculture, social affairs, and education. They looked to their ministries for guidance, promotions, and transfers, but their salaries (except for teachers) were paid by the Higher Council for Combined Centers, a national agency. The plan was to have the ministries decentralize authority to their senior officers on the staffs of the provincial governors, and for councils to be formed at both provincial and combined unit levels, consisting of both technical personnel and representatives of the people. This plan was followed during the early years and 250 combined centers were established. However, some practical problems have arisen: (1) The units cost too much. (2) The allocation of costs was not determined. (3) There was no clearly defined jurisdictional direction under which the combined units operated, either provincial or village. (4) There were problems in applying local government legislation to units of different size, i.e., single villages or combined villages.[6]

The establishment of field stations of central ministries in order to carry out their functions at the local level raises a number of problems. Should there be separate field stations for each ministry or should they be stationed in the provincial headquarters under the administrative direction of the governor of the province? Certainly, from an administrative point of view, the latter would be preferable if the provincial areas

[5] Ralph H. Smuckler et al., *Recommendations Concerning the Department of Interior, the Regions and the Provinces (Vietnam)*, Michigan State University Press, East Lansing, Mich., 1956.

[6] Emil J. Sady, United Nations *Memorandum*, Feb. 20, 1961.

were suitable. If separate field units for national ministries are set up, should they be transformed into local government units at some future time? Are there any sound criteria for size that apply to the administration of various technical services such as road building, health, social services, and education? Could existing local units be utilized for subdistricts and for the more routine tasks in administration of the major central functions? How will administration be coordinated if each ministry has its own field stations? [7] These and similar questions confront the architects of local government and administrative structure in every nation. The solutions must depend upon local conditions and basic needs.

COMPETENT PERSONNEL

In nations bent upon improving standards of living through government effort, the problem of getting competent personnel to assist local government is one of major importance. There is always a critical shortage of qualified administrators and technicians available for work in the field. One of the reasons is that the capital city and urban areas offer more attractions: better living conditions, more prestige, higher salaries, and greater chance for individual preferment and promotion. The nearer to the top, the greater the advantages. To offset this imbalance, many nations are looking for ways and means to equalize conditions of employment between the center and the outlying areas.

Several different approaches have been made. The first is where the central government and local authorities come under a single civil service system. Recruitment, compensation, promotion, transfer, dismissal, retirement, and other fringe benefits are the same for one and all. For example, in *Morocco,* national and municipal civil servants are all recruited by the Ministry of Interior and have the same benefits and conditions of work. Municipal officials belong to a separate cadre within the ministry and can be moved from one town to another. In *Yugoslavia,* local authorities employ their own staffs but salaries and conditions of work are established by law and are the same for all personnel throughout the nation doing comparable work.

[7] *Decentralization for National and Local Development, op. cit.,* pp. 20–21.

Another approach has been the formation of a unified local government staff separate from the central staff but under the control of the Ministry of Interior, which is empowered to make appointments, transfers, and promotions. Such an arrangement exists in *Ceylon* and *Western Nigeria.* The establishment of a unified service could lead to the transformation of central field personnel into local executives and administrators. This has been contemplated both in *India* and in the *United Arab Republic.*

A third approach is where a separate personnel system exists for each local government authority but where certain aspects are regulated by central government. Under such arrangement, conditions of employment might be uniform between local units, but the opportunity for transfer would be unlikely, and the attraction for competent, trained personnel would be slight.

Still another method to strengthen local government personnel is where the central agency loans or "seconds" administrative and technical personnel to specific local units to get things under way, to train local staff, and to stimulate local activity. In all cases where central personnel operates in a local unit, the problem of dual responsibility arises. To whom is such personnel loyal: to the central ministry under whose supervision it operates, or the local council for whom it works? Or does this matter if the administrative process is improved?

There are a number of interesting developments in the transition from the older colonial to the newer and more democratic systems of administration. In *India* and *Pakistan,* district officers, once representing central authority, are now available for service as local government administrators, although in India their future in the district seems to be in coordination, not in administration. In *Eastern Nigeria,* they have become supervisors and advisers of local authorities; in *Western Nigeria,* they are considered unnecessary; in *Senegal,* governors act as coordinators of development programs and technical services. In *Yugoslavia,* the municipal secretary is the executive officer of the people's assembly and his work is supervised by the president of the assembly. In the *Sudan,* the local government inspector, an agent of the central government, exercises local powers until he can appoint a council, and his power diminishes as the council takes on increased responsibilities, the broadest being when the

Council of Ministers issues a warrant setting up a local unit and specifying its powers, and the council elects its own chairman. In *Burma,* district officers became chief executives of local councils in charge of departments headed by representatives of central technical ministries. But here, dual responsibility did not work, and the councils established by 1953 legislation were suspended by presidential decree.[8]

In *Ceylon,* the Local Government Service Ordinance of 1945 established a unified and transferable service for staff of all types of local government. It provided for a Local Government Service Commission, chaired by the Commissioner of Local Government and composed of eight other members appointed by the Minister of Local Government, four directly and four after consideration of nominees from different types of local units. The Ordinance vests with the Commission full powers over methods of recruitment, conditions of employment, appointments, transfers, classification, salaries, and other personnel matters. The Commission makes all appointments to local scheduled posts, those over a certain annual salary minimum, while local units pay the salaries. In *Western Nigeria,* a Unified Local Government Service was established by law in 1952 with a Local Government Service Board which has jurisdication over "superior posts" for those in the career service.[9]

Programs to improve local personnel through preservice and in-service training are widespread. In Southeast Asia, for example, there are many institutions of learning which give training in public administration and local government.

In *India,* Nagpur University offers a diploma course in local self-government administration, and a two-year program for a master's degree in public administration. The Indian Administrative Service Training School of the Ministry of Home Affairs recruits trainees for government posts by examination; they are given a year of training before becoming full-fledged members of the Indian Administrative Service. The Local Self-Government Institute of Bombay offers courses to councilors and local government officials and also to those who aspire to local government service.

The Civil Service Academy of *Pakistan* controls the training of officers

[8] *Ibid.*, p. 154.
[9] *Ibid.*, p. 73.

appointed to the civil service. The Institute of Public and Business Administration at the University of Karachi, Pakistan, offers work in public administration leading to a master's degree.

The Institute of Public Administration of the University of the *Philippines* conducts academic course work in public administration, and offers short courses to in-service government personnel.

Chulalongkorn University of *Thailand* gives training to young men and women looking forward to government service. The University of Thammasat of Thailand offers a master's degree in political science for students going into the government service, especially into the Ministry of Interior.

The National Institute of Administration of *Vietnam* trains cadres of high administration for the government especially in finance, administration, economic development, and foreign affairs.[10]

In *Kenya,* in-service training courses in local government are given both for the executive staff and for the councilors by the Ministry of Interior in schools for adult education. Subjects include general government, economics and social studies, local government structure, local government history and law, minute writing, council procedure, finance, bookkeeping, typewriting, office management, and national-local relations. According to one of the professors, Dr. R. C. Prosser: "It may be relevant to draw attention to one of the greatest difficulties that face local government, namely that on the whole the standard of efficiency of the executive staff is far higher than that of the councillors themselves." [11]

In the *United Arab Republic,* the Institute of Public Administration, which had developed an extensive curriculum in public administration for the training of personnel of the various national ministries and the governorates, recently inaugurated courses of instruction in comparative local government, local government in the United Arab Republic, and municipal administration.

In *Yugoslavia,* there are three categories of civil servants in the people's committees: administrative officers responsible for functions deriving from state organs; executive officers responsible for carrying out ad-

[10] Public Administration Clearing House, *Training for Public Administration, Southern Asia,* Chicago, 1955.

[11] R. C. Prosser, "Training for Local Government," *Journal of African Administration,* April, 1961, pp. 98–107.

ministrative business; and clerical officers. A system of in-service training, where attendance is for two years with full-time pay, includes a college for municipal affairs, a school of finance for collectors and accountants, an administrative staff college, and several other administrative schools which are operated by the various republics of the nation.[12]

Agencies that can contribute to the influence of local government in the national picture are associations of local authorities. Such organizations have been established in at least 42 countries in all parts of the world. They represent the local government interests before the legislative and administrative authorities of the national government, act as clearinghouses for local government information, hold conferences of local officials, undertake training programs, and do a variety of things that are helpful to local officials. There are also organizations of national associations on a regional and international level, namely, the Inter-American Municipal Organization and the International Union of Local Authorities.[13]

INTERNAL ADMINISTRATIVE ORGANIZATION

The *internal organization* of local units of government becomes a problem of increasing importance as deconcentration and decentralization from the center to the lower units are applied, and as new activities, especially in the field of economic enterprise, are added. The natural development when functions increase is to make a new department, a new bureau, or a new section for each new function. The result is that there are soon too many heads reporting directly to the chief executive—the governor, prefect, or mayor—and it is impossible for him to supervise them properly or even to know what is going on. In other words, the "span of control" of the chief executive becomes much too broad.

This calls for administrative reorganization involving the regrouping of functions into fewer but larger departments. Ideally, the chief should deal with no more than ten and possibly no less than five subordinates. These should constitute his administrative cabinet or council; its members should not only administer their own departments, but should collectively advise

[12] "The Training of Officials of the Administrative Organs of the People's Committees," *International Social Science Journal,* vol. 13, no. 3, 1961, pp. 435–438.

[13] International Union of Local Authorities, *National Associations of Local Authorities throughout the World,* The Hague, 1956.

the chief on overall administrative progress and problems. Exactly how this should be applied to each individual type of local government must be a matter for each country to work out. There is no set pattern. The principle, however, is clear—give the chief executive a workable departmental organization, one with which he can effectively deal, one that can and will enforce his commands. Within each of his departments there should be a similar arrangement. The department head should have no more than ten and no less than five bureau chiefs with whom he administers the affairs of the department, and in turn these bureau chiefs should have no more than ten or no less than five section chiefs in charge under them. However, when subordinate units are all the same—like regional police, welfare, or public works units, this number may be increased. All units of this kind will receive more or less similar instructions and directives, and their reports will be on the same forms so as to be more easily consolidated and coordinated by the chief. Thus, personnel at the front line of action would be required to report to the section chief, the section chief to the bureau chief, the bureau chief to the departmental head, and the departmental head to the chief executive. In smaller organizations there need not be as many tiers of administration. The main objective to be kept in mind is that there should be adequate channeling from the top down for commands, and from the bottom up for reports.

The *organization of staff services* is another problem inadequately dealt with in developing systems of local administration. Staff functions must be differentiated from those of the line. Line functions are those that represent direct services to the people, the real reason for the existence of local government. For example, education, health, social welfare, public works, police protection, fire protection, and similar services are of the line. In the economic enterprise field, the production and sale of various items of manufacture, as well as agricultural activities, may be considered line functions.

On the other hand, there are a number of administrative functions which do not render services to the people but which help the line agencies to do a better job. In this category are finance, personnel, legal, research, evaluation, and organization and management activities. In the early days of modern administrative evolution, each department or even each bureau had its own finance, personnel, and other staff activities, usually carried on by the chief with limited clerical personnel to assist him in his own office. Thus, while the chief might be an outstanding health authority or public works administrator, he was bogged down with details of activities about which he knew little and often cared less; and as a result many fine programs were hopelessly emasculated because of inadequate staff work.

This general condition led to the evolution of the principle of separation of line and staff functions, with the objective of relieving line agencies from responsibilities in these fields. In some jurisdictions, staff functions are concentrated in one department, reporting directly to the chief executive and various bureaus established under him, notably budget, accounting, personnel, evaluation, purchasing, and legal. At the head of each one of these bureaus is a man or woman who should be considered an expert in the particular field, with subordinate personnel qualified for the work they do. The head of all staff services has the same rank as the heads of the line departments and reports directly to the chief executive. This arrangement also develops difficult problems even though it is theoretically correct. One of these problems is the relation between the various staff personnel and the heads of the line departments. In preparing the budget, for example, personnel of low rank may be dealing with the head of a department, a situation that calls for a great deal of understanding and diplomacy on both sides. While there is no perfect solution of this dilemma, the general principle should be that the head of staff services is dealing with the head of the line department in the name of the chief executive even though subordinates are doing the actual work, and these two heads should agree on the budget or on personnel changes before reporting to the chief executive.

On the other hand, a recent theory has been enunciated that takes in consideration the actual facts of day-by-day administrative operation. For example, the head of a bureau in a department is responsible to his line superior, and he must also bow to the demands and regulations of numerous staff agencies such as the budget, personnel, legal, and evaluation bureaus; horizontal as well as vertical lines of communication are always open. This is, of course, true, but the only way to handle such a situation if it is not to become chaotic is to recognize that the superior in command has endorsed these staff activities, and that when the bureau chief accedes to these demands and regulations, he does it because his superior officer so ordered. For it must always be understood that both line and staff officials are subordinate to the chief executive, and that he must take responsibility for all decisions and activities within his organization.

10 The Government of Large Cities and Metropolitan Areas

THE MODERN CITY is a recent and worldwide phenomenon. In 1800, less than 2 per cent of the world's population lived in fewer than 50 cities with more than 100,000 inhabitants; in 1950, more than 900 cities had populations of 100,000 or more. These cities accounted for one-eighth of the world's population. Between 1800 and 1950, urban population (towns with more than 5,000 population) grew four to five times as fast as rural population, and three to four times as fast as world population. Between 50 and 60 million people are being added to the world's population each year, and at the current rate population is doubling every twenty-three years. The largest share of this growth is centered in urban places; in some countries the entire net increase is in the metropolitan areas. The United Nations has calculated that about 200 million new inhabitants will be added to the cities of Africa, Asia, and Latin America in the ten-year period between 1960 and 1970. Already, 26 per cent of the population of South America is living in cities of 20,000 or more, in the Caribbean and Central America 21 per cent, in Asia 13 per cent, and in Africa 9 per cent. While in the less industrialized countries of Asia, Africa, and

Latin America, smaller percentages now live in urban areas, their urban growth rates are higher. In these nations, the pace of urbanization is faster than that of industrialization. As a result more people now live in urban areas than can be supported by the present productivity of industry and agriculture. A disproportionate amount of the limited resources of the nations must be used to repair existing social ills caused by excessive urbanization rather than for efforts to increase productivity, and this further reduces the standard of living.

The reasons for the general movement of people from rural to urban areas are many: mechanization of agriculture, pressure of increased rural populations, employment expectations in cities, as well as better educational, medical, and cultural facilities are part of the "push" of the countryside and the "pull" of the big city. In developing countries, the urban environment is affected most adversely by this movement. Physical congestion, blighted areas, shanty towns, poor housing, inadequate urban services, congested traffic, disease, squalor, delinquency, and crime are common under such conditions.

For purposes of local government, a metropolitan area may be defined as a central city or cluster of cities surrounded by urbanized areas outside city borders, and not unified under one local government. That populations of cities and metropolitan areas of the world today develop faster than their governments is obvious, for in most cases present local units are based upon conditions long since passed. The metropolitan area has not been visualized as a single entity in government, although in economic and social affairs its unity has long been accepted. The time is fast approaching, however, when governmental unity and coordination in metropolitan areas must be achieved in view of the pressures for services of government for the rising populations of urban areas.

All over the world, and especially in developing countries, the recent increases in urban population which spill over municipal boundaries have made it obvious that drastic alterations should be made in the structure of local government units in areas of rapid urban growth. In most countries, metropolitan areas are governed by numerous local units: the central city, the outlying towns and villages, the provinces, the districts, and sometimes the subdistricts. All but the central city are too small and financially weak to provide modern urban services that their inhabitants require, and the central city is unable to service inhabitants across its boundaries even though they are part of the urban complex. As a result of local inadequacy, the central governments often fill in with direct services of varying kinds, thus adding confusion to the already confused administrative picture. In order to obtain functional and geographic unity in administration in these areas, municipal boundaries of the central city should be enlarged to include the entire metropolitan area or some federation of all existing local units should be established. A recent and significant recommendation was made to the effect that existing provincial boundaries, especially in urban areas in the United Arab Republic, should be redrawn. They should coincide with the present population pattern of metropolitan areas in order that the provisions of the 1960 local administration law setting up governorates, towns, and rural units for the decentralization of national functions may be successful.[1]

If the village in developing countries is a traditional social and political unit, the modern city is a Western institution transplanted on native soil. It came with modern commerce, business, industry, and government. Therefore, its government right from the start was Western in character. It consisted of a council, generally elected, and a municipal executive, sometimes elected but more often appointed by the council. However, there was more or less strict control from the national government, and the urban municipalities, although given the status of juristic persons, never blossomed as autonomous units of local government. In fact, the national government in many areas undertakes the direct administration of many local functions, and in most South American countries, the capital cities have been declared national responsibilities and are administered directly by the Ministry of Interior.

CITY GOVERNMENT IN LATIN AMERICA

In *Argentina,* cities are the creatures of the provinces. Municipal home rule does not exist. In most of the provinces, the municipal chief executive is the *intendente* chosen by the governor with senate approval. The city council is elected by popular vote. The capital city of Buenos Aires was

[1] Luther Gulick and James K. Pollock, *Government Reorganization in the United Arab Republic,* a report submitted to the Central Committee for the Reorganization of the Machinery of Government, Cairo, June, 1962, pp. 44–46, 100–106.

made a federal district in 1880. Four times an elective city council was established, four times it was abolished. The people have no voice in their city government. The national Congress acts as the lawmaking body, a nationally appointed *intendente* administers.

In *Brazil,* Rio de Janeiro, the former capital, is also a federal district administered by a prefect named by the President and approved by the Senate. Congress enacts its laws. But there is a district council elected by the people, and the district has representation in both houses of Congress.

In *Mexico,* the capital, Mexico City, is a federal district with twelve municipalities outside city boundaries. The municipal council which existed for four centuries was abolished in 1928. The Department of the Federal District is headed by the chief appointed by the President. There is a consultative council made up of representatives of organized groups within the district. The twelve smaller municipalities, which used to have their own councils, now are merely administrative districts. Each is headed by a delegate under the direction of the chief of the district.

In *Chile,* while in provinces and rural areas there is little or no popular participation, cities have popularly elected councils ranging in size from five to fifteen members. The mayor is chosen by the council in all but the three largest cities, where he is appointed by the central government. However, most administration is in the hands of the *intendentes* of the provinces and their subordinates in departments and districts. Santiago, the capital, is a province, a department, and a city. The city contains 60 per cent of the people of the department, which has twenty other municipalities.

In *Peru,* there is no municipal government, only that of departments, provinces, and districts governed according to the French system.

In *Colombia,* the municipalities have an elected council and a mayor appointed by the governor. The governor has an absolute veto on all municipal acts. Bogotá, the capital, has no special status.

In *Venezuela,* cities have a substantial measure of autonomy. The national constitution devotes a thousand words to municipal affairs, declaring their autonomy and rights. City councils are elected, and they elect the mayor. However, the capital city, Caracas, with its suburbs, is a federal district in the hands of an appointed governor. There is an elected council with limited powers.

In *Ecuador,* municipalities have elected mayors and councils and they perform a considerable number of routine functions.

In *Uruguay* and *Paraguay,* there is no local self-government. In *Bolivia,* each municipality has a popularly elected council. The mayor is chosen by the President from a list of three names given to him by the council. One of these names must represent the minority on the council. La Paz, the capital, has the same government as other cities.

The Constitution of *Cuba* stresses municipal autonomy. Every municipality may choose its own form of government: mayor-council, commission, or council-manager, showing American influence. However, no enabling legislation has been passed allowing this to be done. There is a mayor-council government in the municipalities, both elected by the people.

In *Haiti,* communes have elected councils but their authority is small. A local magistrate, appointed by the central authorities, dominates the administration. The same applies to the *Dominican Republic.*

In *Guatemala,* municipalities have their own popularly elected mayors and councils, and exercise a measure of self-government. The same is found in *El Salvador.* In *Nicaragua,* there are no municipal councils. The capital city, Managua, is a federal district. In *Honduras,* there are popularly elected councils, but in large cities, the mayors are chosen by central authority. In *Costa Rica* and *Panama,* municipalities choose their own mayors and councils.[2]

MUNICIPAL GOVERNMENT IN THE NEAR AND MIDDLE EAST AND NORTH AFRICA

Modern municipal government in the Near and Middle East began in Istanbul early in the last century of the Ottoman Empire's existence. Before 1830, the government of the city was largely in the hands of military officers and the religious professionals who divided the responsibility for public security and public morals between them. Both were agents of the sultanate. But about this time the Ottomans were looking to the West, and many foreigners came to live in the city, settling mostly in the districts of Pera and Galata. After a while these persons demanded

[2] Austin F. MacDonald, *Latin American Politics and Government,* Thomas Y. Crowell Company, New York, 1954.

the Western urban amenities: wider streets, water supply, sewage disposal, and street lighting.

The reforming Sultan Mahmud II set up a central inspectorate to take over the duties formerly held by men of religion. He appointed mukhtars as headmen in the various neighborhoods of the city and gave them the responsibility of keeping vital statistics and property records, and a short while later a council of elders was established to assist them. This arrangement had existed in villages in the Near and Middle East for centuries, but for the first time it was given city status. Today the mukhtar still exists in Turkish and Arabic cities as a routine and low-level agent of the national government, and in some places an informal council of elders still assists him.

In 1854, the office of city prefect was established along French lines. The prefect was assisted by a council (*majlis*) appointed by the imperial authorities from the guilds and merchants. In the same year, a study was made on city services and it was decided that a district should be established for Pera and Galata, fashioned on the lines of the French *arrondissement,* as a pilot plan. This district was governored by an unpaid council of thirteen appointed by the imperial authorities, and they in turn appointed city officials paid from taxes levied on the residents. The council was given the power to establish all needed services and facilities. Later this plan was extended to all of Istanbul. Furthermore, municipal affairs for the whole city were placed under the administration of a prefect assisted by an elected assembly and an administrative council. Progress along this line was halted by the reactionary Sultan Abdul-Hamid II who came to power in 1876. He abolished the elections and the local councils, and appointed a mudir as an administrative officer of each of ten districts. The revolution of 1908 revived elections in districts for a short time, but in 1912 all district governments were abolished and the city was constituted a single municipal entity under a prefecture with nine divisions, each with an appointed head. The prefect was assisted by a council of 54, six elected from each of the nine subdivisions of the city. The prefect was both head of the municipality and governor of the city, appointed by the Minister of Interior.[3]

[3] Bernard Lewis, "Municipal Reform in the Ottoman Empire: The Legacy to the Independent Arab States," an international seminar sponsored by the Egypt Society of Engineers and the Congress for Cultural Freedom, Cairo, Dec. 17–22, 1960.

This form of government is, in the main, that which exists at present in Istanbul. One of the problems has been the union or separation of the municipality and the province where the boundaries are almost identical. In 1930, they were merged under the single administration of the vali, or governor, but in 1954 they were again separated; the mayor was elected by the municipal council and the vali appointed by the central government. The municipal and provincial councils were also separated. Adding to the administrative confusion brought on by this arrangement, there were within the city national officials stationed in city districts who reported directly to central authorities. There were also separate public utility commissions under the supervision of the national ministries.[4]

The present organization of city government in the Moslem Near and Middle East and North Africa is based upon the dual organization of the municipality and the province. In some cities such as *Cairo, Alexandria,* and *Beirut,* the municipalities are also provinces, and the chief executive, the *muhafiz,* is also mayor. However, his responsibilities as provincial governor far outweigh those of a municipal character. In other cities such as *Baghdad, Amman, Jerusalem,* and *Damascus,* the chief executive, while not the provincial governor, comes under the direct authority of the Minister of Interior. He has many of the attributes of the governor and, like him, is appointed by central authority. Some places, including *Casablanca,* have a mayor elected by council, who by law is supposed to approve expenditures from communal funds and execute the decisions of the council; all personnel is under the governor of the prefecture, personnel of the municipality and the prefecture being one and the same. Sometimes, as in *Damascus* (1963), the law states that the council should elect the president, who is the chief of the municipality, but he is in reality not elected at all but appointed by the Minister of Interior. For all practical purposes the municipal executive is an official of the national government and responsible to it in the same way as the prefect of the French department. Being also a municipal mayor is of secondary importance. But as a provincial governor, he is all-powerful within the municipality except as he is subservient to the national authorities.

While most of the national constitutions of the Moslem nations of the

[4] H. Hanson, "Municipal Administration," *Studies in Turkish Local Government,* Public Administration Institute for Turkey and the Middle East, Ankara, 1955, pp. 106–126.

Near and Middle East and North Africa recognize municipal councils as basic institutions of local government, councils play a subordinate role in most municipalities. Their decisions, at least the most important of them, must be approved either by the chief executive of the municipality or the Minister of Interior or of Local Government. In some cases, councilmen are even appointed by the central authorities and, as in Damascus, hold office by their authority as a municipal committee pending the advent of regular elections. In most cases, councils may be dissolved and elections postponed.

In the *United Arab Republic,* the Local Administration Law of 1960 establishes three types of local councils: governorate, town, and rural. The five largest cities of the United Arab Republic, including Cairo and Alexandria, are governorates and have provincial councils and status. Each national ministry is represented in the governorate administration by a department whose personnel accepts technical direction from the separate ministries but is under the administrative direction of the governor.

The most salient feature of municipal as well as of rural government in the Near and Middle East is the extensive scope of national control. While this is a legacy of the Ottoman Empire handed down in the French form, it is also dominant in such places as Saudi Arabia, Iraq, Jordan, and the Sudan, where the English-type municipal council was established. While this control is primarily concerned with the supervision of administration, finances, and physical planning, national ministries also perform an extensive number of functions which by their very nature should be locally administered. Supervisory control is exercised mainly by the Ministry of Interior or of Local Government as the case may be. Other ministries such as those for education, public works, health, social welfare, and agriculture operate in local areas and often have certain specific powers over the local units. As a result, local government, even the municipalities of large cities, has become emasculated. Local units are considered unimportant while their problems are becoming more intense and the demands made on them are greater as populations continue to increase. In Syria, for example, only five cities outside of Damascus, the capital, offer any municipal services at all.

Government in urbanized areas outside municipal boundaries in the

Near and Middle East and North Africa is as complicated as it is in the rest of the world. The larger central municipalities usually have no power, activities, or interest in the rest of the metropolitan area. The municipalities and villages that do exist outside are usually not set up for the provision of urban services of government, especially in those places which have experienced rapid urban growth. Thus, urban services are likely to devolve upon the national ministries and to be operated through their local administrative units: the provinces, districts, and, subdistricts. While theoretically under the administrative supervision of the governor, local services often bypass him and operate directly, blithely unconcerned as to what other ministries and local agencies are doing in the same territory. At best, there is a confused pattern of authority which results in delay, inefficiency, and downright neglect. However, in many metropolitan areas, public utilities such as water and electricity are administered by semi-autonomous boards under the jurisdiction of a national ministry rather than the central municipality. It must be remembered that in this part of the world, large municipalities are still struggling to provide their inhabitants with the basic urban amenities. The increases in population since World War II have added materially to their burdens.

Administrative deficiencies in metropolitan areas in this region are many: (1) There is no functional coordination—national ministries, municipalities, governorates, and other public entities divide and diffuse governmental power. (2) There is no metropolitan or geographic governmental unity. (3) Urban local governments are restricted in powers and finances. (4) Popular participation is at a minimum; (5) national control dominates the scene; and (6) adequate and trained personnel is lacking.[5]

URBAN GOVERNMENT IN AFRICA

In East and Central Africa, it was not usual for Africans in pre-European days to live in towns. These developed as foreign creations established for purposes of government, trade, and industry, and were European in character. Governmental administration was modern from

[5] United Nations Regional Social Affairs Office for the Middle East, *Public Administration and Finance Problems Associated with Rapid Urban Growth in the Arab States,* Beirut, Lebanon, 1963.

the start. Later, Africans flocked to these towns in overwhelming numbers. In West Africa, large towns often had pre-European existence. But they were administered by the British as rural areas, as parts of provinces or districts. Ibadan in *Nigeria* with a population over a million was separated from its district only in 1961. Administration in these urban areas was largely that of tribal chiefs and councils. Governmental services to the people were provided either by *ad hoc* agencies or by the central government itself.

In East and Central Africa, there appear to be four principal patterns of urban government. The first is where there is a division of responsibility between the modern type of municipal council and a traditional African government. For example, Kampala and Jinja in *Uganda* have local councils that provide the initiative and administer local services, but Africans living within the municipalities pay their taxes to an African agency and are subject to native courts of law. In a second pattern there is a modern type of municipal council with an African advisory council, the latter having no executive powers. This was found throughout *Kenya* and *Tanganyika.* However, the Royal Commission recommended a "two-tier" structure in which administrative organizations should be established for the areas now occupied by Africans inside and immediately surrounding the town. A third pattern, typical of *Northern Rhodesia,* is the combination of a modern municipal council with an African Affairs committee which has executive powers. Here there are two councils operating in the same area, often with two administrative units having the same functions. A fourth pattern obtains in *Southern Rhodesia,* which might be called dual administration. Here native urban areas are outside municipal areas but are administered by the municipal councils to which they are adjacent through municipal directors of native administration.

In West Africa, three different patterns occur. The first, where there is a division of responsibility between the central government and an elected municipal council, is typical of most medium-sized and large towns in West Africa. *Ibadan,* the largest African city on the continent, has an elected city council, only recently modernized from the traditional tribal form, which is responsible for such services as sanitation, markets, water supply, and the administration of bylaws. The central government is responsible for such services as education, town planning, housing, and electricity, the last three through special national commissions. A second pattern is illustrated in *Lagos,* where there is a division of responsibility between the central government, an elected council, and special agencies. Here the administration of the city is in the hands of four agencies: the federal government, the executive development board, and the Port Authority and the Electricity Corporation of Nigeria, the last two being autonomous federal bodies. The Lagos Executive Development Board operates under the authority of the Lagos Town Planning Ordinance and within the direction of the federal Minister for Lagos Affairs. A third pattern is where responsibility is mainly within the orbit of local government as in *Kano,* a Moslem city in Northern Nigeria. Native authorities and subordinate native agencies, well equipped and organized, handle most local functions both within and outside the old city walls. However, water and electricity are provided by regional and federal agencies, and the central government retains town planning powers.

In African urban areas, the main problems are the complexity and overlapping of administrative units, the ceaseless population growth which makes it impossible to provide necessary urban services to all sections of the urbanized area, and the need for trained administrators and technicians.

As can be expected, financial needs in rapidly growing African urban areas are greater than financial resources. The principal taxes raised locally include taxes on land and buildings and personal taxes. Land and building taxes are the most important, although there are many towns in West Africa, notably Ibadan, with no property tax. Other sources of revenue include charges for services rendered, profits from commercial enterprises such as transport, water and other public utilities, license fees, rents of property, grants from the central government, and loans for capital expenditures.

The city of *Leopoldville,* formerly capital city of Belgian Congo, illustrates the development of local government in tropical Africa. In 1932, a purely Belgian urban advisory committee was set up. In 1945, its Congolese counterpart, the *conseil de cité,* was formed. In 1957, the territory of the city was divided into thirteen communes, each with an elected council but supervised by the district commissioner who had headed Leopoldville administration since 1922. The Belgian central government gave Leopoldville a separate budget in 1953. It was made up of $888,000 in local revenue, $1,574,000 in state subsidies, $400,000 in loans, and $500,000 for the capital budget. Twenty-two different local taxes were levied, including a poll tax on men, and a special tax on women "living theoretically alone." In Leopoldville, the city maintained its own police force. Before independence, it was one of the twenty-five administrative districts of the Belgian Congo.[6]

Dakar, the capital of Senegal, is governed by a special act. It is divided into six administrative districts, each of which has an elected municipal district council and an elected district mayor and his deputy. The district mayor acts as registrar. The city of Dakar is administered by a municipal council consisting of all the municipal district councilors. This assembly elects the mayor, whose office has been in existence since 1914, and his deputies from among its members. By an act of January 14, 1961, the central government has taken over Dakar's public services, reserving the right to choose between direct operation and management through concession. These services include street cleaning, minor roads, water, street lighting, and fire protection. The central government has taken over all the property of city services and brought them under full state control. The commune is bound to bear the operating costs and the mayor is provided with a statement of the expenses incurred.[7]

MUNICIPALITIES IN INDIA

In India, there are four kinds of municipalities: (1) city corporations, big cities such as Calcutta, Madras, and Bombay; (2) municipalities, or the smaller cities; (3) town areas, small towns in rural areas; and (4) notified areas in the suburbs. In 1956, there were 12 city corporations, 1,453 municipalities, 383 town areas, and 82 notified areas. To round out the local government picture, there were 309 districts and 123,670 *gram panchayats* for rural areas. In 1951, India's urban population was 17 per cent of the total, and the 15 largest cities had a total of 16 million people.

Each of these municipal units is governed, English style, by a council or

[6] United Nations, Workshop on Urbanization in Africa, *Introduction to the Problems of Urbanization in Tropical Africa,* part 1, New York, Mar. 7, 1962.
[7] *Ibid.*

committee which numbers from 5 to 80 councilmen. Terms are from three to five years. In India there are three kinds of municipal executives: (1) those directly elected by the people and partly responsible to the council; (2) those chosen by the council and completely responsible to it; and (3) salaried officials largely independent of the council and responsible to the state government.

In the municipal corporations, which are established under specific acts of the state legislature and enjoy greater powers than the smaller municipalities, the elected presidents are known as mayors. There is a general council of the corporation, standing committees, and a commissioner who acts as the executive officer. The council appoints all officials except the commissioner, who is usually appointed by the state. Councilors are elected by adult suffrage from wards of the city. In addition, there are reserved seats for scheduled castes and for special interests such as business and labor groups and women's organizations. Councils may co-opt citizens of the community for special services and assistance on committees. In the municipal corporation, the deliberative and executive functions are separated. The deliberative agency consists of the council, the mayor, his deputy, and committees of the council. The executive agency includes the municipal commissioner, the deputy commissioner, the municipal secretary, the municipal engineer, and the health officer. The entire executive power is vested in the commissioner who, although appointed by the state, may be removed by a vote of 60 per cent of the council.

The general powers of municipalities include street cleaning and lighting, registration of births and deaths, burials, hospitals, medical relief, primary education, regulation of dangerous trades, and water supply—all of which are obligatory. Discretionary powers include libraries, rest houses, public buildings, and welfare measures. However, over all actions of the municipality there is rigid central control from the state.

Municipal finance is characterized by the variety of sources of revenue, the small amount of public utility revenue, the growing importance of state and national grants-in-aid, and the general inadequacy of amounts available in comparison to the obvious needs of the people for services. Taxes on property, which include both house and service taxes, are the mainstays of city corporations and municipalities. The fast-growing urban population almost breaks down the municipal facilities; roads, drainage, water supply, and transport are inadequate, and blight is developing at a rapid pace. Satellite towns are springing up without the facilities for urban services of government.

India has been conducting experimentation in structuring new kinds of local units in order to achieve better service, integration, economy, and efficiency. One such in Pradash, known as *Janpada,* is like the English county, composed of both rural and urban areas, in which all municipalities are integrated. This agency has been given all functions of state administration except police and justice, acts as an agent of the state, and operates with state personnel. Another experiment is the *Anchal Sasan* scheme in Orissa, where the entire state is divided into eighteen "anchals," usually containing ten village panchayats, each of which coincides with a national extension block. The council is indirectly elected by village panchayats, municipalities, and notified areas. Functions of this unit include education, medical relief, health, veterinary services, agriculture, forests, irrigation, roads, and the collection of land taxes and cesses. Another type of unit is established at the community block level, with a statutory, elected popular body called the *panchayat samti* (union) and *zilla panchayat* (district council) consisting of all the local presidents, members of the assembly and parliament from that district, and the principal district officials. The normal block contains about 100 villages with about 66,000 population and covers an area of 150 square miles.

There are a number of semiautonomous bodies, either state corporations or government companies, which furnish various utilities. In addition, many local units have undertaken water supply, electricity, gas production, and transportation services.[8]

GOVERNMENT OF METROPOLITAN TOKYO

Tokyo is the largest city in the world. Furthermore, it is the largest city in the history of the world. As of January 1, 1962, it had 9,984,821 people, about 10 per cent of the national population. It is now well over the 10 million mark. During the seventeen months before January, 1962, it increased 301,019, or more than 17,000 per month. Of this increase 30

[8] Eastern Regional Organization for Public Administration (Eropa), *India,* prepared by the Indian Institute of Public Administration, 1960.

per cent is natural; the rest represents migration from rural areas to Tokyo where employment and educational facilities are deemed to be better. A high percentage of Tokyo's increase of population is in the suburban areas; the latest census estimated that there were 500,000 more people in the city in the daytime than at night. In some city wards the density of population is as high as 31,000 per square kilometer. The city is experiencing the common ailments of a growing metropolis: traffic congestion, housing shortage, insufficient open areas, and deficiencies in urban amenities.

In 1943, at the height of World War II, the prefecture of Tokyo and the city of Tokyo were consolidated into the Metropolis of Tokyo. This public entity has prefectural authority over the cities, towns, and villages within its borders. These are ordinary local public bodies. On the other hand, it has municipal administrative authority over its wards, which are also local public bodies.

The legislative body of the Metropolis of Tokyo is the metropolitan assembly, which consists of 120 assemblymen with four-year terms, elected directly by the citizens from 36 constituencies in the wards, cities, towns, and villages. The assembly has the following general powers: enactment of ordinances, their amendment and repeal; authority over revenues and expenditures; approval of balance sheets; assessment and collection of local taxes, fees, charges, and allotments; signing of important contracts, acquisition of property, flotation of bonds, and other powers given by law and national regulations. The assembly also has the right to appoint certain high officials and to approve the appointment of others by the governor. Its regular sessions are four times a year, lasting about seven days. It has eight standing committees corresponding to the governor's major bureaus.

The governor is elected for a four-year term. He is the chief administrator. Under him are three vice-governors appointed by him and approved by the assembly. Also under him are about twenty-five bureaus or commissions covering all fields of local administration. Commissions are appointed by the governor with the approval of the assembly, or are elected by the assembly. Commissions administer such functions as education, elections, civil service, public safety, labor relations, and real estate assessment examination.

The wards, cities, towns, and villages within Tokyo are given certain powers under the Local Autonomy Law. They have a council and a chief administrator appointed by the council. They are under the supervision of the governor.

The 1961–1962 budget for Tokyo amounted to 342,547 million yen, the largest in history. The general account totaled 236,052 million yen, and of this 60 per cent came from metropolitan taxes and 17 per cent from national grants (much lower than in most Japanese local units). Education took 21 per cent of the general account, while public works took 20 per cent, general administration 9 per cent, police 8 per cent, public welfare 7 per cent, public housing 6 per cent, public debt 6 per cent, economic affairs 4 per cent, fire protection 3 per cent, grants to wards 2 per cent, labor affairs 3 per cent, public cleansing 2 per cent, and the rest miscellaneous.

The metropolitan taxes were on inhabitants, business, real estate acquisition, tobacco, amusement, food, automobiles, property, electricity, and other items of a minor nature. Public utilities and facilities assumed to be self-supporting had separate accounts; they included hospitals, slaughterhouses, markets, racing enterprises, transportation, waterworks, and sewerage. Local units within the Metropolis may levy taxes and collect revenues for local purposes subject to the governor's supervision.

The Law of National Capital Region Development of 1956 comprehends not only the Metropolis of Tokyo but also a number of prefectures surrounding it, and aims at making Tokyo a suitable place for the capital of Japan by removing many drawbacks and nuisances in the area. Uncontrolled urban sprawl is to be prevented, urban renewal promoted, zoning enforced, new housing projects fostered, industry decentralized, and satellite cities developed. All this is to control the growth of Tokyo during the next decade.[9]

SUBMUNICIPAL UNITS AND URBAN COMMUNITY DEVELOPMENT

In some municipalities with large populations or large areas, submunicipal units of government have been established to bring government closer to the people by providing means whereby the public may

[9] The Governor of Tokyo Metropolis, *An Administrative Perspective of Tokyo,* 1962, pp. 3–11.

better be heard and represented in the governmental process. In *Yugoslavia,* villages or settlements may form local committees when size and dispersion allow no direct participation of citizens. Committee members consist of municipal councilmen from the territory involved and members elected by the people. Funds and administrative work and supervision are provided by the central council.[10]

In the *Philippines,* the submunicipal unit is the barrio, which in 1960 was made a corporate local unit of government in rural areas with specific powers, financial resources, and governmental organization within the framework of the municipality. In the chartered cities, the barrio exists as a submunicipal unit in which a barrio lieutenant is elected by the people and is chairman of an advisory committee of three plus a deputy barrio lieutenant. The barrio lieutenant is the contact with a city councilman, who has one or more barrios as his responsibility.

In *Turkey,* the mahallas with a four-member council of elders headed by a popularly elected mukhtar carry out routine central government functions in neighborhood areas of Istanbul and other large cities.[11]

In *Poland,* there are submunicipal units in cities over 200,000, each of which have popularly elected councils, committees, and an executive board. These units act as electoral districts and also carry out administrative duties given to them by the municipal council. In 1954, a new unit called the settlement was created to accelerate the work of urbanization in residential suburbs; these settlements have their own councils.[12]

In South American countries, the municipality is the most viable local unit of government outside of cities. It resembles the American county in that sometimes it encompasses a large area which contains both urban and rural settlements. Submunicipal units have therefore been established in various countries. In *Brazil,* there are submunicipal units in rural areas in which the chief administrator is the submayor appointed by the mayor of the municipality with the approval of council.[13]

In *Ecuador,* municipalities are divided into cantons. There is a three-member board elected by the municipal council, and the chief executive

[10] Samuel Humes and Eileen M. Martin, *The Structure of Local Governments,* International Union of Local Authorities, Martinus Nijhoff, The Hague, 1961, p. 306.

[11] *Ibid.,* pp. 370–372.

[12] *Ibid.,* pp. 294–297.

[13] *Ibid.,* p. 343.

of both urban and rural subunits is the political deputy, the *jefe,* who is appointed by the municipal executive.[14]

In *Colombia,* the *corregimentos* are the municipal subunits with a deputy as agent of the municipal mayor. In large cities the barrios are the subunits.[15]

Casablanca in *Morocco* has fourteen administrative districts with no elected representatives, under the authority of a caliph who is appointed by the governor. The caliph is responsible for law and order and acts as registrar of vital statistics. All large towns in Morocco are divided into districts, but important matters are dealt with at the prefecture level or by municipal officials headed by a pasha or caid, under the Ministry of Interior.[16]

A number of other countries have urban wards which are local government units having their own elective councils. These are generally administrative or election subdivisions. In a number of countries this subunit may have its collective patrimony, even though the management of it is entrusted to organs of the municipality as a whole.

In some countries, an urban community development program has brought into existence or revived submunicipal units of government. In Dacia in *Pakistan,* the unit of administration was initially the municipal ward, comprising a population of approximately 20,000 to 25,000. Each ward has been divided into ten mahallas, or localities, whose committees serve as "basic democracies." At the ward level, "neighborhood councils" have been set up, consisting of representatives from mahalla committees and voluntary agencies. Ward community development teams are led by a male project leader and a female social worker, who supervise the work of the mahalla level, and who use their good offices to coordinate the government activities in that area.

In Delhi, *India,* citizens' developmental councils (*vikas mandals*) have been set up on the basis of 10 to 15 *katias,* each of 15 to 25 families. Officers are elected by residents of the block who are dues-paying members.

In Cali and Bogotá, *Colombia,* neighborhood areas (barrios) have

[14] *Ibid.,* p. 349.

[15] *Ibid.,* pp. 354–355.

[16] Henry Mourer, *Administrative Problems of Urbanization in Africa,* United Nations Workshop on Urbanization in Africa, New York, Feb. 22, 1962.

organized juntas nominated by the municipality and confirmed by a plebiscite of votes. Each junta acts through various committees and is assisted by the municipality.

In Saigon, *Republic of Vietnam,* the problem of squatters' settlements is being handled by a representative neighborhood committee appointed by the municipal administration and including religious and labor leaders. The committee serves as a channel between the people and the city authorities.[17]

The municipality of Bogotá, *Colombia,* in 1959 inaugurated a program of urban community development under a law authorizing such programs throughout the nation. In setting up this program, the municipal council of Bogotá recognized "the belt of poverty," a commonplace condition of all Latin American cities, composed of squatter settlements which were without most of the city facilities and services. The resources of the city itself were insufficient to provide the services by normal means in a reasonable time. Many residents of these areas were driven to the city by the miseries of rural existence and had nothing in the way of ability and experience to adapt themselves to the hard realities of urban life. The program was based on the hope that much could be done by voluntary action and support. Plans were made to establish community action councils in each barrio of the city, and four pilot areas were started. The staff consisted of a sociologist, a housing expert, an engineer, and three social workers. Accomplishments, despite obstacles and lack of interest, included projects completed for school construction, bus facilities, sewer facilities, park lighting, and electrical service extension. These successes have shown the possibility of community development in urban areas of Bogotá.

The experience of four months showed that urban community development is characterized by special factors: (1) Urban people are less isolated than those in rural areas, are less resourceful, and expect more from city officials. (2) City people are more mobile, less rooted in their community, and more exposed to outside currents, often without understanding them too well; (3) they live more anonymously and are less neighborly; (4) they want the facilities that they see all around them. (5) People must be persuaded that they can do some things for them-

[17] Report by the Secretary General United Nations, Department of Economic and Social Affairs, *Community Development in Urban Areas,* New York, 1961, pp. 16–23.

selves; (6) programs in urban areas cannot do much to increase economic well-being; and (7) urban programs must often adjust uprooted people to city life. The Bogotá city ordinance establishing urban community development specified that each community action council should include a priest, a teacher, a police inspector, and a social worker. The most popular projects were for housing improvement, education, recreation, and health. The Bogotá office of community development was lodged in the city planning board. In such a program investigators, organizers, technical advisers, administrators, cooperators, and volunteers are needed. All these workers need intensive training, according to an evaluation of the program.[18]

In addition to the foregoing examples, there are many experiments in popular participation in more specialized local undertakings such as housing and the development of local industry, in which national projects are assisted by nongovernmental and nonproject agencies in urban neighborhoods. For example, in the *Russian Soviet Socialist Republic* workshop trade-union committees select workers who participate in self-help projects on the basis of their need for housing and their length of service. In the *Republic of China* (Taiwan) the workers' union formed a housing committee which supervised and assisted in specific housing projects.

Beginning in the nineteenth century, when the awareness of the blighted urban areas and its problems became widespread, the neighborhood center developed as an important urban institution. Lewis Mumford, in *The Culture of Cities* (1938) said: "It was, then, precisely out of the most degrading poverty and the most disorganized environment, that the new conception of an organized neighborhood with a central building adapted to a varied round of communal activities took shape." He believed that this conception would remain as the most fundamental contribution to the metropolis of the new order.

An increasing number of centers have been founded since that time. In the Soviet nations, trade-union-managed cultural centers are established. In African countries, for example, Nigeria and Algeria, community centers, *centres communicataire* and *foyers social,* have come into being. Furthermore, there are many countries in which neighborhood organizations

[18] Caroline F. Ware, "Community Development in Urban Areas, Initial Experience in Bogotá, Colombia," *Community Development Review,* June, 1962, pp. 43–56.

are initiated and administered by the people themselves without any governmental assistance or legal existence. Mention is made of the *asociaciones de barvadas* in Lima, Peru, *juntas progresistas* (improvement boards) in Costa Rica, *kaifongs* in Hong Kong, and mutual benefit associations in areas of rapid urban growth, based on tribal ties in community of origin, in West Africa. These examples show the "felt need" for neighborhood organization and may point the way to the recognition of the neighborhood in future municipal organization.[19]

PLANNING IN METROPOLITAN AREAS

In order to solve the various and complicated problems of metropolitan areas, comprehensive and detailed study and planning are necessary. It is interesting to note what is being done in some of the developing countries of the world today in this regard.

In *Ghana,* for example, planning has been done by the central government. Plans have been drawn up for the development of municipalities by the Town and Country Planning Division of the central government in consultation with the municipalities.

In *India,* metropolitan planning falls within the jurisdiction of states, which take the initiative but discuss their recommendations with municipal authorities. Furthermore, all large schemes involving the expenditure of substantial sums of money must be integrated into national plans and policy, but they will be executed by the states. The city of Delhi is under the direct jurisdiction of the central government and its master plan was evolved by the central government, which created the Delhi Development Authority.

In the *United Arab Republic,* the governorate is responsible for preparing plans for urban and rural areas, and the central government must approve these plans.

Among the more visible consequences of rapid urbanization in *Latin America* is the decadence of urban environment, which is evidenced by shanty towns and slums, excessive population densities, uncontrolled land use, inadequate urban services, deficient educational and recreational facilities, and inefficient commercial and marketing services. But housing

[19] *Ibid.,* pp. 28–38.

is the most difficult and important problem. While public housing programs have been initiated in most Latin American countries, they have benefited mainly the families of moderate income. However, there are examples to the contrary as in Barranquilla, Colombia, where the entire slum population was resettled. The town planner in Latin America is faced with huge problems: low income levels, monetary devaluation, and rapid growth, both urban and rural. Measures that would improve the situation involve decentralization, the encouragement of village industries, and the resettlement of rural immigrants. However, the Latin American governments have much to do to improve their administrative practices so that planning can be implemented and brought to fruition. Planning now is concentrated in the few large and capital cities.[20]

In *Venezuela,* Caracas is the only city which is the center of a metropolitan area. In 1960, by mutual agreement between the two municipalities that comprise the metropolitan area of Caracas, a planning office for the metropolitan area was established. This agency is only an advisory body. Previous planning for the area had been done by the national government.

In *Israel,* 72 per cent of the population in 1948 lived in three large towns. Planning since then has decreased the percentage to 50, but there is still an increase of overall figures. Population in the other towns increased 12 to 30 per cent of the total population. Planning started off and still is carried on in a centralized fashion. So-called "development towns" have been encouraged by investments in order to provide a better urban-rural balance. Efforts are being made to integrate social, economic, and government activities by providing a system of service centers so that urban benefits can be distributed over wider areas.

In *Poland,* according to the act of 1961, physical planning is divided into national, regional, and local levels, and is the overall responsibility of the Planning Commission of the Council of Ministers. The work on regional planning is directed by the Long-term Plans Department of the Planning Commission; it is being carried out in the regional planning offices attached to the economic planning commissions in each province and in the city of Warsaw. Local planning is in charge of the Committee

[20] United Nations, *Report of the Seminar on Urbanization Problems in Latin America,* New York, July 6–18, 1959.

for Building, Town Planning and Architecture, and is conducted in local offices which, although subordinate to the central committee, are controlled by local people's councils, and act on their behalf.

In *Yugoslavia,* the adoption of a physical plan and its implementation are in the hands of elected bodies of the local governments such as the municipal people's committees and the district people's committees. Before a decision is made it is discussed by professional organizations and by the citizens themselves. State and federal institutes of planning disseminate information to local bodies and prepare studies for them. The decentralized urbanization in Yugoslavia offers a new solution to housing and other urban and socioeconomic problems. Regulation and prevention of urban problems is achieved not only through physical planning but also through the coordinated functioning of the entire economic and political system. The main difficulties lie in the limited material resources of the nation.

According to Minour Yoshida, a prefect governor of *Japan,* the administrative machinery of government in Japan has been enlarged and has become so complicated that coordination between several departments is necessary. Thus, in the construction of a factory one must deal with the Departments of Industry, Agriculture, and Civil Engineering. A new horizontal system has been introduced to facilitate local coordination. This includes the planning board, the general development department, the office of coordination, and the chief executive's office.[21] The only region with a formal planning organization is Tokyo, which has a metropolitan planning commission of four members with the Minister of Construction as chairman. However, it has only advisory powers. Each city and prefecture has its own planning sections, also advisory. Implementation depends on national financial assistance.

NEW AND RAPIDLY GROWING TOWNS

New towns, according to a United Nations report on Asia, may be classified under four categories: (1) overspill towns to relieve congestion

[21] Minour Yoshida, "Trends in the Administrative Machinery of Local Government in Japan," *Local Government Structure and Organization: Problems of Metropolitan Areas,* World Conference on Local Government, Washington, D.C., 1961, pp. 81–82.

in large cities; (2) single-industry towns; (3) administrative towns; and (4) *agrovilles* (literally "land towns," those created out of a scattering rural population which is resettled near its field of work). The need for new towns is based upon the circumstances of the region involved, the pressures of a growing population, rural poverty, and the congestion of old towns. Many questions must be answered in the planning stage. For example: Should the new towns provide shelter only or complete urban services? Should there be a National Development Authority for the planning of new towns on a regional basis? What is the optimum size in area and population? Should old towns be expanded or new ones created to take care of the increased population in metropolitan areas? Should the planning organization be a part of the national or local executive authority of the town, or should it be independent? What elements should be included in the master plan? How should the establishment of new towns be financed? These and many other problems arise in such a complex and costly effort.

The principal methods of financing are loans made by central or state governments, investment of banks and insurance companies, the use of social security and retirement funds, and capital budgeting as part of national economic development. In *Japan,* residential towns are developed with loans obtained by the Japanese Housing Corporation from the central government, while industrial towns are financed from the capital budget and from the companies involved. Slum clearance is financed equally by central and local governments. In *Indonesia* and the *Federation of Malaya,* the muncipal banks offer financing services, and social security and retirement funds are used. In *Thailand,* a corporation finances the new towns, while in the *Republic of Vietnam* a special reconstruction lottery is used to raise money. In *Ceylon,* the central government, and in *India,* the state governments finance new towns. In *Pakistan,* there is a House Building Finance Corporation, and private parties are encouraged to build houses under national regulations and fixed prices.

The problem of managing new towns has been answered in the United Nations report as follows: "It is desirable to set up from the beginning a separate authority for the construction and management of towns in such a way that gradual municipalization develops as new towns grow and as citizens occupy the towns." The report continues by stating: "In all instances it is necessary to avoid paternalism in administration because it undermines the foundations of democracy, namely self-respect and self-reliance." It concludes by preferring "multipurpose" rather than "single-purpose" new towns, moderate-sized rather than large towns, and provincial-local rather than national planning.[22]

Several examples of new towns and rapidly growing urban areas in developing countries will illustrate the problems involved in their governmental administration.

Rajpura in Punjab, India, is a small settlement built to rehabilitate displaced persons who migrated from Pakistan after the partition of the subcontinent in 1947. It was originally intended to be a large town of 100,000, but owing to a limited water supply, the population had to be restricted to 16,000. The new settlement has 1,160 acres and consists of three neighborhoods. The town is administered by a development board consisting of the chief minister of Punjab as chairman, and six members, four official and two nonofficial. The town administrator is the secretary of the board. This board has built 2,600 houses. The working population is 80 per cent labor. The total outlay for the town was about 12 million rupees, divided between the cost of the land, the refugee housing, and the roads and other utility services.

Chandigarh, also in the Punjab, is a town being built for 150,000 people. There is a town center, a capital complex (it is an administrative capital of East Punjab), and an industrial area. Each sector is self-contained with shops, schools, and other amenities. A wide green band called a leisure center runs through the center of the town. The administration of the town is entrusted to the chief administrator, who is directly under the control of the state government, and is authorized to exercise the powers of a municipal council. The execution of the project is included in the India Five-Year Plan, while the master plan was evolved in 1951 by the famous architect Le Corbusier.

Under the second Five-Year Plan, India established three large steel plants in the public sector and is building *Durgapur,* a new town, in which to locate one of these plants and to house its workers. Its ultimate

[22] United Nations Technical Assistance Programme, *Public Administration Problems of New and Rapidly Growing Towns in Asia,* New York, 1962, pp. 3–16.

population will be about 125,000, including 10,000 employees at the steel plant, who will need about 10,000 housing units. The town is divided into five zones and a civic center. Each zone is divided into neighborhoods, and each zone has three shopping centers. The general manager of the steel plant is also general administrator of the municipality, with all municipal powers in his hands.

Chittaranjan in West Bengal is a similar town built for locomotive manufacturing workers by the Indian Ministry of Railways. While these towns are to be considered as pioneer projects, it appears that much needs to be done to develop them into real communities. Local government is almost absent; management is either directly from the central authorities or in the hands of the industrial officials—the existing village panchayats having been abolished.[23]

[23] *Ibid.*, pp. 17–22.

11 Community Development and Local Government

COMMUNITY DEVELOPMENT is a concept that in recent years has undergone widespread exploration, experimentation, and application in developing countries throughout the world. The term as defined by the United Nations means "the processes by which the efforts of the people themselves are united with those of governmental authority to improve the economic, social and cultural conditions of communities, to integrate these communities into the life of the nation, and to enable them to contribute fully to national progress." [1]

In most countries the national governments (or the states in federal governments) have taken the initiative in community development through appropriate ministries or special national community development agencies. They are responsible for supplying trained community workers, for giving technical advice and assistance, for furnishing material assistance in terms of money, materials, and personnel, and for establishing viable local governments and cooperative organizations to maintain

[1] United Nations Technical Assistance Programme, *Public Administration Aspects of Community Development Programmes,* New York, 1959, p. 2.

the voluntary initial efforts. The community development workers serve as catalysts of self-help in communities and as liaison between the communities and the assisting governmental agencies. There are several types of community development programs: (1) those countrywide in scope, coordinated with technical services of the government, which are administered by special agencies of government; (2) those countrywide in scope which place emphasis on community organizations without any change in the governmental machinery; and (3) those multifunctional and limited in geographic scope.[2]

The program developed in India has set the pattern for similar programs in Afghanistan, Iran, Indonesia, Pakistan, the United Arab Republic, the Philippines, Thailand, and Vietnam. In this type of program, the organization responsible for its administration is a separate national agency attached either to the national planning office or to the office of the president or chief executive of the nation. Policy making and guidance are done through a cabinet-level or an interdepartment-level committee. At the state, regional, provincial, and district levels there is usually a development committee with the chief executive officer of the unit as chairman and a community developmental official as secretary. On this committee may be national or state members of the legislature from the district, representatives of national ministries in the district, and representatives of private welfare organizations. If the administrative districts of the government cover too large an area, if they do not suit for developmental purposes, or if the villages are too small, new types of units are set up. In India these are called "developmental blocks," in Pakistan "developmental areas," and in the United Arab Republic "areas of combined units." Trained community workers and monetary grants are furnished for the various local projects and activities.[3]

In *India,* the program aims at an all-round development of the rural sector of the nation in a "planned democratic manner." This indicates an interest not only in the increase of food production, but also in the proper land distribution; not only in the development of community organizations, but also in the promotion of local self-government as a permanent democratic institution; not only in the improvement of the general stand-

[2] *Ibid.*, pp. 5–9.
[3] *Ibid.*, p. 6.

ard of living, but also in the promotion of self-reliance, cooperative action, community solidarity, and a change in attitude from a negative to a positive approach. The program in India is multipurpose, aimed to meet all the major needs of the rural people. It consists of activities in agriculture, animal husbandry, irrigation, village industries, cooperatives, health, sanitation, education, communications, arts and crafts, and rural housing. The means used are extension education and community organization. Peoples' institutions at the village level are important and basic: the panchayat (democratically elected council), the cooperative (economic in character), and the village school (for art and culture). The "block" is a new territorial unit above the village level, which plans and administers the regional program; it is the coordinating agency for the various state departments that contribute to the program. Financial grants from higher authority flow through it and are allocated by it to villages and projects. The National Extension Service has been created for community development purposes. At the block level, its staff consists of a block development officer, eight extension officers—one each for agriculture, animal husbandry, cooperation, panchayats, rural industries, rural engineering, social education, and programs for women and children. At the village level there are ten village men workers and two village women workers. Each block has a primary medical center headed by a medical officer. The block development officer is the captain of the team and the coordinating officer. The village-level worker is a multipurpose worker with emphasis on agriculture. Above the block levels are the district, divisional, and state levels, and at all levels there are nonofficial advisory bodies. At the top is the national Ministry of Community Development, a consultative committee of Parliament, and a top coordinating committee made up of appropriate members of the cabinet headed by the Prime Minister. The entire community development program is geared into the Five-Year Plans of the nation and is based upon the ideology of the welfare state. The Indian program is countrywide in scope and had by 1959 been extended to 290,000 villages out of the total of 850,000, with almost half of the proposed 5,000 blocks having been set up. The average size of a block is about 250 square miles with a population of between 60,000 and 80,000 people and 100 villages.[4]

[4] *Ibid.*, pp. 71–82.

The second general type of community development, popular in Africa and in the Caribbean, is found in *Ghana,* where it is known locally as "mass education." It is under the direction of the Department of Social Welfare and Community Development located in the Ministry of Health and Welfare. It operates in four main fields: adult education, home economics, self-help construction projects, and general extension work for national departments. An important aspect of the program is getting the cooperation of the local leaders and people. The main aim is to improve the standard of living of rural dwellers. Village-level workers participate in multipurpose activities; there are more than 1,000 salaried staff workers. Their task is to stimulate enthusiasm among the voluntary village leaders and to coordinate their efforts.[5]

The third type of program predominates in Latin America and is exemplified by the National Indian Institute of *Mexico.* Of the 30 million inhabitants of Mexico, 10 per cent are Indians, and the government is most anxious to integrate them into the national stream of life. The National Indian Institute was created for this purpose in 1948, and is an autonomous federal agency of government, headed by a director and a council. It is entrusted with the development of projects for the improvement of Indian communities. It integrates the work of various competent ministries relating to Indian life. It has its own staff and its budget is made up of contributions from interested ministries. The work is channeled into regional projects through coordinating centers, which are headed by a director and technical personnel including agricultural engineers, medical doctors, anthropologists, agronomists, nurses, and *promotores,* the last being bilingual Indians who are trained in the centers for the job of introducing into the Indian communities new ideas, practices, and techniques. Educational workers teach in the rural schools; most of these as well as some of the technicians live in the villages.[6]

LOCAL GOVERNMENT AND COMMUNITY DEVELOPMENT

The problem of integrating community development with local government is illustrated by the program which was initiated in *Pakistan* in

[5] *Ibid.*, pp. 93–99.
[6] *Ibid.*, pp. 100–105.

1953. Here the program is known as Village AID (Village Agricultural and Industrial Development Programme). Its objectives are to raise the productive output and real income of the villager, to increase community services, and to create a spirit of community self-help, initiative, and leadership. Local government institutions in Pakistan are known as basic democracies. The lowest tier in rural areas is the union council (10 to 15 villages with 10,000 to 15,000 population); the next higher tier is the tehsil or thana council (150 to 200 villages and about 250,000 people); and the next higher levels are district, division, and provincial councils. The lowest rung of the community development program is the village community; its organization is voluntary and not statutory; its activities depend on cooperation, not authority. But these two institutions, Village AID and the union council, supplement each other and cooperate each in its own sphere so they will not duplicate each other's efforts. According to a ranking Pakistanian official, the answers to the problem of integration should be along the following lines: (1) Village AID must work at the village community level. (2) The village worker must limit his activities to nonregulatory development functions and sponsor only "felt-need" projects of the village council. (3) Village AID funds should maintain their separate identity. (4) Village AID should be the developmental agency recognized by all levels of the basic democracies. (5) All elected members of union councils should be trained in AID work.[7]

In the *Philippines,* a presidential assistant for community development was first appointed in 1956. His duties included the planning and implementing of the President's community program in barrios (villages), municipalities (counties), and chartered cities, and integrating the work of national ministries and departments with local activities. To each of the provinces there was assigned a provincial community development officer and a provincial community development council composed of representatives of the various national ministries in the province and municipal officials, headed by the governor. Likewise, in each municipality there was organized a municipal community development council with the mayor as chairman and the community development officer of the municipality as executive secretary. At the barrio level is the barrio

[7] H. B. Minocher Homji, "Community Development and Local Government," *Community Development Review,* March, 1961, pp. 59–81.

community development worker who assists the barrio council and other local organizations in the development of projects.[8]

The *United Arab Republic* has set up 250 "combined centers" of local administration for the provision of extension and demonstration of agricultural services, primary education, and health and welfare services on the basis of serving between 15,000 and 20,000 people per center. This has been the UAR answer to the problem of field coordination of technical services in rural areas. Before this, there were separate multifunctional social centers administered by the Ministry of Agriculture and the Ministry of Social Welfare. These centers were located in different areas and were directly administered from Cairo with little or no liaison between ministries at top level and no joint planning. The "combined centers," established in 1955, were staffed with professional personnel in health, agriculture, social affairs, and education.

In *Vietnam,* municipalities, provinces, and villages have some semblance of self-government but play a secondary role in community development. The program is almost entirely nationally administered with technical, planning, and financial leadership from the top. However, local units collaborate with the technical services in working out detailed plans for local action. They conduct on-the-spot investigations for the evaluation of projects and their progress. They also may submit to the appropriate national ministries proposals for local development and may carry out projects on their own initiative or may assist with funds and personnel nationally administered projects in their areas.[9]

AGRARIAN REFORM AND COMMUNITY DEVELOPMENT

Community development, the establishment of local self-government, and agrarian reform are the three main prongs in the worldwide drive to improve rural conditions. Without all three, ultimate stability and progress cannot be complete. Throughout the world today, great strides have been made on all three fronts, but still much remains to be done.

[8] Ernest E. Neal, "Community Development in the Philippines," *Community Development Review,* September, 1957, pp. 24–44.

[9] Eastern Regional Organization for Public Administration (Eropa), *Vietnam,* answer to questionnaire on "Government Administration of Rural Development," prepared by National Institute of Administration, Manila, Nov. 24, 1960.

Several examples of recent efforts in agrarian reform will indicate both the general problem and the ways in which it is being attacked. The two extreme conditions of landownership in rural areas are *latifundia* (large land holdings) and *minifundia* (small land holdings), each one militating against the improvement of the economic condition of rural people. In the areas from which the following examples are taken, 70 per cent or more of the population is dependent upon agriculture. In many such places, rural overpopulation is the predominant feature of the economy, and the agrarian organization is characterized by large numbers of fragmented and uneconomic holdings, high rents, and excessive debt costs. Unequal distribution of landownership, coupled with shortage of land, enables the owners to collect excessively high rents. The shortage of capital prevents improvement in agricultural practices. In regions where there is a high ratio of land to labor, the outstanding feature is the wasteful utilization of land. In both cases, exploitation and inefficient use of labor are common.

In *India,* land reform is within the legislative power of the states. However, the principles of land reform were laid down by the government of India, and laws passed by the states must have the approval of the President of India. Before recent reforms, zamindari was one of the three main forms of landownership. Its characteristic feature was the vesting of proprietary rights in the tax collectors, the zamindars, to whom, in the late eighteenth and early nineteenth centuries, the British farmed out the collection of revenue from the cultivating peasants occupying the land. The condition has now been abolished in every Indian state, and has been replaced by the system of ryotwari, in which the cultivator pays revenue directly to the state and enjoys proprietary rights. The general policies of Indian land reform, which are by no means completely carried out at this date, include limitation of area to that which owners can resume for personal cultivation, and conferring on the tenant of land in excess of the resumable area security of tenure and the right to acquire ownership. For the smaller holders, the development of cooperatives is encouraged. Maximum rents are being fixed at rates one-fifth to one-fourth of the annual produce, and landless workers are being settled on land available for distribution in cooperative groups. Ancillary industries for the unemployed are being developed in villages. But in spite of progress since independence in 1947, there is still great overcrowding, shortage of land, uneconomic and fragmentary holdings of land, and a low level of agricultural output both per acre and per man.[10]

In *Pakistan,* following independence and partition from India in 1947, the government enacted laws abolishing private agricultural estates, bringing them all under public ownership. In spite of the high cost involved in settling liquidation with the absentee landlords, land reform has proceeded in the interest of those who till the soil. Laws have been passed in various parts of the nation ensuring tenure for the agricultural workers and securing for them an equitable share of the produce. Progress has also been made in establishing cooperatives and in consolidating fragmented holdings of agricultural land.[11]

In the *United Arab Republic,* the law on agrarian reform which followed in the wake of the 1952 revolution provided that land held in large estates exceeding a maximum of 100 feddans must be redistributed to cultivators in parcels not to exceed 5 feddans. Likewise, multipurpose cooperative societies were formed among the beneficiaries of land distribution, subdivision of properties below a minimum area was prohibited, relations between landlord and tenant were laid down, maximum rents and minimum wages for agricultural workers were fixed, entailed estates were dissolved (these covered a substantial acreage throughout the nation), and agricultural workers were granted freedom to form trade unions.[12]

In *Iraq,* the objective of the government lands development law was to provide adequate income for landless peasants by enabling them to cultivate their own land. Land also was to be distributed to other low-income groups besides farmers, such as industrial laborers, retired civil servants, and military personnel. Measures have also been taken to form cooperative groups. Iraq enjoys favorable conditions for agricultural development because it has large areas of irrigable land, plenty of low-cost water, and

[10] United Nations, Department of Economic Affairs, *Progress in Land Reform,* New York, 1954, pp. 20–23. E. Gordon Alderfer, "The Engineer and the Minifundio: The Challenge of Technology for Peasant Societies," Paper no. NA63-103, Care, Inc., New York, August, 1963.

[11] *Ibid.,* pp. 23–24.

[12] *Ibid.,* pp. 29–30.

adequate national revenue from oil royalties. The agricultural policy therefore is one mainly of extensive land settlement.[13]

In *Latin America,* the agrarian structure is characterized by a high degree of inequality in landownership and wastage of land. Land is abundant in relation to population, but concentration of ownership reduces a large part of the rural population to the status of laborers with a low standard of living, or of small cultivators with precarious conditions of tenancy. In two countries, however, policies representing complete land reform have been adopted. In *Mexico,* since the revolution of 1910, the basic principles of land reform have been in the direction of eliminating latifundia and of raising the living standards of rural workers. Reforms have included the granting, restitution, and development of *ejidos,* which can be described as land held by a town or village, either for collective use or distribution among the inhabitants for cultivation in small plots, to which each individual has the right to occupancy and use so long as he keeps the land under cultivation. In colonial times, villages had received grants of land of this kind, but during the nineteenth century had lost them to the owners of large estates. The restitution of *ejido* land has thus involved the splitting up of large latifundia and the return of this land to village or town ownership. Also agricultural education, machinery, and credit have been extended and improved. In *Bolivia,* a decree on agrarian reform was passed in 1953, implementing the constitutional provision relating to the regulation of landownership. The objectives of the new decree aimed at the provision of arable land to landless peasants, the expropriation of owners not working their land, the restoration of land to Indian villages, the liberation of rural workers from bonds of financial servitude, the migration of settlers to better regions, and the encouragement of greater agricultural productivity.[14]

In tropical *Africa,* natives under traditional customary tenure possess complete security of tenure and usufructuary rights in land. Land here is the basis of social organization and not only of production, so that reforms of a purely economic-agricultural kind would run the risk of disrupting the entire social organization. Land held under indigenous ten-

[13] *Ibid.,* p. 32.
[14] *Ibid.,* pp. 37–40.

ures in Africa is not subject to ownership; it is not owned by a small number of large landholders, and security and property rights are not denied to large numbers of cultivators and occupants. While this system deters the development of large-scale agriculture and the increase of productivity, it has the merit of providing security of tenure and land use to those who cultivate the land and live off it. However, improvement in agriculture in tropical Africa has taken the form of better utilization of land, the development of cooperatives, and settlement schemes for large areas still not under cultivation.[15]

In *Japan,* land-reform legislation was enacted in 1946 and substantially amended in 1950. The main provisions were as follows: (1) The state was to purchase all agricultural land of absentee owners. (2) The state was similarly to purchase all the agricultural land of village landowners in excess of certain ceilings, differing in various prefectures and under different conditions, but usually from 4½ to 11 acres. (3) Landlords were to be paid compensation in government bonds redeemable in thirty years and bearing 3.6 per cent interest, the price being arrived at by capitalizing the annual return on land per acre. (4) The land thus acquired was resold to the tenant who cultivated it at the same price that was paid to the landlords, payable over thirty years at 3.2 per cent interest. (5) Tenants were given almost complete security of tenure on the untenanted land which remained, with rents fixed but never more than 5 per cent of the gross yield. (6) The reform was administered by land committees established in each town and village.[16]

[15] *Ibid.*, pp. 33–36.

[16] R. P. Dore, "The Administration of the Japanese Land Reform," *Journal of Local Administration Overseas,* October, 1962, pp. 231–238.

12 Local Government and National Progress

IF LOCAL GOVERNMENT in developing countries is to have a vital role in the general drive toward national progress that is evident in the world today, it must do so on the basis of recognizing and accepting certain basic trends inherent in modern society. These are: (1) toward urbanization; (2) toward national control; (3) toward the welfare state; (4) toward a higher standard of living; and (5) toward democracy. These trends, following the historical evolution of our time, are being translated into the pronouncements of political leaders and parties who want to be successful in the foreseeable future. They are, moreover, fairly uniform throughout the world, especially in developing countries where the pace is often fast and furious. They represent perhaps the outermost limits of the three-century surge toward liberty, equality, and fraternity that has characterized the democratic movement in Western culture that has now engulfed the entire world, as well as the more recent mass striving for materialistic gains in everyday life. Actually, there are no alternatives to these trends; the problems that arise will be solely those of leadership, procedure, and administration.

This is not to say that these trends will come to perfect fruition and that all the latent possibilities will develop to their fullest, for there can be many diversions, bypasses, frustrations, and downright failures. The road ahead will be strewn with good intentions and mangled plans. Within the framework of destiny, there will be ample time and space for freedom of choice, decision making, politics, and war. In fact, conditions being what they are today, the chances of getting to the end of this road seem doubtful to many. But be that as it may, there is good work to be done by one and all, and this is where local government can be useful.

In suggesting the form of local government in developing countries only the barest outlines should be sketched, for each nation has its own problems, conditions, and background. Important elements, as well as minor details, may vary from place to place. However, it should be emphasized that all nations today are living in practically the same modern world, and that the fundamental objectives of governmental activity are identical all over. In urban areas there must be adequate water, electricity, sewerage, transport, schools, hospitals, streets, markets, housing, and other commonplace amenities. In rural areas the need for improved education, health, cleanliness, agriculture, and general welfare is uniformly apparent. Therefore, governments to be successful must be positive, constructive, forward-looking, and active, and in so doing will face the same administrative problems wherever they may be. Moreover, there are no ancient forms and practices to fall back upon. Never in history have there been such large urban agglomerations. They are new, their problems are new, and these must be solved by new methods. The same can be said about the rural scene. The ancient concept of the village, socially, economically, and almost politically autonomous, is simply not geared to modern times. Such a village cannot bring its inhabitants modern benefits. The new governments of developing nations have opted for the welfare state; they have promised the people higher standards of living. To get them, modern practices of administration are required; to get them, the national governments must share their responsibilities with the leadership and citizenry of localities. Local government, democratic, modern, and efficient, holds the key to national success and progress.

TOWARD EFFECTIVE METROPOLITAN LOCAL GOVERNMENT

Urbanization is a worldwide phenomenon. There is no way it can be stopped by the hand of man. The strongest national government cannot drive more than a small percentage of the excess urban population out of the cities or keep rural dwellers from coming in. If it were to try, it would be submerged by new demands, tensions, and problems even greater than those that have been brought about by urbanization. The fact is that no one has the least idea about what to do with the present metropolitan populations any more than anyone knows what to do about the population explosion that has helped it on its way. Nor can the national leadership put out the lights of the city that attract the rural dwellers in such countless numbers. The expectation of jobs, the chance to get ahead, the opportunity for education, and the excitements of city life are all pervasive. The radio via the transistor has done its job well. Not even the slums and the blighted areas, the hopeless position of the proletariat, the actual poverty and lack of urban facilities, or even the threat of the atom bomb can scare them or keep them out. They, and millions more to come, are in the cities of the world to stay. What, therefore, is there to do? More specifically for our purpose, what can local government do?

Local urban government can help to govern cities and their metropolitan areas, and render the services that urban dwellers need much better than it is now doing, especially in developing countries. In these nations, the present position of municipal and local government in urban areas is minor and secondary in importance. The national government has controlled it down to the minutest detail, has reduced its powers to the very minimum, and has impoverished it financially by absorbing its natural sources of revenue. In exchange, it has ladled out pennies in grants-in-aid where dollars are needed, and where this was not enough, it has taken over functions that are strictly local in character. Cities, moreover, are impeded by antiquated forms of government that simply cannot work effectively under modern pressures. Moreover, there is little or no popular participation in the process of urban government—councils are either nonexistent as policy-making bodies, or else their decisions may be ignored and disapproved at will at the executive or higher level of government. Nor is there much encouragement for the development of modern administrative practices under the direction of capable and trained public administrators. Professional and technical personnel are offered poor and scant rewards for their efforts. Municipal boundaries are not in line with actual urban population, with the result that there is no geographic unity in governmental activity throughout the metropolitan area. Nor is there functional unity. Municipalities, villages, provinces, districts, subdistricts, and local echelons of national ministries all vie with one another in the same geographical area without coordination or integration of effort.

How can urban local government be revitalized for its great tasks? *First,* the national government and its ministries should divest themselves of all line and service functions within metropolitan areas. They should not be agencies for direct administration. They should not administer schools, build streets, construct municipal buildings, dig sewers, operate clinics and hospitals, or render any service to the people that is local in character. All of these functions should be carried on by local government in the metropolitan areas.

However, there must also be national guidance and policy making, for local government is an integral part of the nation. The national government should set the guidelines of local government, inspect its administration, approve its budgets, audit its accounts, train its personnel, and make uniform regulations that will chart the general outlines of local administration. In short, the national government might well take over many of the staff responsibilities for local governments in urban areas, allowing them to concentrate on the line and functional services rendered directly to the people.

Furthermore, these national policy and staff functions for local government should be concentrated in the hands of one ministry whose sole interest would be the welfare of the local units of government. This ministry, either the Ministry of Interior or of Local Government, should be the coordinating agency for local government on the national level, subject, of course, to the will of the national executive or the national parliament as the case may be.

Second, urban areas must be given a modern form of government which will include the entire metropolitan area. Within the boundaries of this metropolitan unit of government there should be no other local government or administrative units—no municipalities, villages, provinces, districts, subdistricts, or special *ad hoc* commissions carrying on local functions. All local government should be unified in this metropolitan unit. However, this large area should be broken down into administrative districts which would coincide with councilmanic electoral districts; it should follow indigenous neighborhoods as much as possible and include approximately an equal number of people.

Third, the basic governmental agency of this metropolitan government should be a council elected from single-member districts on the basis of universal suffrage on nonpartisan tickets for four-year terms, half of the council membership being elected every two years. The council should elect a president who should be the titular head of the municipality without having any administrative powers. The council should have the power to enact ordinances for the government of the metropolitan city, which could be disapproved by the central authorities only on the basis of illegality and if an ordinance would incur expenditures over and above the annual budget as approved by the Minister of Interior or of Local Government. The council should also have the power to approve the appointment of the chief administrator of the metropolitan unit, but should have no other administrative powers.

Fourth, the chief administrator should be a prefect, manager, chief of service, or governor, depending on the local nomenclature. He should be a qualified public administrator appointed by the chief executive of the nation upon the recommendation of the Minister of Interior or of Local Government and with the approval of the council of the metropolitan government. He should be the chief agent of the state in the metropolitan area, should enforce national laws and regulations as well as the ordinances of the council. He should be in supreme command of all the employees of the metropolitan government. All employees should be within the national civil service. The chief administrator should have as an administrative cabinet or council under his chairmanship the heads of his major departments. They and their subordinates should be appointed by the chief administrator from lists prepared by the civil service commission of the national government. The chief administrator should have the power to appoint his own deputy administrators for each administrative district within the metropolitan unit, subject to the approval of the Minister of Interior or of Local Government. Each of the major departments of the metropolitan administration should have a chief in the administrative district under the direction of the deputy administrator. The organization chart of the metropolitan unit of government should be made and approved by the Ministry of Interior or of Local Government.

Fifth, the finances of the metropolitan unit of government should be consonant with its needs. It should have its own sources of revenue independent from those of the national government. These sources should include taxes on real property, both buildings and land, either upon the assessment of market value or upon annual net productive income, but they should not include taxes upon personal property. Revenues should also include taxes and fees for the privilege of doing business within the metropolitan area. These taxes should be assessed and collected by the finance department of the metropolitan unit, and be levied by the local council. However, maximum limits should be prescribed by law. Another source of revenue could be the earnings from the various public utility enterprises owned and operated by the metropolitan unit, as well as a percentage of the profits or franchise rentals from private companies which operate public utilities. All public utilities within the metropolitan area should be within the jurisdiction of the metropolitan government under terms provided by law, and power to provide service outside the metropolitan unit boundaries should be given.

Grants-in-aid from the national government should be made on a uniform basis throughout the nation, for specific purposes, under terms of legislation rather than regulation, and without the necessity for local matching. The metropolitan unit should also be allowed to make loans for capital improvements, with the procedure for financing the debt service provided by law within a reasonable period for amortization and with as low an interest rate as possible. Such loans should be made, if possible, through a revolving fund established and administered by the national government. The annual budget of the metropolitan unit should be prepared by the chief administrator and approved by the council, and then submitted to the Ministry of Interior or of Local Government for final approval. This ministry should also be responsible for making quarterly allotments and enforcing the overall budget provisions, but not for passing upon expenditures made within budget limits.

Sixth, the metropolitan unit should be constituted by law as a municipal corporation and should be given powers and duties consonant with the needs of the metropolitan areas of the nation. Additional powers and responsibilities might be devolved upon the units by the Council of Ministers upon the recommendation of the Minister of Interior or of Local Government. However, any such additional powers should be accompanied by the provision of additional sources of revenue necessary for their administration.

The practical effect of such a system would be to make the metropolitan unit not only a municipality but also a province, both a vehicle for local administration and an agent of the state for national administration. The foregoing system of urban government should apply to all places within the nation that could be considered as metropolitan areas by the Ministry of Interior or of Local Government. It should be approved by the Council of Ministers, the national legislative assembly, and the national executive. All other areas within the nation would be governed under a provincial-local government system.

TOWARD EFFECTIVE PROVINCIAL AND RURAL GOVERNMENT

In ascribing the areas of a nation not in any metropolitan area to the system of provincial local government, it must be understood that the province is a local administrative unit of government. It is a unit of deconcentration of the national government, that is, the unit to which the administration of many national functions can be delegated. One of these is the supervision of local government within its jurisdiction. The functions of the province should be twofold. First, it should support and supervise all government activity within its jurisdiction; and second, it should administer directly those functions devolved upon it by the national ministries, those which are too large or cover too wide a territory to be undertaken by the local units within the province. In other words, the province should be a multipurpose unit of local government and administration.

The form of government for the province might well follow the same general lines in use today in many nations. The provincial governor, appointed by central authority, could be the chief administrator of the region including the smaller towns and rural villages. He would enforce national law and regulations; he would supervise town and rural government within the framework of the government for them as established by law. The provinces should have an administrative council consisting of all heads of major departments of the province, plus some representatives of local units. There should also be a legislative assembly elected by the people with power to enact ordinances, approve the annual provincial budget, and suggest measures for the welfare of the province. Their decisions should be approved by the Ministry of Interior or of Local Government only on the basis of legality and budget limitations, and the governor would be bound to carry out their decisions.

The United Nations Working Group on Decentralization suggested that local authority areas under the province should be as large as might be appropriate for the functions they have to perform. To this group, two levels of rural local government seemed ideal. On the lower or village level, the authority should cover the largest area at which a sense of community exists and direct participation of local government is possible; at the higher level, the authority should cover the largest area from which most technical services can be provided efficiently, but the area should not be so large that councilors cannot meet frequently. The higher authority should include both urban and rural populations with the central town or village serving as the local authority headquarters. It is this unit which should be established as a municipal corporation, and this unit might well be the municipal unit for smaller cities and towns that would not qualify for metropolitan status. This larger local unit is a necessary local government unit because if anything fundamental has been learned during the present century it is that the small traditional units are too poor and ineffective to perform the newer functions of government. Furthermore, joint administration by contiguous but minuscule units of government is too cumbersome and difficult. When the need for larger areas of local government remains unfulfilled, the provincial, state, or national levels take over, and centralization, even when not sought for as a national policy, increases.

From a Western point of view, direct and free local elections seem desirable as fundamental bases of democracy. However, there are other means by which popular participation in the process of local government may be obtained, as for example, (1) through elections within a one-party system; (2) through indirect elections by electoral committees elected by the people; and (3) through elections, where the people elect the council at the lowest level, and that council elects membership to the council of the next higher level. Another device for obtaining the expression of popular opinion and decision at the grass-roots level is in the assembly of the village, consisting of all adult inhabitants, which meets regularly to elect members of the council and to decide major problems of village concern which the council in turn carries out.

In developing countries, it is extremely difficult to staff rural and smaller town units of local government with competent personnel. The attractions of work and living in capital cities and other larger urban areas are great in comparison to those in remote and rural places. Ways to encourage higher standards of personnel must be sought by national and state governments in an effort to decentralize governmental activity. Facilities for training auxiliary rural helpers should be set up in rural areas; young persons making a career of government administration should get early experience outside the capital. Professional and technical personnel in rural areas should be given ample opportunities to keep in contact with the larger world. There should be a unified civil service with equal pay, status, retirement, and other benefits for national and local employees, with opportunity for rotation and transfer.

Financing small town and rural local government in developing countries might well follow the same pattern as that outlined for metropolitan areas. There should be a separation of tax sources between the national government, on one hand, and the provincial, town, and rural units on the other. To the local units should go the revenues from buildings and land, and from agricultural land or produce, at maximum limits established by law. Revenues should be assessed and collected by the finance department of the provincial government and divided according to a formula provided by law or agreed to by all units concerned. Miscellaneous sources of revenue such as license fees and taxes on commercial establishments should go to the lower unit of government in which they are located. Grants-in-aid for facilities and activities concerned with community development should go to the larger town and rural unit, which should also be authorized to make loans from the national government for particular projects.

In summarizing the national reports made for the International Union of Local Authorities at its Jubilee Congress in 1963 held in Brussels, Sir Harold Banwell said: "Local authorities have more to do than ever before." During the past fifty years, their expenditures and personnel have grown enormously even with the concomitant growth in activities of the central and provincial governments. Other outstanding changes in the local government picture which he noted were (1) the development of national social security systems in many countries, (2) increased urbanization and rapid urban growth, (3) the need for local units larger in size because of rapid communications, and (4) the emphasis on modern social and economic development in the newer and emerging countries. While recording increases in local activities, local officials have also complained about stricter central control and a consequent loss of local autonomy. Sir Harold declared: "The day of the really self-governing community has gone." The demand for uniformity of services and the need for money to provide them have made central intervention necessary. But, he goes on: "It is the people themselves who have made the demand." National activity has been largely in the social welfare field and in that which necessitated large capital expenditures. Future emphasis must be on working out ways and means for interdependence between the national and the local units and between local governments with one another.[1]

[1] International Union of Local Authorities, *Local Government in the XXth Century* Martinus Nijhoff, The Hague, 1963, pp. 481–491.

Bibliography

al-Ameri, Abdul-Hussein R.: *Local Government in Iraq: Comparative Study with the French Local System,* master's degree thesis, New York University, New York, 1961.

Alderfer, Harold F.: *Facts on Greek Local Government,* Economic Cooperation Administration, United States Government, Athens, Greece, 1950.

———, Mohamed F. El Katib, and Moustafa Ahmed Fahmy: *Local Government in the United Arab Republic—1963,* Institute of Public Administration, United Arab Republic, Cairo, 1963.

Alexander, Robert J.: *Communism in Latin America,* Rutgers University Press, New Brunswick, N.J., 1957.

Allen, Luther A., and Pham Ngog An: *A Vietnamese District Chief in Action,* Michigan State University Advisory Group, Saigon, National Institute of Administration, Republic of Vietnam, Report no. 5, Provincial-Local Administration Series, 1961.

Anderson, William, ed.: *Local Government in Europe,* Appleton-Century-Crofts, Inc., New York, 1939.

Bedale, Harold: *Establishment, Organization and Supervision of Local Authorities in the Federation of Malaya,* Government Press, Kuala Lampur, 1953.

Bernstein, Marver H.: *The Politics of Israel: The First Decade of Statehood,* Princeton University Press, Princeton, N.J., 1957.

Busey, James T.: *Notes on Costa Rican Democracy,* University of Colorado Studies, Series in Political Science, no. 2, Boulder, Colo., 1962.

Butler, D. E., ed.: *Elections Abroad,* St Martin's Press, Inc., New York, 1959.

Cameron, D., and B. K. Cooper: *The West African Councillor,* Oxford University Press, Fair Lawn, N.J., 1954.

Cardenas, Leonard, Jr.: *The Municipality in Northern Mexico,* Southwestern Studies, vol. 1, no. 1, Texas Western College Press, El Paso, Tex., 1963.

Care, Inc.: *Colombia Community Development: A Survey Report,* New York, 1960.

Carney, David F.: *Government and Economy in British West Africa,* Bookman Associates, New York, 1961.

Carter, Gwendolen M., and William O. Brown, eds.: *Transition in Africa: Studies in Political Adaptation,* American Research Studies, no. 1, Boston University, Boston, Mass.

Castillo, J. G.: *Property Tax Administration in the Philippines, 1956,* Bureau of Printing, Republic of the Philippines, Manila, 1957.

Chapman, Brian: *Introduction to French Local Government,* George Allen & Unwin, Ltd., London, 1953.

———: *The Prefects and Provincial France,* George Allen & Unwin, Ltd., London, 1955.

Cowan, L. Gray: *Local Government in West Africa,* Columbia University Press, New York, 1958.

Dao, Ngugen Xuan: *Village Government in Viet-Nam,* Saigon, 1958, in Lloyd W. Woodruff, *The Study of a Vietnamese Rural Community,* doctoral dissertation, Michigan State University, East Lansing, Mich., 1960.

Davis, Harold Eugene: *Government and Politics in Latin America,* The Ronald Press Company, New York, 1958.

Davis, Helen Miller: *Constitutions, Electoral Laws, Treaties of States in the Near and Middle East,* rev. ed., The Duke University Press, Durham, N.C., 1953.

Donoghue, John D., and Vo-Hong-Phuc: *My-Thuan: The Study of a Delta Village in South Viet-Nam,* Michigan State University Advisory Group, Saigon, Report no. 1, Provincial-Local Government Series, 1961.

Drakakis, Alex.: *Local Government in Greece,* Ministry of Interior, Kingdom of Greece, 1958.

Eastern Regional Organization for Public Administration (Eropa) First General Assembly, *National Reports,* Manila, 1960.

Emerson, Rupert: *Representative Government in Southeast Asia,* Harvard University Press, Cambridge, Mass., 1955.

———, Lennox A. Mills, and Virginia Thompson: *Government and Nationalism in Southeast Asia,* Institute of Pacific Relations, New York, 1942.

Finer, Herman: *English Local Government,* Columbia University Press, New York, 1934.

Fitzgibbon, Russell H.: *The Constitutions of the Americas,* The University of Chicago Press, Chicago, 1948.

Furnivall, J. S.: *The Governance of Modern Burma,* Institute of Pacific Relations, New York, 1960.

Gibb, H. A. R., and Harold Bowen: *Islamic Society and the West,* Oxford University Press, Fair Lawn, N.J., 1950.

Gibson, William M.: *The Constitutions of Colombia,* The Duke University Press, Durham, N.C., 1948.

Goethals, Peter R.: *Aspects of Local Government in a Sumbawan Village,* Department of Far Eastern Studies, Cornell University, Ithaca, N.Y., 1961.

Golay, Frank H.: *The Philippines: Public Policy and National Economic Development,* Cornell University Press, Ithaca, N.Y., 1961.

Gomez, Rosendo A.: *Government and Politics in Latin America,* Random House, Inc., New York, 1960.

Gomme, G. L.: *The Village Community,* Charles Scribner's Sons, New York, 1890.

Governor of Tokyo Metropolis: *An Administrative Perspective of Tokyo,* 1962.

Green, L. P.: *History of Local Government in South Africa,* Juta and Co. Ltd., Capetown, South Africa, 1957.

Gudoshnikov, L. M.: *Development of the Organs of Local Government and Administration in the People's Republic of China,* United States Joint Publications Research Service, Washington, D.C., 1958.

Gulick, Luther, and James K. Pollock: *Government Reorganization in the United Arab Republic,* United Arab Republic, Cairo, 1962.

Hailey, Lord Malcolm: *Native Administration in the British African Territories,* part 4, "A General Survey of the System of Native Administration," Colonial Office, London, Her Majesty's Stationery Office, 1951.

Haring, C. H.: *The Spanish Empire in America,* Oxford University Press, Fair Lawn, N.J., 1947.

Harris, G. Montagu: *Comparative Local Government,* Longmans, Green & Co., Inc., New York, 1948.

Hicks, Ursula K.: *Development from Below: Local Government and Finance in Developing Countries of the Commonwealth,* Oxford University Press, Fair Lawn, N.J., 1961.

Hinden, Rita: *Local Government and the Colonies,* George Allen & Unwin, Ltd., London, 1950.

Horrigan, Frederick James: *Local Government and Administration in Thailand: A Study of Institutions and Their Cultural Setting,* doctoral dissertation, Indiana University, Bloomington, Ind., 1959.

Hoven, W., and A. van den Elshout, *Central Services to Local Authorities,* International Union of Local Authorities, The Hague, 1962.

Humes, Samuel, and Eileen M. Martin: *The Structure of Local Governments,* International Union of Local Authorities, Martinus Nijhoff, The Hague, 1961.

International Union of Local Authorities: *Local Government Finance and Its Importance for Local Autonomy,* reports for the Rome Congress, The Hague, 1955.

———: *National Associations of Local Authorities throughout the World,* The Hague, 1956.

———: *Local Government in the XXth Century,* Martinus Nijhoff, The Hague, 1963.

Jha, Chetakar: *Indian Local Self-government,* 3d ed., Novelty Company, Patna, 1958.

Jorrin, Miguel: *Governments of Latin America,* D. Van Nostrand Company, Inc., Princeton, N.J., 1953.

Kahin, George McTurnan, ed.: *Major Governments of Asia,* Cornell University Press, Ithaca, N.Y., 1958.

Karnjanaprakorn, Choop: *Municipal Government in Thailand as an Institution and Process of Self-government,* doctoral dissertation, Indiana University, Bloomington, Ind., 1959.

Kirby, E. Stuart: *Rural Progress in Taiwan,* Republic of China, Taiwan, 1960.

Kovačević, Živorad: *Communal System in Yugoslavia,* Belgrade, 1958

Kraines, Oscar: *Government and Politics in Israel,* Houghton Mifflin Company, Boston, 1961.

Kropotkin, P.: *Mutual Aid: A Factor in Evolution,* Penguin Books Limited, Middlesex, England, 1902.

LeBar, Frank M., and Adrienne Suddard: *Laos, Its People, Its Society, Its Culture,* Hraf Press, New Haven, Conn., 1960.

Legge, John D.: *Problems of Regional Autonomy in Contemporary Indonesia,* Cornell University Press, Ithaca, N.Y., 1957.

Maass, A.: *Area and Power: A Theory of Local Government,* The Free Press of Glencoe, New York, 1959.

MacDonald, Austin F.: *Government of the Argentine Republic,* Thomas Y. Crowell Company, New York, 1942.

———: *Latin American Politics and Government,* Thomas Y. Crowell Company, New York, 1954.

Malaviya, H. D.: *Village Panchayats in India,* All India Congress Committee, New Delhi, 1956.

Marquard, Leo.: *The Peoples and Policies of South Africa,* 2d ed., Oxford University Press, Fair Lawn, N.J., 1960.

Marshall, A. H.: *Financial Aspects of Urban Local Government in English-speaking Africa, Excluding South Africa,* United Nations, New York, February, 1962.

Maryanov, Gerald Seymour: *The Establishment of Regional Government in the Republic of Indonesia,* abstract of doctoral dissertation, Indiana University, Bloomington, Ind., 1959.

Morse, Richard M.: *From Community to Metropolis: A Biography of São Paulo, Brazil,* University of Florida Press, Gainesville, Fla., 1958.

Morsink, Hubert: *Rapid Urban Growth in the Arab States,* Beirut, Lebanon, 1963.

Mourer, Henry: *Administrative Problems of Urbanization in Africa,* United Nations Workshop on Urbanization in Africa, New York, 1962.

———: *Les Problèmes Administratifs de l'Urbanisation au Maroc,* United Nations, Department of Economic and Social Affairs, Document no. 15, Rabat, 1962.

Munro, William Bennett: *The Government of European Cities,* The Macmillan Company, New York, 1927.

Nehru, Jawaharlal: *Glimpses of World History,* Lindsay Drummond, Ltd., London, 1945.

Palmer, Norman D.: *The Indian Political System,* Houghton Mifflin Company, Boston, 1961.

Papastathopoulos, Catherine D.: *Local Government in Greece,* master's thesis, University of Minnesota, Minneapolis, 1961.

Public Administration Clearing House: *Training for Public Administration, Southern Asia,* Chicago, 1955.

Public Administration Institute for Turkey and the Middle East: *Studies in Turkish Local Government,* Ankara, 1955.

Pylee, M. V.: *Constitutional Government in India,* Asia Publishing House, London, 1960.

Rao, V. Venkata: *The Administration of District Boards in the Madras Presidency, 1884–1945,* The Local Self-government Institution, Bombay, 1953.

Romani, John H., and M. Ladd Thomas: *A Survey of Local Government in the Philippines,* Institute of Public Administration, University of the Philippines, Manila, 1954.

Royal Institute of International Affairs: *Nigeria: The Political and Economic Background,* London, 1960.

Ryan, John William: *Bangkok Government and Administration: Appearance and Reality,* doctoral dissertation, Indiana University, Bloomington, Ind., 1959.

Scott, Robert E.: *Mexican Government in Transition,* The University of Illinois Press, Urbana, Ill., 1959.

Sharma, M. P.: *Local Self-government in India,* 3d ed., Hinds Kitabs, Ltd., Bombay, 1961.

Short, Lloyd M.: *The Relationship of Local and National Government in the Philippines,* Institute of Public Administration, University of the Philippines, Manila, 1955.
Shoup, Carl S., et al.: *The Fiscal System of Venezuela,* The Johns Hopkins Press, Baltimore, 1959.
Siffin, William J.: *Towards the Comparative Study of Public Administration,* Indiana University, Bloomington, Ind., 1957.
Smith, T. E.: *Elections in Developing Countries,* St Martin's Press, Inc., New York, 1960.
Smuckler, Ralph H., et al.: *Recommendations Concerning the Department of Interior, the Regions and the Provinces (Vietnam),* Michigan State University Press, East Lansing, Mich., 1956.
Spengler, Oswald: *The Decline of the West,* Alfred A. Knopf, Inc., New York, 1934.
Staley, Eugene: *The Future of Underdeveloped Countries,* 3d ed., Harper & Row, Publishers, Incorporated, New York, 1961.
Stokes, William S.: *Honduras: An Area Study in Government,* The University of Wisconsin Press, Madison, Wis., 1950.
Sweet, William Warren: *A History of Latin America,* Abingdon Press, Nashville, Tenn., 1919.
Tinker, Hugh: *The Foundations of Local Self-government in India, Pakistan and Burma,* The Athlone Press, London, 1954.
———: *The Union of Burma,* Oxford University Press, Fair Lawn, N.J., 1959.
Tucker, William P.: *The Mexican Government Today,* The University of Minnesota Press, Minneapolis, 1957.
United Nations: *Community Development in Urban Areas,* Department of Economic and Social Affairs, New York, 1961.
———: *Introduction to the Problems of Urbanization in Tropical Africa,* Workshop on Urbanization in Africa, New York, 1962.
———: *Progress in Land Reform,* New York, 1954.
———: *Report of the Seminar on Urbanization Problems in Latin America,* New York, 1959.
United Nations Regional Social Affairs Office for the Middle East: *Public Administration and Finance Problems Associated with Rapid Urban Growth in the Arab States,* Beirut, Lebanon, 1963.
United Nations Technical Assistance Programme: *Decentralization for National and Local Development,* New York, 1962.
———: *Public Administration Aspects of Community Development Programmes,* New York, 1959.
———: *Public Administration Problems of New and Rapidly Growing Towns in Asia,* New York, 1962.
Wallich, Henry C., John H. Adler, et al.: *Public Finance in a Developing Country, El Salvador: A Case Study,* Harvard University Press, Cambridge, Mass., 1951.
Woodruff, Lloyd W.: *A Study of a Vietnamese Rural Community,* Michigan State University, East Lansing, Mich., 1960.
World Conference on Local Government: *Local Government Structure and Organization: Problems in Metropolitan Areas,* Washington, D.C., 1961.
Zink, Harold, Arne Wahlstrand, Feliciana Benvenuti, and R. Bhaskaran: *Rural Local Government in Sweden, Italy and India,* Frederick A. Praeger, Inc., New York, 1958.

Index